Made Flesh

Made Flesh

Sacrament and Poetics in Post-Reformation England

Kimberly Johnson

PENN

UNIVERSITY OF PENNSYLVANIA PRESS

PHILADELPHIA

Published by
University of Pennsylvania Press
Philadelphia, Pennsylvania 19104-4112
www.upenn.edu/pennpress

Printed in the United States of America on acid-free paper
10 9 8 7 6 5 4 3 2 1

Library of Congress Cataloging-in-Publication Data
Johnson, Kimberly.
   Made flesh : sacrament and poetics in post-Reformation England / Kimberly
Johnson.—1st ed.
      p. cm.
   Includes bibliographical references and index.
   ISBN 978-0-8122-4588-2 (hardcover : alk. paper)
   1. Christian poetry, English—Early modern, 1500-1700—History and criticism.
2. Christianity and literature—England—History—17th century. 3. Lord's Supper in
literature. 4. Theology in literature. 5. Symbolism in literature. 6. Transubstantiation in
literature. I. Title.
PR545.R4J64 2014
821'.409382—dc23

2013042034

For my children,
Bennett Zion Greenfield and Elijah West Greenfield

Contents

Eucharistic Poetics: The Word Made Flesh

This is a book about how poems work, and about how the interpretive demands of sacramental worship inform the production of poetic texts.

If it seems impolite for a book to declare its intentions so brashly in its first gesture, such insolence has nevertheless been made necessary by the publication of several critical texts that set out to investigate what they term the *poetics* of the post-Reformation period, particularly in conjunction with a consideration of eucharistic theology. In what has become a minor fad in Renaissance literary criticism, a number of studies advertise themselves as engaged in an examination of the relationship between the sacramental theologies of the early modern period and the representational strategies of poetic texts; but too often these critical examinations seem to lose track of, or fundamentally to misunderstand, the terms in which they frame their projects. While a number of well-meaning critics have trafficked in phrases like "eucharistic poetics," "sacramental poetics," and "the poetics of immanence," and have acknowledged, either explicitly or implicitly, the interpretive overlap between sacramental worship and the processes of signification, their attention remains focused not on poetics—that is, not on *the way poems work* as literary artifacts—but rather on whatever opinions concerning sacramental theology Renaissance literature seems to offer. The present study, by contrast, concerns itself primarily with poetics, with the ways in which poems communicate information beyond denotation and in addition to the referential content of words rather than with whatever thematic commentary poems may offer on the subject of the Eucharist. I am most urgently interested, in other words, in *how* poems say as opposed to *what* poems say. For it is in their concern with the success and failure of language to provide interpretive experiences that these poetic texts reveal and respond to the challenges of eucharistic worship. The Eucharist is after all a ritual fundamentally involved with the mechanisms of representation, and the question of how exactly Christ is presented in the bread and wine is one of the animating debates of the Reformation. This book demonstrates the ways in which the sacramental conjunction of text and materiality, word and flesh, in the ritual of Communion registers simultaneously as a theological concern and as a nexus for anxieties about how language—particularly poetic language, with its valences of embodiment—works.

In advancing these claims, I do not seek to rehearse the arguments made by Malcolm Ross in his stealthily enduring 1954 study *Poetry and Dogma*. That book takes a dim, not to say curmudgeonly, view of post-Reformation poetry (as well as post-Reformation dogma), lamenting that what Ross identifies as Protestantism's "outright abandonment of Eucharistic sacramentalism" constitutes nothing less than the "declension of symbol into metaphor," with disastrous aesthetic effects.[1] Ross's thesis suggests that such a shift—or, in his oft-repeated term, a "deterioration"—is at once the inevitable consequence of Reformed eucharistic theologies, which Ross argues make a "drastic separation of the sign from the thing signified" (51), and the ineluctable cause of poetic decline over the course of the seventeenth century. Leaving aside the tendentiousness of Ross's approach to his subject, his argument is puzzling in its apparent indifference to the ways in which the work of John Donne, George Herbert, Richard Crashaw, Edward Taylor, and other devotional poets of the period explicitly engage—in the thematic content of their poems, to be sure, but also in their poetic strategies—issues of signification, sacrament, worship, and the ontological value of the material world and of the flesh, concerns whose purported decline in seventeenth-century poetry most vexes Ross. Indeed, the flowering of English poetry in the seventeenth century, which this study will argue stands in response to the challenges, tensions, and potentialities of sacramental worship, eventuates not, as Ross seems to think, in the thin broth of poetic godlessness but in the establishment of an aesthetic that underwrites the composition of poems even to the present day, an aesthetic that relies upon the capacities of poetry to express and to embody, in which the word is continually made flesh.

Until fairly recently, Ross's book was virtually the only critical study devoted to poetic treatments of the Eucharist in Renaissance poetry. But the last several years have seen the publication of a number of studies that acknowledge the proximity of sacramental worship and literary encounter in the early modern period. Investigations such as Regina Schwartz's *Sacramental Poetics at the Dawn of Secularism*; Robert Whalen's *The Poetry of Immanence: Sacrament in Donne and Herbert*; Eleanor McNees's *Eucharistic Poetry*; and Theresa M. DiPasquale's *Literature and Sacrament: The Sacred and the Secular in John Donne* have contributed to an increasing critical awareness that the interpretive strategies inherent in a sacrament that relies on the presentation of one modality of objects (the material artifacts of bread and wine) which refers to another (the substance, either corporeal or spiritual, of Christ) necessarily ramify into a cultural approach to literature.[2] Still, a full assessment of the ways in which eucharistic worship informs literary production in that crucial period of doctrinal reformulation has been preempted in part by an overwhelming critical focus on determining a precise confessional identity for the poets under investigation, a schematic approach whose obvious attractions of definition and certainty do not provide for what Molly Murray has described as "the more fluid and provisional reality" of Christian experience in the early modern period.[3] Despite this urge among modern readers to fix early modern poets within coherent and defined doctrinal positions, early modern poets do not always cooperate. While many critics tend to be reductively content to let Crashaw stand as uncomplicatedly, even simplemindedly, committed to an identifiably Catholic ceremonialist sacramentalism, or to view Taylor as so strong and unanxious a champion of nonconforming Calvinism that he exiled himself to the American wilderness to administer both his faith and its Suppers, such confessional stability has eluded scholarly treatments of the two major devotional poets of the theologically jumbled Stuart church, Donne and Herbert—which elusiveness explains in part why the question of confessional identity has so dominated Donne and Herbert studies.

Much critical energy has been devoted to trawling through the literary output of post-Reformation religious writers generally, and of Donne and Herbert especially, in order to determine whether the true theological allegiance of each author lies most properly with Catholicism, Anglo-Catholicism, crypto-Catholicism, high or low Anglicanism, *via media* Anglicanism, Protestantism, Calvinism, Puritanism, or some combination thereof. And while there is certainly more than a little slippage among these designations, owing in part to the hodge-podge nature of English church doctrine during the period and in part to inconsistencies of usage, it has occasionally seemed as if twentieth- and twenty-first-century critics were bent on perpetuating the confessional quarrels of Reformation and post-Reformation divines in their claims about early modern poets, imagining Renaissance views on the Eucharist as merely dichotomous (pitting the literalism of transubstantiation against bare memorialism) and reinscribing those binaries in their treatment of poetic texts. The modern debate is framed on the one hand by the intellectual heirs of Louis Martz, whose influential view of seventeenth-century religious poets located their greatest aesthetic sympathies with the practices of Catholic worship and meditation, and on the other hand by the school of "Protestant poetics," whose view, seminally articulated by Barbara Lewalski, is that the work of those same devotional writers accomplishes a distinct departure from continental Catholicism in both style and substance.[4] Not surprisingly, the Eucharist has come to serve for modern critics, as it did for early modern divines, as a kind of litmus test for confessional allegiance, as when Richard Strier's *Love Known: Theology and Experience in George Herbert's Poetry* considers a passage from Herbert's poem "Love Unknown." Of his problematically hard heart, the speaker reports,

> I bathed it often, even with holy blood,
> Which at a board, while many drank bare wine,
> A friend did steal into my cup for good,
> Even taken inwardly, and most divine
> To supple hardness.[5]

Strier writes that in these lines "Herbert goes out of his way to present a strongly receptionist view of the Eucharist," which understands sacramental transformation as occurring through the exercise of the communicant's faith rather than by means of priestly consecration, and he concludes that "the central point" of these lines is to declare Herbert's Reformed conception of "the religious life as entirely a matter of 'the heart.'"[6] For Strier, in other words, the poem's narration of its eucharistic encounter indicates Herbert's decided rejection of the Catholic doctrine of works in favor of a brand of Protestantism inspired by Luther and Calvin in which man is justified by faith alone. The events of Herbert's poem provide, in Strier's reading, a key into the poet's larger theological affinities, and disclose something about how Herbert defined his doctrinal position within the religious turmoil of the Stuart church.

But Strier's effort to establish Herbert's theology through the evidence in "Love Unknown" does not allow for the poem's own complication of that theology, for even as the poem's drama argues against the efficacy of labor—or, to use the theological terminology that Strier invokes, of "works"—in the pursuit of grace, its language foregrounds the labor of its own telling. The speaker's tale, as he introduces it to an unidentified interlocutor in the poem's first line, "is long and sad," and the telling of it hard, for as the speaker importunes his audience, "in my faintings I presume your love / Will more complie then help" (2–3). Here, the term "faintings" collapses the speaker's narrative of past afflictions into his present relation of that narrative, marking the tale itself as an effort, an exhaustion. This sense is reaffirmed throughout the poem, as the speaker interrupts his narrative with parenthetical expressions of its difficulty: "(I sigh to say)" (8), "(I sigh to tell)" (24), "(I sigh to speak)" (50), the tale and indeed the very regularity of the poem's iambic pentameter disrupted by these short, gasping lines. Strier claims that the poem expresses "Herbert's rejection of works," and he seeks to extract from the poem's apparent conviction about "the pointlessness of effort" a stable eucharistic theology for the poet: "Herbert does not want to present taking communion as either a good work in itself or a way of cooperating with God in suppling the heart," Strier concludes, arguing that "Herbert's insistence on the action of a friend in stealing the 'holy bloud' into the speaker's cup eliminates all suggestion of cooperation" in a thoroughly Reformed sacrament.[7] However, the ostentatious labor of the poetic utterance here works precisely in cooperation with the interlocutor's response to achieve the poem's redemptive lesson, which is offered in the poem's concluding lines as an interpretation of the speaker's recounted afflictions: the heart's having endured being "washt and wrung" (17) is reframed in the interlocutor's reading as a sign of baptismal renewal, the heart's time in the "scalding pan" (35) served but to soften it, the bed of "*thorns*" (52) works in this new perspective to "quicken what was dull" (65), each and every challenge revalued by the speaker's auditor as a gracious gift of God to make the soul "new, tender, quick" (70). That is to say, as the unnamed, unknown "Deare Friend" (1) explicates the narrative's spiritually fraught picaresque, so difficult to be told, what that interpretation produces is an apprehension of grace: the *work* of utterance is a crucial activity toward apprehension, and this regenerate understanding of the self is produced in cooperation with the divine perspective of the unnamed friend.

I have focused on this poem and this critic not to posit a theological counter to Strier's Calvinist reading of Herbert—not, that is, to claim "Love Unknown" for the theology of works set—but rather to indicate how such a doctrinally definitive approach may prevent even acute readers from appreciating how adaptable, porous, and sometimes inconsistent Christian worship was in the post-Reformation period, for both communities of worship and individuals alike. Studies that ground textual analysis within historical context have done much to illuminate the complexity of belief in the period, and have helped demolish any notion that post-Reformation doctrine, institutional or otherwise, was consistent. And yet the persistent assumption that a poem declares any given writer's creed or that it presents a stable articulation of a doctrinal position threatens to reduce poetic utterance to a transparent referential instrument, a straightforward and aesthetically naïve expression of the spiritual life of the poet. But as we shall see, poetic utterance itself works ever against the referential impulse, emphasizing the surface of its discourse in a way that both invites and occludes a referential encounter. And in this quality, holding invitation and interruption in tension one with another, poetic utterance corresponds to nothing so much as the sacramental event of the Lord's Supper.

My concern here is to chart the ways in which poetic texts of this period explore the expressive capacities of their own discursive surfaces, a practice that transcends doctrinal divides and defies nice theological categories. This study is far less interested in jumping into the fray of doctrinal dispute; it resists focusing its claims on whether, say, Donne is more a Roman churchman or some stripe of "Protestant," however variously defined—more a secret papist with an enduring fondness for his ancestral Catholicism, or a restive apostate from his family faith, or rather a full-throated participant in some "Calvinist mainstream."[8] Instead, *Made Flesh* addresses the phenomenal and epistemological overlaps between textuality and sacramental worship to demonstrate that in the period following the religious Reformation of the sixteenth century, the lyric poem becomes a primary cultural site for investigating the capacity of language to manifest presence. In poems that employ the presentational, and representational, strategies of Communion, seventeenth-century writers assert the status of poems as artifacts with corporeal as well as symbolic resonances, such that the poems themselves embody the shifting and precarious relationship between materiality and signification—which, not incidentally, is precisely the issue that produces conflicting accounts of the operation of the Eucharist.

The Eucharist is distinct among sacraments for a number of reasons, including that it is celebrated across the wide field of Reformation-era Christian churches, though some denominations prefer to call the ritual by other names, including Holy Communion, the Lord's Supper, and the Sacrament of the Altar.[9] Where Catholic doctrine identifies seven sacraments, the sacramental theologies that developed out of the Reformation reduced that number substantially. The Thirty-Nine Articles of Religion (1563), which codified the creed of the English church under Elizabeth, rejected the Roman sacraments of confirmation, penance, the taking of orders, marriage, and unction as "corrupte" because they did not have "any visible signe, or ceremonie, ordeyned of God."[10] But even to Reformed theologians who break to a greater or lesser degree with the view articulated by Thomas Aquinas that "Nam in sacramento Eucharistae id quod est res et sacramentum est in ipsa materia" [In the sacrament of the Eucharist what we call the "thing and sign" is in the very matter],[11] the material valences of the rite—its activity of making the invisible visible through the concrete and objective reality of the physical world—are crucial to its special status. In manifesting the incomprehensibility and imperceptibility of the divine as corporeally present and perceptible, the Eucharist reenacts the mystery of Christ's Incarnation. But that reenactment, as it occurs in the performance of the rite, is self-consciously symbolic, accomplished through the operation of signs. That is, beyond considerations of doctrine and the evolving parameters of observance, this sacrament explicitly engages incarnational concerns from the remove of a symbol that advertises itself as such. In effect, the Eucharist is a sacrament that stages its correspondence to the Incarnation, regardless of the nature of that correspondence, as a set of figures.

It is not at all surprising, then, that literary texts should have been affected by the eucharistic debates of the sixteenth century, given that the ceremony at the ritual center of Christian observance across the confessional spectrum is unavoidably bound up with interpretive practices. The perplexed hermeneutics of sacramental worship extend beyond the representational status of the eucharistic elements to the very narrative of the ritual's institution. Indeed, no sentence has provoked more, or more anxious, readerly commentary in the history of Christian theology than the one Jesus is reported to have uttered at the Last Supper, which insisted upon a radical new relationship between spirituality, reading, and corporeal experience: *This is my body*. Theological disagreements over the nature and operation of the sacrament rest on fundamental questions about interpretation, and the long history of doctrinal conflict about the operation of the Eucharist dramatizes the consequences of Christ's own verbal ambiguity. Are we to understand that the verb *is* (Greek ἐστιν) denotes true identity between *This* and *my body*? Or is Jesus speaking metaphorically, playing on the association of bread with nourishing staple food (as in Matthew 6.11: "Giue vs this day our daily bread")[12] or, in the festive context of the Last Supper, making use of the operative symbolism of the Passover matzoh as the bread of both affliction and deliverance? Or does the significance of the rite inhere in some combination of these referentialities? That the words of institution lend themselves to a range of figurative and nonfigurative readings is compounded by inconsistencies across different biblical accounts of the Last Supper, as when the version reported in Matthew 26.26, where Christ merely instructs his disciples, "Take, eate, this is my body," is expanded in Luke's report: "This is my body which is giuen for you, this doe in remembrance of me."[13] Seemingly from the moment of this ritual's institution, interpreters have disagreed about the precise meaning of Jesus's words, and that history of controversy and division regarding the nature of sacramental worship has ensured that the Eucharist is experienced primarily as a ritual engagement with signs.[14]

The earliest commentaries on the sacrament indicate the harrowing stakes by which the rite foregrounds the interpretation of signs. When Paul writes to the early Christian community at Corinth in an effort to promote unity of practice and belief among their nascent sect, he relates Jesus's actions at the Last Supper, reminding his audience of the injunction to repeat the ceremony: "And when he had giuen thanks, he brake it, and sayd, Take, eate, this is my body, which is broken for you: this doe in remembrance of mee. After the same manner also hee took the cup when he had supped, saying, This cup is the new Testament in my blood: this do ye, as oft as ye drinke it, in remembrance of me." Paul's phrasing at the end of this passage, which seems to frame the sacrament as a memorialist ritual, the symbol of a new covenant, would make him a favorite among reformers. But just a few lines later, Paul warns that "hee that eateth and drinketh vnworthily, eateth and drinketh damnation to himselfe, not discerning the Lords body."[15] Classifying as unworthy unto damnation the partaker who participates in the sacrament "not discerning the Lord's body," Paul's caution communicates the tremendous pressure that the sacrament put on both the signifying capacities of the sacramental elements and the interpretive faculties of the worshipper. For Paul is not advocating a literal and sensibly perceptual encounter between the communicant and Christ's body but rather a hermeneutic action that locates real and efficacious significance in the substance of the ritual.

As Paul's commentary indicates, one of the challenges facing even the earliest Christian communities with regard to the eucharistic meal involved that ritual's mediation between meaning and materiality. As Christianity evolved, theologians remained alive to the ways in which the Eucharist elides referentiality and immanence, pointing toward divine principles even as it instantiates divine presence. Beginning in the ante-Nicene era, exegetes register this simultaneity of signification and immanence in commentaries on the Eucharist, as when Origen links the corporeal presence of Christ in the ritual meal with the principle of Christ's providing spiritual nourishment to the worshipper through the nexus of the word: "Carnibus enim et sanguine verbi sui tanquam mundo cibo ac poto, potat et reficit omne hominum genus" [Surely by the flesh and blood of his word as clean food and drink, he refreshes and provides drink to the whole race of men].[16] When Ignatius of Antioch, writing in the second century, speaks of "πίστει ὅ ἐστιν σάρξ τοῦ Κυρίου, καί ἐν ἀγάπῃ, ὅ ἐστιν αἷμα Ἰησοῦ Χριστοῦ" [faith, which is the flesh of the Lord, and charity, which is the blood of Jesus Christ] and advocates "προσφυγὼν τῷ εὐαγγελίῳ ὡς σαρκὶ Ἰησοῦ" [taking refuge in the Gospel as the flesh of Jesus], he imagines the body of Christ as a metaphor for Christian doctrine itself, permeating all of Christian worship through the effectual mechanism of sacramental participation.[17] A century later, Tertullian describes the rite in terms that collapse interpretation into the bodily encounter of ritual eating: "Itaque sermonem constituens vivificatorem, quia spiritus et vita sermo, eundem etiam carnem suam dixit, quia et sermo caro erat factus, proinde in causam vitae appetendus, et devorandus auditu, et ruminandus intellectu, et fide digerendus" [Establishing his word as vivifying, because his word is spirit and life, Christ also spoke of his flesh in the same way, because the Word became flesh; accordingly, to obtain life, we ought to crave him, and to devour him with our hearing, and to ruminate on him with our understanding, and to digest him by faith].[18] And in the early third century, Clement of Alexandria offers a vivid sense of the Eucarist as a kind of immanent sign, a figure that makes use of the capacity of the flesh itself to serve as a site of representation: "σάρκα ἡμῖν τὸ Πνεῦμα τὸ ἅγιον ἀλληγορεῖ· καὶ γὰρ ὑπ' αὐτοῦ δεδημιούργηται ἡ σάρξ. Αἷμα ἡμῖν τὸν

Λόγον αἰνίττεται· καὶ γὰρ ὡς αἷμα πλούσιον ὁ Λόγος ἐπικέχυται τῷ βίῳ" [The Spirit uses flesh as an allegory for us; for by him was the flesh created. Blood signifies through a veil the Word for us, for as rich blood the Word has been poured forth into our life].[19] Clement's use of "σάρκα," whose carnal connotations are akin to "meat," to describe the embodiment of spiritual ideas, locates in corporeal flesh the function of representing divine interventions into the world. In a later passage from the same treatise, Clement returns to the same terminology to elaborate on the ways in which the particular enfleshed signs of the sacrament manifest not only the body of Christ, but the abstract meaning of sacramental worship:

Διττὸν δὲ τὸ αἷμα τοῦ Κυρίου· τὸ μὲν γάρ ἐστιν αὐτοῦ σαρκικόν, ᾧ τῆς φθορᾶς λελυτρώμεθα, τὸ δὲ πνευματικόν, τοῦτ' ἔστιν ᾧ κεχρίσμεθα. Καὶ τοῦτ' ἔστι πιεῖν τὸ αἷμα τοῦ Ἰησοῦ, τῆς κυριακῆς μεταλαβεῖν ἀφθαρσίας· ἰσχὺς δὲ τοῦ λόγου τὸ πνεῦμα, ὡς αἷμα σαρκός. Ἀναλόγως τοίνυν κίρναται ὁ μὲν οἶνος τῷ ὕδατι, τῷ δὲ ἀνθρώπῳ τὸ πνεῦμα, καὶ τὸ μὲν εἰς πίστιν εὐωχεῖ, τὸ κρᾶμα, τὸ δὲ εἰς ἀφθαρσίαν ὁδηγεῖ, τὸ πνεῦμα, ἡ δὲ ἀμφοῖν αὖθις κρᾶσις ποτοῦ τε καὶ λόγου εὐχαριστία κέκληται, χάρις ἐπαινουμένη καὶ καλή, ἧς οἱ κατὰ πίστιν μεταλαμβάνοντες ἁγιάζονται καὶ σῶμα καὶ ψυχήν, τὸ θεῖον κρᾶμα τὸν ἄνθρωπον τοῦ πατρικοῦ βουλήματος πνεύματι καὶ λόγῳ συγκιρνάντος μυστικῶς· καὶ γὰρ ὡς ἀληθῶς μὲν τὸ πνεῦμα ᾠκείωται τῇ ὑπ' αὐτοῦ φερομένῃ ψυχῇ, ἡ δὲ σὰρξ τῷ λόγῳ, δι' ἣν ὁ λόγος γέγονεν σάρξ.

[The blood of the Lord is double in nature. In one sense it is fleshly, that by which we have been redeemed from destruction. In another sense it is spiritual, that by which we have been anointed. To drink the blood of Jesus is to share in the Lord's immortality; and the force of the Word is the Spirit, as the blood of the flesh. Thus as wine is mixed with water, just so is the Spirit mixed with man; the one, the mixture, quenches us to faith, and the other, the spirit, leads us to immortality; the mingling of both—of the drink and the Word—is called the Eucharist . . . and those who partake of it with faith are sanctified in both body and soul. . . . For truly the Spirit cleaves to the soul that is moved by it, and the flesh to the Word, for which purpose the Word became flesh.][20]

Clement's reading exemplifies the interdependence of figuration and corpo-reality in the sacrament. He identifies the different senses by which the Eucharist manifests the divine as physical and spiritual, and argues that the partaker experiences a transformation in both body and soul. That is to say, Clement, like other early thinkers about the Eucharist, views the sacra-ment as both a fleshly and a referential event, signifying both in the drink and the word.

Though these early Christian writers tend to display a notable, almost programmatic, reserve regarding the operation of the Eucharist, preferring mystery to speculation on the precise mode of sacramental physics, their commentary consistently recognizes the special significative status of the eucharistic elements. The ritual has ever been understood as a ceremony deeply invested in representation, and historical divisions in eucharistic theology arise precisely over questions of signification—that is, of how a sign manifests meaning. And while the variety of opinion on the manner and mode of signification in the sacrament dispels any illusion that Chris-tianity enjoyed, even long before the Reformation, a monolithic and uncomplicated understanding of the rite, much of the diversity of opinion from the early medieval church through the era of Reformation can be traced to the competing influences of Ambrose of Milan and Augustine of Hippo.[21] In his fourth-century treatise on the Eucharist, *De sacramentis*, Ambrose emphasizes the identity of sign and signified as the sacrament's primary event: "Ergo, tibi ut respondeam, non erat corpus Christi ante consecrationem, sed post consecrationem dico tibi quia iam corpus est Christi. Ipse dixit et factum est, ipse mandauit et creatum est" [Thus, so that I answer you, there was no body of Christ before the consecration, but after the consecration I say to you that there is now the body of Christ. He himself said it and it is done; he himself commanded and it is established].[22]

Ambrose commits his understanding of the Eucharist to a kind of her-meneutic certainty, in which the sign is secured to its signified: the ritual elements are substantially identical to the body of Christ, the words of institution are identical to their accomplishment. But writing as a rough contemporary to Ambrose, Augustine proposes a formulation of the ritual that allows for a degree of referentiality, the sign indicating its signified as a figure or metaphor, as when he recalls that the Last Supper was a festive event "in quo corporis et sanguinis sui figuram discipuis commendavit et tradidit" [in which he delivered and entrusted to his disciples the figure of his body and blood].²³ In his *De Doctrina Christiana*, Augustine elaborates on his use of the term "figuram" to describe the sacramental event:

> Si praeceptiva locution est aut flagitium aut facinus vetans, aut utilitatem aut beneficentiam jubens, non est figurate. Si autem flagitium aut facinus videtur jubere, aut utilitatem aut beneficentiam vetare, figurate est. *Nisi manducaveritis*, inquit, *carnem filii hominis, et sanguine biberitis, non habebitis vitam in vobis (Joan. VI, 54)*. Facinus vel flagitium videtur jubere: figura est ergo, praecipiens passione dominicae communicandum, et suaviter atque utiliter recondendum in memoria quod pro nobis caro ejus crucifixa et vulnerata sit. [If a commandment prohibits that which is shameful or villainous, or orders what is useful or beneficial, it is not figurative. But if it seems to order what is shameful or villanous, or to prohibit what is useful or beneficial, it is figurative. *Except ye eat the flesh of the Son of man*, scripture says, *and drink his blood, ye have no life in you* (John 6.54). This seems to order what is villainous or shameful: it is a figure, therefore, commanding communion in the passion of the Lord, and that there is to be a sweet and useful recollection in the memory that for us his flesh was crucified and wounded.]²⁴

Here, Augustine foregrounds the referential qualities of the sacramental rite, designed to activate in the worshipper an awareness of sacrifice and mercy. And yet this figure is distinct from other kinds of signs because of the ways in which it commands "communicandum"—both *communication* and *communion* together—a representational and experiential sharing in Christ's passion that is unavailable in other signs. Indeed, Augustine argues, "Diximus enim, fraters, hoc Dominum commendasse in manducatione carnis suae et potatione sanguinis sui, ut in illo maneamus, et ipse in nobis" [We have said, brothers, that the Lord commended to us the chewing of his body and the drinking of his blood, so that we might remain in him, and he in us].²⁵

Despite his affirmation of a materially efficacious sacrament containing the corporeal presence of Christ, Augustine's discomfited reflection that the conversion of the elements of bread and wine to Christ's body seems shameful helped, a millennium later, to fuel Reformation attacks on what was canonized during the thirteenth century as the Catholic doctrine of transubstantiation. According to this doctrine, whose articulation is as much indebted to Ambrose as to Aristotle, the substance or essence of the elements undergoes a change while the bread and wine remain present to the senses as accidents or forms. As Thomas Aquinas explicates it, in the *Summa Theologiae*'s meticulous and definitive codification of transubstantiation, Christ "per veritatem corporis et sanguinis sui nos sibi conjungit in hoc sacramento" [joins us to himself in this sacrament in the reality of his flesh and blood]. Aquinas distinguishes the Eucharist as a special category of signs, differing even from other sacraments in that "in aliis sacramentis non est ipse Christus realiter, sicut in hoc sacramento" [In the other sacraments we have not got Christ himself really, as we have in this sacrament]. He makes clear that he is not speaking about Christ's being represented in the elements in some figural fashion: "Per quod non intelligimus quod Christus sit ibi solum sicut in signo, licet sacramentum sit in genere signe: sed intelligimus corpus Christi hic esse, sicut dictum est, secundum proprium modum huic sacramento" [In saying this we do not mean that Christ is only symbolically there, although it is true that every sacrament is a sign, but we understand that Christ's body is there, as we have said, in a way that is proper to this sacrament]. And yet, Aquinas explains, the sacramental presence of Christ in the eucharistic elements relies on the operation of a figure, the bread and wine serving as a means by which Christ can be comprehended. Aquinas defines sacramental signs as serving a particular significative function, one that communicates a sacred term to human perception:

Signa dantur hominibus, quorum est per nota ad ignota pervenire. Et ideo proprie dicitur sacramentum quod est signum alicuius rei sacrae ad homines pertinentis, ut scilicet proprie dicatur sacramentum, secundum quod nunc de sacramentis loquimur, quod est signum rei sacrae inquantum est sanctificans homines.

[Signs are given to men. Now it is characteristic of men that they achieve an awareness of things which they do not known through things which they do know. Hence the term "sacrament" is properly applied to that which is a sign of some sacred reality pertaining to men; or—to define the special sense in which the term "sacrament" is being used in our present discussion of the sacraments—it is applied to that which is a sign of a sacred reality inasmuch as it has the property of sanctifying men.]

As Aquinas stipulates, the sacramental sign does not present its signified to the senses, but like any other sign, it requires interpretation: "Dicendum quod duplex est oculus scilicet corporalis, proprie dictus et intellectualis, qui per similitudinem dicitur. A nullo autem oculo corporali corpus Christi potest videri prout est in hoc sacramento . . . sed solo intellectu, qui dicitur oculus spiritualis" [There are two kinds of eyes, the eye of the body, properly so called, and the eye of the intelligence, called so by analogy. The body of Christ, as it is under this sacrament, cannot be seen by any bodily eye. . . . It is only open to the intellect, which may be called a spiritual eye]. For Aquinas, Christ's body, which is substantially present albeit patently *not* perceptible by means of the senses, is apprehended by means of a "similitudinem" or figure. Aquinas locates the effective power of the sacrament in the virtue of christic presence even as he delineates the ways in which the communicant engages interpretively with the sacramental elements. This is to say that in the Thomist formulation, the sign is understood simultaneously as a figure or similitude and as an object whose value is inherent by virtue of its identity with the substance of Christ's body. Even as this formulation invites an interpretive encounter with the eucharistic elements, which indicate figurally the principles of spiritual nourishment, charity, mercy, and sacrifice, as well as the abiding presence of Christ during what Aquinas calls the "peregrinatione," or pilgrimage, of life,[26] it also asserts that the sign has essential and efficacious meaning in and of itself because it has become sacramentally identical to the body of Christ.

Throughout the centuries of Christianity leading up to the Reformation, the Sacrament of the Altar is treated as an event in which corporeal experience is not extricable from hermeneutic activity, the perceptible sign not disseverable from its holy signified. Early exegetical writings on the Eucharist display a remarkable willingness to allow the materialist and figural valences of the ritual to maintain themselves in fruitful tension with one another. Indeed, the doctrine of transubstantiation is, as Thomas makes clear, entirely dependent upon a set of analogical associations: the body of Christ is unavailable to the bodily eye, but it is made present by means of a symbolic figure; likewise, the more figural perspective on the sacrament's effects, described so influentially by Augustine, is secured by the good bishop's insistence on the substantial reality of the divine body figured forth in bread and wine. And while it is plainly inaccurate to consider sixteenth-century Protestantism as a cohesive organization united in doctrine and creed, or to imagine, as Ross seems to do, that the sacramental program of the Reformation was to create irremediable lines of division between body and spirit, yet it is not too much to observe that as currents of receptionism and memorialism were introduced ever more fervently into the theological conversation over the course of the sixteenth century, it became increasingly possible to conceive of a sacramental system in which the referential meaning of signs may be divorced from the signs themselves. Where in the Lateran Council's doctrinal canonization of transubstantiation the elements of the sacrament are transformed in essence into the body of Christ, sixteenth-century challenges to that formulation called into question the manner of association between corporeality and the spirit, and interrogated the material reality of Christ's presence in the sacramental signs. In working through shifting conceptions of the significative status of the physical world, Reformation debates about the sacrament—the defining controversy of the Reformation itself—focus precisely on the relationship between signs and signifieds, presence and representation, materiality and tropology. To put it another way, the history of eucharistic theology in the sixteenth century is a history of theories about the operations of signification and figuration.

The shared investments of sacramental theology and language are confronted directly by Swiss reformer Huldreich Zwingli, whose paradigm-shifting assertions about the nature of the Eucharist are based explicitly in the figural qualities of linguistic representation. Zwingli and his followers contend that the sacrament functions as a trope, as "sacrae rei, hoc est factae gratuae signum. Credo esse invisibilis gratiae, quae scilicit dei munere facta & data est, visibilem figuram sive formam, hoc est visibile exemplum, quod tamen fere analogiam quandam rei per spiritum" [a sign of a sacred thing, i.e., of grace that has been given. I believe that it is a visible figure or form of the invisible grace, provided and bestowed by God's bounty; i.e., a visible example which presents an analogy to something done by the Spirit].[27] He elaborates:

Ex his enim fit manifestissimum quod veteres semper symbolice locuti cum corporis Christi in cœna esui tantum tribuerunt, puta, non quod sacramentalis manducatio mundare animum posset, sed fides in deum per Iesum Christum, quae spiritualis est manducatio, cuius externa ista symbolum est & adumbratio. Et quemadmodum panis corpus sustinet, vinum vegetat, et exhilarat, sic animum firmat & certum facit de misericordia dei, quod filium suum nobis dedit.

[It becomes very evident that the ancients always spoke figuratively when they attributed so much to the eating of the body of Christ in the Supper meaning, not that sacramental eating could cleanse the soul but faith in God through Jesus Christ, which is spiritual eating, whereof this external eating is but symbol and show. And as bread sustains the body and wine enlivens and exhilarates, thus it strengthens the soul and assures it of God's mercy that he has given us his son.][28]

For Zwingli, the communicant, while considering the sacramental elements, is provoked to reflect on the divine principles of cleansing and sustenance to which the signs refer, an association that even in its evacuation of divine presence endows the signs of bread and wine with special value. As Zwingli explains elsewhere,

Res arduas significant. Ascendit autem euiusq; signi pretium cum aestimatione rei cuius est signum. Ut si res sit magna, pretiosa, et amplifica, iam signum eius rei eo maius reputetur. . . . Sic panis & vinum amicitiae illus quo deus humano generi per filium suum reconciliatus est, symbola sunt, quae non aestimamus pro materiae oretuim sed iuxta significatae rei magnitudinem.
[They signify sublime things. Now the value of every sign increases with the worth of the thing of which it is the sign, so that if the thing be great, precious, and sublime, its sign is, therefore, accounted the greater. . . . So the bread and wine are the symbols of that friendship by which God has been reconciled to the human race through his Son, and we value them not according to the price of the material but according to the greatness of the thing signified.][29]

By amplifying the concept of referentiality in the Eucharist, Zwingli paradoxically foregrounds the sign *qua* sign—that is to say, in correlating the objective value of the sign to the thing it signifies, Zwingli also recognizes that a sign itself *has* an objective value. Indeed, the intrinsic value of the sign as a material object provides the means by which we comprehend the signified:

Visus cum panem videt ac calicem . . . Christum enim velut ante oculos conspicit, quem mens eius inflammata pulchritudine deperit.

Tactus panem in manus sumit, qui iam nō panis sed Christus est
significatione. Gustus Olfacts'q; & ipsi huc advocantur, ut odorent
quam suavis sit dominus, quam'q; beatus sit qui in illo fidit.
[When the sight sees the bread and cup . . . it sees Christ, as it were,
before the eyes, as the heart, kindled by His beauty, languishes for
Him. The touch takes the bread into its hands—the bread which is
no longer bread but Christ by representation. The taste and smell
are brought in to scent the sweetness of the Lord and the happiness
of his that trusteth in Him.][30]

Though those opposed to Zwingli's sacramental theology dismiss his ritual
symbolary as "bare tokens,"[31] Zwingli's explication of the tropes of the
Eucharist postulates the sign as crucial because it is the material object of
encounter, because it must be confronted as the apprehensible term of a
hermeneutic act distinct from but assistive to its content. His formulation,
shifting from one model of interpretive event to another, from sensorily
imperceptible corporeal change to figurative memorialism, asserts the matter of the bread and wine as objects for meaningful sensory engagement,
an approach that recognizes the sign itself—in and beyond its referential
function—as a legitimate site of sacramental participation.[32]

Zwingli's contentions turn the attention of Reformation theologians
upon the question of the precise manner in which a sign interacts with its
content, and upon the phenomenon of signification generally; in one way
or another, each of the developing strains of sacramental theology over the
course of the sixteenth century responds to the Zwinglian perspective, and
thereby engages in a debate about the significative qualities of materiality.
A generation after Zwingli's period of greatest productivity, John Calvin
situated his own view of the sacrament against what he considered the
errors of both Zurich and Rome, warning, "ne aut in extenuandis signis
nimii, a suis mysteriis ea divellere, quibus quodammodo annexa sunt: aut
in iisdem extollendis immedici, mysteria interim etiam ipsa nonnihil ob-
scurare videamur" [neither let us be seen diminishing the signs overmuch
by wresting them from the mysteries to which they are in some fashion
connected; nor extolling them immoderately so as to obscure in some way
the mysteries themselves]. As he defines his position against these perceived
misformulations of the sacrament, Calvin reveals that his primary anxiety
concerns, again, the status of the sacramental elements as signs. The Lord's
Supper, Calvin argues, offers a tangible symbol or seal of grace, which "rem

illic signatam effert et exhibet" [offers and exhibits the reality there signi-
fied]. It is against the specter of Zwingli's argument that Calvin commits
himself most explicitly when he takes up the question of referentiality and
metaphor, parsing out the immanent meaningfulness of the eucharistic
signs in and of themselves. It is worth quoting Calvin's rather lengthy articulation of the relationship between the "symbolum" of bread and the "res,"
or real thing, it symbolizes:

> Nec est, quod obiiciat quispiam figuratam esse loquutionem, qua
> signatae rei nomen signo deferatur. Fateor sane, fractionem panis
> symbolum esse, non rem ipsam. Verum hoc posito, a symboli tamen
> exhibitione rem ipsam exhiberi, rite colligemus . . . . Itaque si per
> fractionem panis Dominus corporis sui participationem vere
> repraesentat, minime dubium esse debet, quin vere praestet atque
> exhibeat. Atque omnino istaec piis tenenda regula est, ut quoties
> symbola vident a Domino instituta, illic rei signatae veritatem adesse
> certo cogitent ac sibi persuadeant. Quorsum enim corporis sui sym-
> bolum tibi Dominus in manum porrigat, nisi ut de vera eius partici-
> patione te certiorem faciat? Quodsi verum est, praeberi nobis
> signum visibile ad obsignandam invisibilis rei donationem, accepto
> corporis symbolo, non minus corpus etiam ipsum nobis dari certo
> confidamus.
>
> [Nobody can object that this is a figurative expression by which the
> name of the thing signified is given to the sign. Indeed, I acknowl-
> edge the breaking of bread to be a symbol, not the thing itself. But
> having posted this, we nevertheless infer that by the showing of the
> symbol the thing itself is also shown. . . . Therefore, if through the
> breaking of bread the Lord represents the participation of his body,
> there ought not to be the slightest doubt that he truly presents and
> shows himself therein. And the pious ought by all means to hold to
> this rule, that whenever they see symbols appointed by the Lord,
> they should think and be persuaded that the truth of the thing signi-
> fied is certainly present there. Why should the Lord put in your
> hand the symbol of his body, except to make certain his true partici-
> pation in it? But if it is true, that to us a visible sign is offered to seal
> the gift of a thing invisible, when the symbol of the body has been
> received, let us trust with just such a certainty that the body itself is
> also given to us.][33]

As Calvin takes care to distinguish the "figuratum" of Zwingli's referential sacrament from the "symbolum" of a sacrament in which God is actually present, he lays out a ritual in which signs become mysteriously and efficaciously substantial. In asserting elsewhere that "the inward substance of the sacrament is annexed to the visible signs," Calvin argues for a material encounter with the signs themselves because the reality they signify inheres in them.[34] Where Zwingli argues that the sign demands to be addressed as a distinct and assistive reality, Calvin insists that the "symbolum" manifests the fullness of the "res." This recognition leads Calvin into an argument that has aesthetic implications: "Hac ratione Augustinus sacramentum verbum visibile nuncupat: quod Dei promissiones velut in tabula depictas repraesentet, et sub aspectum graphice atque εἰκονικῶς expressas statuat" [For this reason Augustine calls a sacrament a visible word: because it represents the promises of God just as if they were depicted in a picture, and places beneath our gazes an *icon*, a verisimilitude masterfully expressed].[35] Calvin's comparison registers the proximity between the symbolic action of the sacrament and the symbolic action of art, a similarity that does not differentiate the literary from the pictorial. Indeed, by understanding both eucharistic and verbal signs as kinds of icon, Calvin foregrounds their physical valences, offering a conception of signs that maintains their visual presence, their perceptible materiality. From this perspective, the sacramental elements are experienced as aesthetic objects of devotion, appealing to the spiritual precisely because they are material.

It is this legacy to which the English divines of the late sixteenth and early seventeenth centuries are heir. As the Elizabethan church formulates its developing position out of wildly divergent confessional affinities, its theologians are at pains to justify a persistent sense that the eucharistic signs *matter*, in both senses of that term—that the bread and wine are both significant and significantly material. Mid-century reformer Nicholas Ridley, who rejects a doctrine of Real Presence, also rejects a view of the sacramental elements as "common baken bread . . . a bare sign, or a figure, to represent Christ, none otherwise than the ivy-bush doth represent the wine in a tavern; or as a vile person gorgeously apparelled may represent a king or a prince in a play"; rather, he asserts, Christ is effectually present in the bread in "the propertie of hys substance."[36] Edwin Sandys, who would become Archbishop of York under Elizabeth, calls the sacrament "a figure effectual,"[37] and the Thirty-Nine Articles adopt similar language, describing sacraments as "effectual signs" even as they insist that "The body of Christ is given, taken, and eaten, in the supper, only after an heavenly and spiritual manner."[38] Richard Hooker's moderate synthesis of an ecclesiastical standard promotes a clear receptionism, but continues to dwell upon the importance of the sacramental elements for spiritual participation: "The breade and Cup are his body and bloud because they are causes instrumentall vpon the receipt whereof the *participation* of his body and bloude ensueth. For that which produceth any certaine effect is not vainely nor improperly said to be that very effect wherunto it tendeth. Euery cause is in the effect which groweth from it." The bread and wine are here "instrumentall," each conceivable as a cause distinct from but effectually bound to the end it produces: "to us they are thereby made such instrumentes as misticallie yet truely, inuisibliy yet really worke our communion or fellowship with the person of Iesus Christ." And even as Hooker states clearly that the body and blood of Christ are "onely in the very hart and soule of him which receiueth them," the statement immediately following this receptionist declaration emphasizes that the elements are remarkable for the significatory work they do: "As for the Sacraments they really exhibit . . . that grace which with them or by them it pleaseth God to bestow."[39] That Hooker commends the capacity of the sacramental elements to "really exhibit" reveals the peculiar materiality of their instrumental force: it is precisely because the bread and wine are material, apprehensible objects that they can serve a sacramental function, manifesting the divine through their corporeality. Indeed, Lancelot Andrewes explicitly identifies the eucharistic elements as embodying "a kind of hypostatical union of the sign and the thing signified," and extends this association further, determining that the signifying properties of sacramental elements make them akin to Christ in his incarnation: "even as in the Eucharist neither part is evacuate or turned into the other, but abide each still in his former nature and substance . . . each nature remaineth still full and whole in his own kind. And backwards; as the two natures in Christ, so the *signum* and *signatum* in the Sacrament, *e converso*."[40]

Andrewes's sermon makes clear that these questions of how signs mean reflect ultimately on the spiritual status of the material. The perceptible objects of bread and wine in eucharistic worship guarantee the immanence of the divine in the physical world, but in the perceptual absence of their holy signified, the sacramental elements and one's encounter with them become the nexus of spiritual engagement. The sign becomes, in eucharistic worship, the principle of presence, and thus the object not only of interpretation but, as we have seen, of anxiety, obsession, and desire. Ryan Netzley has persuasively argued that the sacrament posits not the problem of divine absence but the problem of immanent desire. His 2011 study *Reading, Desire, and the Eucharist in Early Modern Religious Poetry* investigates the challenge of approaching the sacrament with the appropriate recognition of the fullness of presence, a stance made necessary given that "even the theological underpinnings of this communion ritual foreground the problem of desiring signs and seals in their own right." Netzley uses the model of desire offered by the Eucharist—that is, desiring a sign for its own sake—to explore its effects on reading, and argues that the poetry of the early seventeenth century is invested in treating the activities of both desiring and reading themselves as "intrinsically valuable devotional practices."[41] In its adroit claim that eucharistic theology influences reading practices, Netzley's argument delineates the ways in which receptionism transfers readily from the sacramental to the textual. His work invites the logically prior question of how Reformation eucharistic theology influences *representational* practices by reconceiving the sign as intrinsically valuable. For as religious reformers emphasize the capacity of *signs as such* to be meaningful, or perhaps *meaning-full*, they outline the parameters of a plenitudinous symbology that redounds to the literary. The Reformation drives, and is driven by, an unprecedentedly vigorous and systemic public discussion about signification, one that takes as its central focus of interrogation the vexed relationship between being and meaning. The model of devotion that emerges out of sixteenth century theology is, finally, textual.

In the wake of such a sustained controversy in which sublimity, materiality, and signification itself are fused together, it should come as no surprise that the questions at the heart of these disputes should ramify into poetry. Lyric poetry in general and the devotional lyric in particular are dedicated to the principle of evoking presence, and it is inevitable that such an enterprise would respond to such explicit and enduring pressures on the mode and manner of signification in this ritual of presence. For post-Reformation writers, the Eucharist stands not only as the central sacrament of Christian worship and the fiercest flashpoint of Reformation dispute, but also as the sacrament whose efficacy is understood to be contingent on questions of signification and the matter (again, in both senses of that term) of words. Nor is it adequate to suggest that the poetic effects of this controversy are confessionally limited—to claim, for example, that post-Reformation poetry exhibits a distinctly Protestant poetics in its word-centered pieties, or that it clings bravely to an imperiled Catholic system of valorized materiality. It is more accurate to say that post-Reformation poetry is self-consciously engaged with its own capacities—and failures—to manifest presence, and thus registers vividly the ways in which signification informs and is informed by eucharistic controversy. Indeed, when we consider Schwartz's passing remark that "While theologians argued about the status of signs in the Eucharist . . . the *mysteries* of the Eucharist gave Reformation *poets* little difficulty," that assertion becomes increasingly puzzling.[42] For, as we have seen, the status of signs is inextricable from the central mystery of the Eucharist, and in displaying an obsessive concern with that mystery in its very poetics, the seventeenth-century lyric announces its difficult theological inheritance. Particularly in the devotional lyric of the English seventeenth century, poets confront directly and explicitly the presence-making capacities of the tangible sign, and probe the relationship between the unsublimable materiality of the text and its potential as an instrument of referentiality.

As a genre, poetry is distinguished by the ways in which it generally emphasizes the communicative properties of its nondenotative features to produce a self-aware and objective textuality, a self-affirming textual objecthood.[43] That is to say, poetry is a formal practice fundamentally invested in the substantiality of its own medium, not only as a mechanism for generating referentiality, narration, mimesis, and other discursive acts but for its own sake. Indeed, the dynamic interaction of referentiality and materiality underwrites poetic utterance, as on the one hand the designative function suggests the transparency of the word, while on the other hand the formal conspicuities of poetic language intrude into that designative function, asserting the word as a sonic, rhythmic, and spatial object. As Mutlu Konuk Blasing writes, "The incommensurability of the semiotic/formal and the semantic/symbolic systems is perceivable as an immediate experience in poetic language, for they work at each other's expense. A poem, far from being a text where sound and sense, form and meaning, are indissolubly one, is a text where we witness the *distinct* operations of the two systems. We cannot do both at once, and poetic language will not allow us to ignore either system."[44] As poetry elaborates its devices into the sensorium, it destabilizes the referential function of words, an interplay that trains hermeneutic attention on the linguistic surface, thwarting interpretive transparency. Formal patterns of recurrence rely on corporeally available qualities of language: schemes using rhyme and alliteration, assonance and consonance, and the alternating and variable stress patterns of meter contribute to the semantic meaning of a poem, but they do not themselves constitute semantic meaning. Likewise, the positioning of words on a page, including but not limited to the line breaks that interrupt the horizontal progress of language and activate perceptions of the spatiality of text, intrudes into the accumulation of semiotic information. These features interpose a textual substantiality that resists being "read through" to some stable and defined "real meaning" or content. Similarly, figurative language emphasizes the estrangement or incommensurability of the terms which it links, irrupting as difference into the conciliatory urges of meaning-making.[45] In Blasing's terms, these poetic processes work to "foreground the mechanism of the code" because they present to the apprehension language per se, as an artifact of encounter.[46] It would not be inappropriate here to reframe this theoretics in the language of Reformation theology: such features work to emphasize the sign as effectual, and meaning-full, objects as such—that is, objects in which significance inheres.

Though the field of his primary study is some centuries removed from early modern England, Charles Bernstein's analysis of the extent to which poetry foregrounds its own presence on the page is particularly relevant to the poetics that develops out of the Reformation and is influenced by that era's renegotiations of the capacities of the sign to manifest immanence. (Again, it is precisely to my point to note that Bernstein's diction sounds a strong echo to the theological treatises of the sixteenth century.) The mark on the page, argues Bernstein,

> is the visible sign of writing.
> But reading, insofar as it consumes &
> absorbs the mark, erases it—the words disappear
> (the transparency effect) & are replaced by
> that which they depict, their "meaning" . . . Antiabsorptive
> writing recuperates the mark by making it opaque,
> that is, by maintaining its visibility
> & undermining its meaning, where "meaning" is
> understood in the narrower, utilitarian sense
> of a restricted economy.[47]

As what Bernstein calls "antiabsorptive" writing foregrounds the nondenotative qualities of its language, it impedes "the transparency effect," in which meaning is conceived as somehow standing behind the words, waiting to be claimed. Antiabsorptive writing must be negotiated not merely as a set of referential signs but as an object, which status confers presence rather than implying absence (e.g., the absence, among other things, of the signified):

> The visibility of words
> as a precondition of reading
> necessitates that words obtrude impermeably into
> the world. . . . The thickness
> of words ensures that whatever
> of their physicality is erased, or engulfed, in
> the process of semantic projection,
> a residue
> tenaciously in-
> heres that will not be sublimated
> away.[48]

Moreover, as Bernstein goes on to suggest, as poetic utterance both invites an encounter with semantic absorption and frustrates that encounter by dint of its opaque objecthood, the intersection of those registers of textual experience "is precisely / flesh,"—or, more precisely, it is "the flesh of the word":

> The tenacity of
> writing's thickness, like the body's
> flesh, is
> ineradicable. . . .
> The thickness of writing between
> the reader & the poem is constitutive for the poem
> of its visibility & for the reader
> of the outer limit of his or her absorption
> in the poem; it is not an obstacle
> between them, it is their means
> of communication.[49]

Those features that prevent readerly absorption into a poem, that prevent the poetic text from yielding transparently to "meaning," do not prevent the matter of the poem, as Bernstein observes here; they constitute the matter of the poem.

In the lyric mode, this general poetic investment in presencing capacities of language extends to the manifestation of the lyric subject or "I," the speaker who functions in the poem as the principle of aesthetic presence. That is, in the lyric poem, the speaker serves as an embodiment of the concern with making present to the senses that which is phenomenally absent. Susan Stewart connects the speaker's position with the significative operation of language explicitly. The central concern of the lyric, she argues, is "to make visible, tangible, and audible the figures of persons" as a strategy against what she identifies as the central crisis of the lyric: "the fading of the referent." In this light, those poetic devices of prosody, form, sound, and so forth become strategies of recuperation as well as presence, lineamenting an otherwise perceptually absent speaker in perceptible structures. Stewart calls these elements "The poet's recompense" because the sense impressions they produce ensure that the poetic encounter is an essentially material one; this material encounter is not limited to the matter of the book with its pages and ink (though these qualities certainly shape a literary encounter) but extends to include these strategies by which the signs of language are concrete and perceptible manifestations of the imperceptible.[50] On this point, Stewart's argument is indebted to Allen Grossman's *Summa Lyrica*, whose foundational claim is that "Poetry is language in which the eidetic function is prior to all other functions. Indeed, the meaning of most claims for poetic language (that it is 'divine,' 'primordial,' etc.) is that poetic language, by contrast to other kinds of language, has no other function than the eidetic function."[51] As Grossman articulates it, all the tools of poetic language serve to manifest presence, the presence of the poem itself, and of the speaker whose presence is co-terminous with the poem's. Working to this end, the nonreferential components of poetic speech—again, rhyme, meter, structure, figure, and so forth—become epiphanic instruments in that they constitute and reveal the poem, making it present to the reader.

The lyric's fundamental concern with what Grossman calls "the presence of presence" produces a state of affairs in which the assertively nonreferential mechanisms of poetic devices define the text's substantial form. The principle of presence in the lyric thus is delineated within the energetic exchange between the semantic impulse toward the signified and the irrepressible materiality of the sign. The similarities between the priorities of the lyric poem and the notion of a Real Presence in the sacrament are clear. For the Eucharist too is primarily concerned with "the presence of presence," and with the capacities of material figures to *present* presence, as it were, in recompense for the promised but ultimately imperceptible reality of Christ's physical body.[52] Indeed, following Grossman and Stewart, it might be said that this sacrament is a ritual in which the eidetic function is prior to all other functions. The eucharistic event, at its most basic level, involves the worshipper's encounter with material signs for the substance of the body of Christ. The body of the communicant becomes an apparatus by which Christ's body can be both affirmed and meaningfully manifest, a site wherein presence *matters*. Again, this relational corporeality is reflected in the lyric, in which the structural investments of poetic language mandate a particularly bodily mode of engagement with the text on the part of the reader. Since presence is effected in the poem by means of sensorily apprehensible structures, the reader's body is enlisted as a device for registering that presence. In lyric poetry, as in the Eucharist, corporeality is an intrinsic component of the system of representation. It is, as Bernstein says, "their means / of communication."

Reformation-era sparring over the operation of the Eucharist offers, as we have seen, a range of opinions regarding the status of signs and, by implication, the role of the material in sacramental worship. But as reformers diverge from the Lateran dogma of the Eucharist, it is precisely the mode by which "the presence of presence" is achieved that becomes destabilized. By calling into question the manner of sacramental presence, the eucharistic debates of the early modern period disclose the ontological disjunction between sacramental signs and their divine referents. And while sixteenth-century exegetes were not unaware of what we would now call the semiotic consequences of their controversy (even this chapter's cursory survey of Reformation writings on the Eucharist reads like a veritable primer in semiotics!), it is in the poetry of the post-Reformation period that these consequences are most fully registered. For in their fixation on the perceptual absence of Christ's body and on the mechanisms by which that absence is redressed, and in their reimagining of the Eucharist's underlying assumptions regarding the capacity of signs to manifest corporeal presence, reformers interrogate the very phenomena that animate lyric poetry.

Lyric poetry in early modern England begins to exhibit a suite of characteristics that can only be understood as a direct response to Reformation controversies over the Eucharist. And while the effects of this reaction can be felt in sacred and secular poetry alike, they are most pointedly evident in the devotional lyric, which not coincidentally emerges in English poetry in an extraordinary efflorescence during the early seventeenth century. Certainly, a number of factors contributed to the development of such a strong tradition of devotional poetry, including the availability of the Bible as both a generic sourcebook and a common storehouse of phrases and stories, and the humanist revitalization of the idea that the poet is a kind of inspired prophet, uniquely qualified to address divine things.[53] Such cultural conditions doubtless go some way toward explaining the predominance of devotional writing in the period, but they do not account for the startling development, in the seventeenth-century English lyric, of poetic strategies that simultaneously assert the linguistic sign as an intractable and unsublimable object and the central role of the body as a communicative and a perceptual instrument.[54] The persistence of this trend over the course of the seventeenth century and across confessional divides argues against attributing this development to a broadly defined tradition of Protestant poetics; neither can we align it with some generalized nostalgia for the theological certainties of pre-Reformation religion. Rather, the Reformation's long dispute about the mechanics of sacramental worship catalyzes a poetics that foregrounds the ritual's inherent tensions between material surface and imperceptible substance, between sign and signified, between flesh and spirit, a poetics remarkably attuned to the complicated interdependence of the body and the word.

The phenomenon I wish to address here is, again, not some preponderance of talk about the body in seventeenth-century poetry, nor am I interested in locating in the early modern lyric tradition a set of theological treatises with line breaks. Indeed, if theological argument is the goal, poetry offers a circumlocuting and inefficient means to such an end. Instead, I wish to demonstrate that the seventeenth century witnesses the development in English poetry of particular poetic strategies that directly respond to the hermeneutic challenges of sacramental worship and replicate its conflicts. Though I will naturally attend to the arguments of poems, this study's primary concern involves poetics as opposed to thematic content; for, as Brian Cummings observes, "It is at the surface of discourse that the nexus of grammar and grace is found. It is here that the anxieties and tensions of early modern religion are revealed."[55] The poetry of the period, especially when it addresses devotional concerns, deploys a set of structural and representational tactics that emphasize the objecthood of language, both as material artifact on the page and as representational surface. Seventeenth-century poetry displays a marked unwillingness to allow the word to become a mere transparent conduit to some imperceptible referent, rather asserting the priority of the sign and problematizing its relationship to any signified. The poetry of Donne, Herbert, and other writers of the period exhibits a strange fixation on the physicalizing potentialities of its own language, calling attention to the lineaments of structure, prosody, and sound even as it probes the capacity of language to function symbolically. The effect of these strategies in concert is to arrest readerly absorption—that is, to prevent the dissolution of the sign into the signified, the word into content. The antiabsorptive turn in the post-Reformation lyric asserts the significance of the material in the representational ground, and so conserves in the material a mechanism for presence. To put it another way, by maintaining readerly awareness of the substantiality of words, the post-Reformation lyric provides an event in which reading becomes an encounter with fully present signs.

The substantiality of poetic elements, already crucial to the presencing project of the lyric, are in post-Reformation poetry enlisted into a program of corporealized signification urgently connected to the theological developments of the sixteenth century. By exploring the poetic effects of the materiality of the word, both ontologically and receptionally, the poetics that develops during the early seventeenth century negotiates the same difficulties that animated sacramental reforms. Like the Eucharist itself, such a poetics explores its own capacity to actualize presence, for in the same way that the sacrament is ultimately concerned with reenacting or recalling Christ's Incarnation by manifesting divinity in the material world, seventeenth-century poetry implements a poetics radically invested in plumbing the representational reach of the Word made flesh. And just as Reformation debates about the operation of the Eucharist seek to resolve the ways in which presence inheres in the representational scheme of the sacrament, the devotional poetry of the seventeenth century proclaims its investment in the incarnational capacity of language to realize presence. The seventeenth-century lyric witnesses the development of a set of poetic strategies provocatively resistant to spiritualized readings—that is, readings that would displace the object for its meaning, the sign for the signified. The eucharistic poetics of the seventeenth century react to the rhetorical implications of sacramental discourse in which the presence of the Word becomes extricable from the presentational capacities of the word.

Made Flesh charts the ways in which seventeenth-century poetic practice negotiates the strange triangulation of body, word, and meaning in the

Sacrament of the Altar and effectively reproduces the interpretive challenges of sacramental worship. In the materially invested poetics of the
post-Reformation period in England, presence is asserted as a perceptual
phenomenon, and the axis of presence is relocated from the signified to the
sign itself. In accomplishing such a shift, this poetics ensures the interpretive persistence, the *significance*, of the material in the face of the precarious
sacramentality of the phenomenal world. The material becomes thus a
recourse against the perceptual inapprehensibility of sacramental presence,
and holds out the promise of holy immanence in the world, of the very
kind established by the Incarnation itself. Indeed, it might be tempting to
label this poetics as *incarnational* rather than as *eucharistic* were it not for
the pervasive concern with the activity of representation in both poems and
sacrament—a correspondence amplified when the poems address explicitly
the manner of Christ's presence in the Eucharist and the mode of its operation. Though that theological commentary may be inconsistent from poem
to poem, and though the poetics of a poem often complicates, subverts, or
belies its theological assertions, devotional poetry's thematic awareness of
the theological and representational issues in play in the sacrament of the
Lord's Supper makes it a lively platform for observing eucharistic poetics
at work. These texts provide a richly self-aware sample of peculiar poetic
strategies designed to disrupt the transparent action of interpretation and
to make of reading a bodily event, one that finally sustains the material as
a site of immanent presence.

This study limits the primary field of its survey to the devotional poetry
of the seventeenth century, though, as my concluding chapter will demonstrate, the poetic developments I trace here ramify into the broader poetic
landscape and inform the production of poetry for centuries to come. Chapters 1 and 2 of this book explore one mode of poetic response to the problem
of absent presence, in which the communicative properties of poetic structure
are marshaled as a means of securing the lyric event to its textual substantiality. As a sensorily apprehensible set of signs that lineament presence, the
poetic text has an *a priori* investment in the ways in which form itself communicates, and in how structure offers a kind of significance that precedes
semantics. It is natural that the expressivities of form should become a center
of gravity for eucharistic poetics. Exploiting poetic form as a communicative
end in itself—that is, as an objective textual feature whose meaning is self-
contained rather than referential—the seventeenth-century lyric makes
increasing use of the architectural objecthood of the poetic text and, in so

doing, relocates significance from the strictly abstract and perceptually unavailable sphere of the signified to the sign.

Chapter 1 of this book examines the aggressively corporeal innovations of George Herbert's *The Temple*, a collection of poems characterized by extravagant formal invention, in which the manifestly constructed object-hood of signs secures the material ontology of the incarnate Word. Herbert's verse constantly asserts its own poetic surfaces, emphasizing the sonic and graphic qualities of language so forcefully that the reader becomes radically aware of the experience of encountering signs. This treatment reflects an approach to eucharistic worship, sometimes articulated in Herbert's own pastoral writings, in which the physical aspects of sacramental participation serve to recall and celebrate the Incarnation. Herbert's poetic texts register the incarnational potential of the sign in both language and in sacrament, and I explore the ways in which his assertions of objecthood make of poetry a ritual of material immanence against the absence of the divine.

The signifying properties of form and their implications for the material experience of sacramental worship remain my focus in Chapter 2, which investigates the interventions of poetic structure into eucharistic theology in the poetry of Edward Taylor. Taylor, writing a generation after Herbert and (like so many others) in the shadow of *The Temple*, redirects his anxiety about the absence of God into a suspicion about his own qualification to participate in sacramental worship. In Taylor's nonconforming Calvinist view, the Lord's Supper is a nuptial banquet, effecting a marriage between the soul and God, but even as he in his ministerial position advocates that every worshipper who approaches this "Wedden Feast" should inspect himself to ensure that he is properly regenerate, Taylor necessarily confronts the difficulty of determining regeneracy. For Taylor, the absence of an apprehensible sign from God that the soul is regenerate, which is itself a symptom of God's ultimate inapprehensibility, redounds to the absence of stable signs for the self's righteousness. The perceptual lacuna at the heart of Taylor's sacramental concerns is simultaneously God's and the soul's, each eluding the certainty of the senses. Without the assurance of sense-data, Taylor turns to poetic form, using it as a sensorily legible proxy, a kind of body for the intangible soul. In Taylor's long lyric cycle of *Preparatory Meditations*, the poetic text comes to embody his own process of regeneracy, demonstrating structurally the poem's ever-repeating desire to purge sin and prove ready for Christ's grace. That Taylor models this cyclical project of purgation and desire after the menstrual cycle concords with his view of the "Wedden Feast," in which the soul must become the Bride of Christ, a gendered construct that again flouts the evidence of the senses. Taylor's poetic body offers an alternative physicality in which the gendered valences of sacramental worship can be satisfied even as it offers a knowable embodiment of the unknowable soul.

My initial focus on structure and form as instruments for producing an antiabsorptive textual materiality gives way in the latter chapters of this book to an investigation of what happens when such an approach gets absorbed into the system of symbolic signification. Structural innovation produces one kind of hermeneutic arrest; another occurs when symbol itself responds to this same urge toward objecthood. Certainly poetic form and structure are fundamentally invested in the relationship between linguistic surfaces and semantic meanings, and the status of the text as an object in its own right in addition to a referential instrument aligns it interpretively with the eucharistic elements. But this scheme has implications, too, for the symbolic use of language, particularly when symbol is employed to represent the divine. If the Eucharist, that holiest of symbolaries, resists interpretive access and denies absorption through transparent symbols to the heart of their sacred meanings, how might a poetics informed by such a system negotiate the competing demands of the referentiality and the discursive surface of symbol? In the second movement of this book, I concentrate on two poets whose work explores precisely this question. Chapter 3 reveals that while John Donne shares with Taylor an enthusiasm for biblical metaphor, and like Taylor freely appropriates figurative conventions that have been normalized into the general religious lexicon, his treatment of those conventions is complicated by his stake not in the achievement of its primary symbol (as is Taylor's hope) but in the persistence of unsublimated corporeality such that the referential function of that symbol is obstructed. In other words, Donne's physicalized embroideries of traditional symbols render them no longer functional *as symbols*, no longer conducive to revealing the meanings with which they are conventionally associated. For Donne, the particularizing of the sign renders it more opaque, more substantial, and as a consequence more durable than the ephemeral signified. Donne's recourse to common scriptural tropes upends whatever currency they possess through their familiarity; in Donne's hands, such theological conventions as the Bride of Christ and the glorious resurrection of the flesh become shockingly unfamiliar precisely because they endure as ends in themselves rather than as transparent symbols referring to abstract spiritual principles. In his refusal to allow tropes to transluce into meaning, Donne locates spiritual significance not in the disembodied and abstract sphere but in the body itself.

I finally examine the work of Richard Crashaw, whose rococo aesthetic tendencies have relegated him to the periphery of critical interest in seventeenth-century literature. Indeed, most critics seem not to know what to do with Crashaw: his work is seen variously as grotesque or as hopelessly primitive because of what is perceived as its indecorous integration of discomfitingly physical language into the devotional depiction of sacred scenes. But Crashaw's dissonant style is not, I argue, evidence of his poetic immaturity so much as it is a canny replication of the interpretive problems, as Crashaw himself articulates them, of eucharistic worship. Foremost among these problems, as a number of Crashaw's poems allow, is that the senses are simultaneously activated and defied by the ritual of the Eucharist, a contradiction that prompts in Crashaw a real ambivalence about both the role of the body in sacramental worship and the integrity of sacramental representation. For Crashaw, the material remains vexingly, maddeningly present in a rite that argues against its relevance, and this presence gets recorded in Crashaw's devotional verse as an obstruction to locating divinity in the Eucharist. Moreover, Crashaw sees clearly how the contradictory demands of the rite impinge upon the system of representation itself. The signature excesses of Crashaw's style bring to bear an insurmountably corporeal poetics that expels the reader from the symbolic system of the sacrament. And where Donne compromises the sacramental symbolary at the level of the trope, Crashaw undermines the symbolic function of the word itself, foregrounding disjunctions in the representational project of the Eucharist in order to disclose its limited referential capacities.

Form and structure, trope and symbol: in the seventeenth-century lyric each of these materials of poetic *techne* are subjected to the pressure of a developing aesthetic imperative that would privilege the imperceptible abstract over the perceptible object. This innovation, borne ultimately out of the profound anxiety about reading and the status of the corporeal that attended the semantic revisions of the Reformation, makes of poetry an event that promotes the meaningfulness of the sensual world and argues for the fitness of that world for realizing presence objectively. Though the restoration of meaning to the corporeal transforms the poem into a process in which the sign and signified are estranged, post-Reformation poetics accomplishes what the Eucharist itself, by any confessional definition, cannot: it transforms—we may say *transubstantiates*—absence into perceptual presence. At issue here are the incarnational possibilities of representation and the capacities of the Word to take fleshly expression, which are the fundamental concerns of eucharistic worship.

More alive than any of his contemporaries to the fleshliness of the poem on the page, Herbert recognizes the sacramental quality of poetic form, and he invests his ingenious art with a sometimes playful self-awareness about its own status as an artifact, as a thing made to be present to a reader. Before continuing in later chapters to trace out subtler manifestations of antiabsorptive poetics, this study begins by addressing Herbert's conspicuous application of a sacramental representational scheme to the poetic medium. And though I begin with what some readers have dismissed as Herbert's ingenuous curiosities,[56] I aim in the end to demonstrate that the impulses that animate Herbert's ostentatious technique permeate all aspects of poetic craft in the seventeenth-century lyric—and continue to be felt long past the moment of the seventeenth century. For my conviction is that these strategies remain influential far beyond the period of heightened religious fervor that produced them, and my hope is that *Made Flesh* will suggest the persistence of post-Reformation poetic innovations into the later literary tradition. In short, my slightly immoderate ambition is to suggest that the stable of unsublimable, self-asserting flourishes of technique that we have come, in our enlightened postmodernity, to think of as *poetics* was effectively developed four hundred years ago by devotional poets.

Chapter 1

"The Bodie and the Letters Both": Textual Immanence in *The Temple*

In order to understand the ways in which George Herbert's elaborate experiments in poetic form are informed by the incarnational investments of
sacramental worship, we must first consider the theological landscape in
which Herbert produced *The Temple*. Though Herbert's era had not fully
resolved the controversies of the preceding century, Herbert himself
remains irenically reticent on the mechanics of eucharistic presence.
Indeed, of the poets whose work is examined in the present study, Herbert
is perhaps the least openly engaged in doctrinal and spiritual controversies.
Owing to this doctrinal restraint, the good rector of Bemerton has come to
be seen as an exemplar of the early seventeenth-century *via media*, a moder-
ated position that conflated English national identity with the English
church's ecclesiastical distinction both from Rome and from the fraught
doctrinal wranglings of continental Protestantism. Accordingly, in the decades concluding the twentieth century, as historical and literary studies have
attempted to define the theology of the Stuart church, Herbert studies have
registered these skirmishes as conflict over Herbert's confessional allegiance.[1] The English church's position on the precise mode of Christ's presence in the sacramental elements had evaded consistent definition since
Thomas Cranmer moved to revise the Book of Common Prayer during the
short reign of Edward VI. To appreciate the degree to which such efforts to
define the mysterious operation of the Eucharist had caused divisions
among English divines, we need only review Richard Hooker's handling of
the question: "Let it therefore be sufficient for me presenting my selfe at

the Lords Table to know what there I receiue from him, without searching
or inquiring of the maner how Christ performeth his promise; let disputes
and questions[,] enemies to pietie, abatements of true deuotion, and hith-
erto in this cause but ouer patiently heard let them take their rest; let curi-
ous and sharpe witted men beate their heades about what questions
themselues will . . . what these elements are in themselues it skilleth not, it
is enough that to me which take them they are the body & bloud of
Christ."[2] Though Hooker's call for a shift from disputation over "the maner
how" to affirmation that the sacrament does in truth perform Christ's
promise to offer his body and blood seems to provide a reasoned response
to controversy, it is nevertheless a bit disingenuous because the question of
whether the elements "are the body & bloud of Christ" is deeply entwined
with the manner in which that mystery occurs. And while Herbert seems
never to have explicitly entered into the theological debates surrounding
"the maner how" that flourished as suspicions of crypto-popery ran ram-
pant during the 1620s and beyond, he does not scruple to wrestle with "the
maner how" in a number of poems that consider the Eucharist directly. On
the contrary, Herbert's concern with the relationship between the material
species of bread and wine and the spiritual operation of Holy Communion
is evident throughout *The Temple* as well as in his other writings, both
poetry and prose. For Herbert, the sacrament asserts itself in both spiritual
and material registers, and their very inextricability both repeats the incarnational model of the Word made flesh and influences the representational
strategies of Herbert's poetic practice.

Herbert's literary canon would seem to offer a rich field for investigating
the ways in which the Eucharist informed and inspired seventeenth-century
devotional poetry. The sacrament provides the imaginative center for his
lyric collection, governing its organization as well as its subject matter.
Whether we consider his stable of images, with its reliance on familiar sacramental topoi like grapes, winepresses, vines, veins, and so forth, or regard
The Temple's overarching narrative of sacramental preparation culminating
in the feast of "Love (III)," or examine the poems that explicitly dramatize
participation in Communion, C. A. Patrides's conclusion that "The Eucharist is the marrow of Herbert's sensibility" feels entirely justified.[3] Perhaps
the most obvious place to begin a study of Herbert's engagement with
eucharistic theology is the pair of poems each given the title "The H. Communion," in which Herbert addresses directly the ritual and its operation.

In the version of "The H. Communion" that Herbert did not include in *The Temple,* the poet begins with a survey of theological claims about the mode of christic presence in the sacramental elements:

> O gratious Lord how shall I know
> Whether in these gifts thou bee so
>   As thou art evry-where;
> Or rather so, as thou alone
> Tak'st all yᵉ Lodging, leaving none
>   ffor thy poore creature there.[4]

In its first stanza, the poem presents two competing versions of eucharistic operation: Lutheran ubiquitarianism, which holds that Christ is substantially present in all things and by extension also in the bread and wine, and Roman transubstantiation, in which Christ's substance replaces that of the bread. But after considering these options, the poem adopts a tone of gentle mockery: "ffirst I am sure, whether bread stay / Or whether Bread doe fly away / Concerneth bread not mee" (7–9). Here, Herbert waves off the controversial question of the mode of Christ's presence, and the poem would seem to continue as if it pursued a poetic version of Hooker's counsel, letting disputations rest in the face of mystery: "But yᵗ both thou and all thy traine / Bee there, to thy truth, & my gaine / Concerneth mee & Thee" (10–12). The only matter worth addressing, suggests Herbert as if channeling Hooker, is not "the maner how" but that "Christ performeth his promise."

But Herbert's confidence about that performance seems to waver in the middle stanzas of the poem:

> That fflesh is there, mine eyes deny:
> And what shold flesh but flesh discry,
>   The noblest sence of five.
> If glorious bodies pass the sight
> Shall they be food & strength, & might
>   Euen there, where they deceiue? (31–36)

Herbert here identifies explicitly the fundamental interpretive problem of a ritual that proposes to make the divine present to man by means of a set of physical signs: "mine eyes deny." Herbert's inability to descry Christ's presence in the species of Communion leads him to question both the efficacy of the sacramental elements and the credibility of Christ, whose most glorious body remains most imperceptible in the sacrament that represents it. Michael C. Schoenfeldt reads this uncomfortable questioning as Herbert's discovery of "the wall that divides matter and spirit," and sees Herbert pursuing the consequences of that discovery into the assertions of his next stanza:[5]

> Into my soule this cannot pass;
> fflesh (though exalted) keeps his grass
>   And cannot turn to soule.
> Bodyes & Minds are different Spheres,
> Nor can they change their bounds & meres,
>   But keep a constant Pole. (37–42)

Despite the poem's professions of its own uninterest in "the maner how" Christ might be present in the sacramental elements, it spends twelve lines worrying about precisely that question: how can Christ be present to the soul in the Lord's Supper, especially in light of the fact that he is completely absent to the senses? Herbert's insistence that "Bodyes and Minds are different Spheres" may address the problem of Christ's sensory imperceptibility, but it also forecloses the possibility that God might be transmitted to the incorporeal soul by means of this corporeal ritual.

Herbert returns to the relationship between these "different Spheres" in his later poem also called "The H. Communion," which was included in *The Temple*. This poem opens by rejecting the idea that God employs material finery to communicate himself to man. "Not in rich furniture, or fine aray, / Nor in a wedge of gold" (1–2), Herbert insists, and although the imagery he refuses seems to invoke the ceremonial richness of the Mass, the poem's objection to such stuff has less to do with its confessional extravagance than with the fact that its materiality remains unassimilable: "For so thou should'st without me still have been" (5). The phrase "without me," in its conflation of physical separation and lack of possession, is attuned to the difficulty of apprehending God (in both physical and nonphysical senses of that verb) through a material medium. Though Schoenfeldt concludes that "The H. Communion" resolves this difficulty by

defining divine presence not as if it might be located in any external trappings but as an internal, spiritualized process, the poem nevertheless exhibits a continued preoccupation with the relationship between physical signs
and their immaterial referents:

> But by the way of nourishment and strength
>> Thou creep'st into my breast;
>> Making thy way my rest,
> And thy small quantities my length;
> Which spread their forces into every part,
>> Meeting sinnes force and art.

> Yet can these not get over to my soul,
>> Leaping the wall that parts
>> Our souls and fleshly hearts;
> But as th' outworks, they may control
> My rebel-flesh, and carrying thy name,
>> Affright both sinne and shame. (7–18)

After the poem's opening repudiation of luxurious trappings as a conduit
for Christ, the second stanza prefers a view of sacramental contact in which
the divine presence creeps in by "nourishment and strength," which
Schoenfeldt glosses as "the medium of food."[6] Herbert's echo of Cranmer's
sacramental formulation rings loudly enough here: Holy Communion,
explains Cranmer, is a "visyble sacrament of spirituall nourishment in
bread and wyne." Still, as Cranmer, and later Hooker, must acknowledge,
a conception that the spirit is nourished by means of the sacramental elements makes this process of spiritual sustenance discomfitingly inextricable
from the processes of the body. Cranmer goes on in the same passage to
say that the spiritual nourishment of the bread and wine is "to the intent,
that as muche as is possible for man, we may see Christe with our eies,
smell hym at our nose, taste hym with our mouthes, grope hym with oure
handes, and perceaue him with al our senses. For as the word of god
preached putteth Christe into our eares, so lykewise these elementes of
water, breade and wyne, ioyned to Goddes woorde, doo after a sacramentall
maner, put Christe into our eies, mouthes, handes, and all our senses."[7]
What Cranmer describes is a sacrament of dual significance, body and spirit
alike invigorated by the encounter with the elements of bread and wine. He

advocates that the communicant fuse the spiritual to the sensual, which Herbert's poem accomplishes in the slippage of its language between corporeal and noncorporeal registers. Just as in Herbert's phrase "nourishment and strength," the terminology of the poem's second stanza activates physical and spiritual associations as it charts the progress of the sacramental experience: Christ "creep'st into my breast," the poem reflects, suggesting both the abstracted seat of emotions and the vault of the body that encases those emotions. And when divine power manages to fill the speaker's "length" and to "spread . . . forces into every part," the physical suggestiveness of both "length" and "part" is supplemented by the way that this divine occupation develops at the stanza's end, for what it meets is not bodily substance but "sinnes force and art," a figurative army whose spiritual encampment cannot be pinpointed in fleshly coordinates. As Cranmer yokes the mouth, hands, and eyes to the spiritual apprehension of Christ in his rhapsody on sacramental contact, Herbert joins the physiological to the spiritual, such that the two modes of sacramental experience cannot be distinguished from one another.

In his attentive study *The Poetry of Immanence*, Robert Whalen steps away from the confessional squabbling of much twentieth-century criticism on Herbert in order to recognize (appropriately irenically) the poet's synthesis of sensual ceremonialism and internal spirituality; accordingly, Whalen acknowledges Herbert's investment in a Eucharist that maintains both spiritual and material significance. For Herbert, writes Whalen, it was important "to realize in the sacramental sign an effectual, objective communication of grace and not merely the outward symbol of a process with which it has no material connection." Though Whalen glances at the resemblance between the dual signification of Herbert's Eucharist and the Incarnation's mysterious joining of divine spirit to carnal flesh, Word to body, he seems not to appreciate the implications of that conjunction for Herbert's view of language generally, and of poetry in particular. Whalen rightly declares that "it is through the insistent fleshly status of the eucharistic species that the paradox of the Word become flesh is stubbornly proclaimed," but he does not mark the ways in which his own insight bears upon Herbert's poetics.[8] For both Communion and the Incarnation provide for Herbert a literary model in which the divine Logos gains significance by its material expression, a model that Herbert imitates in his own poetic texts. Whalen acknowledges that the material aspects of eucharistic presence "go to the very heart of [Herbert's] sacramental poetic,"[9] and his close readings are specific and sensitive to Herbert's eucharistic preoccupations, but he does not pursue his insights to discuss the way that Herbert's verse makes use of representational strategies that emphasize his poems as material artifacts—that is, the way they repeat the incarnational model of Communion. Or, to put this problem in the terms with which this book began, Whalen is admirably exhaustive in cataloguing *what* Herbert's poems say about the Eucharist but gives scant attention to *how* they say it.

The distinction I am making between even a careful review of the content of poems and an assessment of their poetic function is particularly germane to a reading of Herbert. I argue that Herbert's sense of the affinity between text and sacrament is recorded in the very representational architecture of *The Temple*. Herbert himself provides in the later version of "The H. Communion" a virtual pronouncement of the way that texts, like sacraments, can operate with an incarnational, instrumental force born simultaneously of the substance of their signifieds and the accidents of their material expression. What usually gets overlooked in critical treatments of the climactic stanza of "The H. Communion" is that "Leaping the wall" is accomplished neither by the material substance of the bread and wine nor by the force of spiritual nourishment. Instead, Herbert concludes,

> Onely thy grace, which with these elements comes,
> > Knoweth the ready way,
> > And hath the privie key,
> > Op'ning the souls most subtile roomes;
> While those to spirits refin'd, at doore attend
> > Dispatches from their friend. (19–24)

Disputations about whether Herbert privileges in these lines a Catholic or a Reformed view of the progress of grace obscure the fact that grace finally manages, in Herbert's explanation, to link body and soul as "Dispatches"—as a message that arrives in expressly written form. As with the communication contained within a packet of letters, grace inheres in the message of the text, a message inseparable from and dependent for its transmission on the material artifact of the page. For Herbert, sacramental efficacy is achieved by the simultaneity of material and spiritual, a correspondence whose ideal, in "The H. Communion," takes the form of a piece of writing.

In putting a sacramental focus here on writing, on the efficacy of the word, my aim is not to revisit the position held by critics like Daniel Doerksen and Gene Veith, claiming for Herbert a conforming Calvinist piety centered on the word, and on the way that the authority of Christ as the Word made Flesh gets refracted into the words of scripture and of preaching.[10] Herbert's term "Dispatches" rather collapses the distinction between sign and signified promoted in the *Institutes*, where Calvin affirms Augustine's definition of the sacrament as "rei sacrae visibile signum" [a visible sign of a sacred thing]:[11]

Sacramenta igitur exercitia sunt quae certiorem verbi Dei fidem nobis faciunt: et quia carnales sumus, sub rebus carnalibus exhibentur: ut ita pro tarditatis nostrae captu nos erudiant, et perinde ac pueros paedagogi manu ducant. Hac ratione Augustinus sacramentum verbum visibile nuncupat: quod Dei promissiones velut in tabula depictas repraesentet, et sub aspectum graphice atque εἰκονικῶς expressas statuat.

[Sacraments, therefore, are exercises that make more secure our faith in the word of God: and because we are fleshly, they are exhibited under fleshly things: so that they may instruct us in our sluggish capacities, and lead us by the hand like the young students of a schoolmaster. For this reason Augustine calls a sacrament a visible word: because it represents the promises of God just as if they were depicted in a picture, and places beneath our gazes an *icon*, a verisimilitude masterfully expressed.][12]

Calvin writes that those who participate in the Eucharist must maintain an understanding of the ontological distinction between the sacramental signs and the spiritual realities they represent. The visible word of the sacrament stands as an accommodation to, and a marker of, the human region of unlikeness from divine things. This formulation, which can be traced from Calvin back through Augustine to Aristotle, imagines the sacrament as an outward seal or sign for the invisible, internal, and finally immaterial operation of grace.[13] But Herbert's engagement with the issue of sacramental representation in the published version of "The H. Communion" is not consistent with the ontological binary that Calvin promotes. Rather, Herbert focuses on "Leaping the wall" between fleshly and spiritual, using the word itself as an instrument for producing indistinguishability between ontological realms. Herbert, after all, is the country parson who praised the Lord of the Altar as "not only the feast, but the way to it."[14] That phrase begins to suggest Herbert's peculiar willingness to collapse sacramental and representational means into ends—that is, to preserve the significance of the sign in itself, in addition to honoring the significance of the principle to which the sign refers.

For Herbert, Communion presents a model for this kind of ontological indistinguishability, offering a text whose spiritual valences endure even as its objectively perceptible substance refuses to be (to use Charles Bernstein's useful terms) "sublimated / away."[15] As "The H. Communion" makes clear, the sacrament is for Herbert both spiritually and materially signifi-cant, and it is striking that his model for eucharistic reception in that poem is figured through the written communiqué of "Dispatches." In Herbert's formulation of the sacrament, Christ graces both the end and the means, the feast and the way to it, in direct echo of the Incarnation's simultaneous valorization of the divine Word and the flesh in which it was made present to man; this principle of holy and meaningful presence effected by the hypostatic union of sign and signified ramifies into Herbert's perception of texts.[16] Over the course of *The Temple*, Herbert consistently and explicitly evokes the function of Christ as Logos in a way that foregrounds the textu-ality of that designation, as when in "Sepulchre" he imagines the crucified Christ as an inscription:

> And as of old the Law by heav'nly art
> Was writ in stone; so thou, which also art
> The letter of the word, find'st no fit heart
> To hold thee. (16–19)

The comparison to the material ground of the engraved Decalogue gestures toward Christ's allegorical associations with rock,[17] and also calls up an uneasy awareness of the engraving of Christ's flesh by the spears and nails during the crucifixion (a concept that Christian readings of Isaiah 49.16, "Behold, I haue grauen thee vpon the palmes of my hands: thy walles are continually before mee," made familiar).[18] The meaning of the "letter" here follows from its having been inscribed in the flesh, and Christ's flesh signifies spiritually because it has been marked materially. Christ is both transparent gospel text and harrowingly, transformatively, unsublimable object.

The consistency with which Herbert foregrounds the sign as a site of substantiality and consequence is a key feature of his poetics. In Herbert's work, this emphasis arises in part out of his extravagant formal experimentation, a set of antiabsorptive strategies that, to return again to the terms of Bernstein's analysis, lends to the poetic text a "thickness" that continues to "obtrude impermeably into the world."[19] Herbert's work is, I argue, radically invested in promoting its own surface, asserting the *sign as such* as an object rather than treating the text as a transparent conduit to content. Herbert's incarnationalist poetics bespeak a fundamental faith in the meaningfulness of the material in general and of the material valences of text in particular. When, in "The H. Scriptures I," Herbert says of the Bible that "heav'n lies flat in thee" (14), he affirms that the physical dimensions of the page parameter heaven itself, and he reacts accordingly with a desire to "Suck ev'ry letter" (2) of that page. Herbert's attention to the topography of text, with all its surface contour and formal architecture, is at bottom a confirmation of the text's objecthood. In this project, Herbert shows himself to be in sympathy with the textual experiments at Little Gidding, the religious community established by Herbert's acquaintance Nicholas Ferrar. The Ferrar household pursued a rigorous devotional life that included communal worship and biblical study; part of this practice involved the construction of Gospel concordances or "harmonies," in which passages from the four gospels were cut and glued into new arrangements in order to harmonize their narratives. "One of these books," reports Ferrar's brother John, "was sent to Mr. Herbert which, he said, he prized most highly as a rich jewel."[20] The book arts projects of Little Gidding, with their endlessly mobile word packets in a variety of fonts, emphasize the physical manipulability of text as well as its hefty substantiality, and argue implicitly that content is contingent on the material. Their emphasis on the physical artifact as an instrument that expresses holy worship claims for words and phrases a meaningfulness that inheres in their very objecthood.

Throughout *The Temple*, Herbert performs a poetics that likewise claims for language a meaningful objecthood, a poetics in which the material of text tenaciously obtrudes into the transparency of semantic projection. The antiabsorptive qualities of Herbert's verse are evident, to be sure, in the extraordinary formal innovation that characterizes *The Temple*, where among other experiments, as Joseph Summers has noted, "Herbert used twenty-nine different patterns with the simple *a b a b* rhyme scheme."[21] Such formal ingenuity should not be regarded as mere ornamentation or even a reinforcement of the "real meaning" of the poem as expressed in its content. Rather, an emphasis on form, on surface, as opaque in Herbert's poetry demands that we confront form *qua* form, that we register the presence of the poem as a material artifact. I mean to echo and refine Whalen's point when I say that to recognize Herbert's stake in the relationship between the objecthood of poems and the incarnational poetics of the sacrament is to go to the heart of Herbert's project.

Herbert treats the signifying capacity of sacramental form itself most conspicuously, of course, in "The Altar," in which the shape of the poem on the page approximates the site of the encounter for which it yearns.[22] Summers identified this poem many years ago as an example of the importance to Herbert's poetry of the hieroglyph, which Summers defines as a figure that "presented its often manifold meanings in terms of symbolic relationships rather than through realistic representation."[23] Summers sees the structure of "The Altar" as "Herbert's attempt to use the shape of a classical altar as a hieroglyph of his beliefs concerning the relationships between the heart, the work of art, and the praise of God,"[24] and though these relationships are undoubtedly interrogated in Herbert's poem, Summers's influential view repeats the distinction between representational means and ends that Calvin articulates in his exegesis on the species of Communion. Such an account fixes the form of "The Altar" as representationally transparent, pointing ever beyond itself to a set of ideas; for Summers, as for many other readers of Herbert, those ideas encompass both the offering of the broken heart in worship and the offering of the poem as an emblem both of praise and of the surrender of the will.[25] While I do not mean to suggest that the shape of "The Altar" does not relate symbolically to the content of the poem, to view the poem's presence on the page as if it merely served a referential function, as if it were simply a vehicle by which we understand the "real meaning" of the poem, is to undercut the poem's powerful emphasis on textual embodiment. Even prior to the drama of the poem's content, the structure of "The Altar" asserts its ontological sufficiency such that Stanley Fish, who turns immediately to the work of discrediting the poem's strident constructedness as "one path Herbert chose not to follow," nevertheless initiates that argument by remarking that "The most notable and noticeable feature of the poem is, of course, its shape. . . . In fact, one might say that the first thing the poem does, even before we take in any of its words, is call attention to itself as something quite carefully made."[26]

In practical terms, the form of "The Altar" interacts puzzlingly with the content of the poem. The physical presence of the poem on the page, rather than reinforcing or supplementing the sense of its words, seems disorientingly resistant to the argument of the language it contains:

> A broken A L T A R , Lord, thy servant reares,
> Made of a heart, and cemented with teares:
>   Whose parts are as thy hand did frame;
>   No workmans tool hath touch'd the same.
>   A H E A R T alone
>   Is   such   a   stone,
>   As   nothing   but
>   Thy pow'r doth cut.
>   Wherefore each part
>   Of my hard heart
>   Meets in this frame,
>   To praise thy Name;
>   That, if I chance to hold my peace,
>   These stones to praise thee may not cease.
> O let thy blessed S A C R I F I C E be mine,
> And sanctifie this A L T A R to be thine.

Even as this poem argues for the replacement of the material altar with the spiritual offering of the heart, of the will, of the potentially idolatrous work of art, of all three together,[27] this repudiation of the physical altar is contradicted by the presence on the page of a perfectly symmetrical and self-consciously constructed arrangement of text, whose structure is made most complete when the last line renounces artistic ownership over the altar of the poem/altar of the self to God. But the inevitable identification of the shape of the poem with an altar introduces a dimension of referentiality to which the poem's textual material is yet prior. Thus, to adapt Fish's claim, the first thing this poem does is advertise its own objecthood, its presence on the page as a physical shape. We need only to consult a handful of critical opinions on the poem's shape to grant that the referential ends of the poem's shape remain uncertain: does it depict a Communion table? A classical altar? A deuteronomic altar of unhewn stones? A pillar? The letter

I? Each of these referents has been defended by readers eager to establish how the ostentatious form of the poem contributes to its semantic content.[28] But the very referential uncertainty of the shape indicates the ways in which it resists stable representation even as it projects its own ineffaceable presence as an object. Moreover, the language of "The Altar" explicitly reflects upon the poem's textuality as a site of immanence, for each piece of the broken heart "Meets in *this frame* / To praise thy name" (emphasis added). In self-reflexively implicating the "frame" of the poem, as well as the larger frame of *The Temple*, these lines point toward the architecture of the texts in which they are embedded and locate conservative efficacy in their materiality.[29] For the frame of the poem—its graphic presence on the page—and the artifact of the book each embody the cries of the heart, making them both permanent and materially apprehensible. By foregrounding its own textuality both in its form and in its semantic self-reflexiveness, the poem invites an encounter in which the textual *is* material, an association recapitulated in the capitalization and expanded spacing of "A L T A R," "H E A R T," and "S A C R I F I C E," which dramatize brokenness in form. Through such formally assertive poetic strategies, the poem insists on itself as a sensible (or perhaps rather *sense-able*) object, and the poem's language hints at the presence that inheres in its formal frame.[30] Poetic form, in "The Altar," *means*—which is to say, *presence as such* means.

The notion that presence means is, to be sure, particularly relevant to the long debate about the mode of divine presence in the eucharistic species. But Herbert's treatment of presence intriguingly avoids engaging the terms of theological disputation, displacing any argument about the operation of signs into his poetics, which exhibits considerable reluctance to divest the corporeal of significance. Herbert's conjunction of corporeality and textuality may well invite comparisons to a kind of *via media* between the word-based pieties of Calvinism and the purportedly sensualist ceremonialism of the Roman church, but I am far more interested here in the way that Herbert collapses the two approaches into one another, regarding text as a kind of presence machine. This emphasis on textual immanence recurs in "IESU," in which the word for the Word, the name *IESU*, is broken into pieces. The poem's conceit asks us again to imagine, as in "The Altar," that the heart is a quasilinguistic "little frame" (3), upon which a variant of the name of Jesus is "deeply carved" (2). When the speaker's heart breaks in pieces, the name likewise breaks into its constituent parts, the poem literal-izing the "parceling" of "thy glorious name" discussed in "Love I" (3). As Martin Elsky explains, "Broken into *I, ES, U*, Christ's name is divided into components of sound" in which "the speaker deciphers lexical units, words, which in turn make up a syntactical unit, 'I ease you' (9)."[31] And yet, even as this narrative of meaning-making plays out in the poem, the word *IESU*, or rather the letters that constitute that word, remain separable into units, materially manipulable—like children's wooden blocks with the alphabet painted on them. The "heart" of line one dissolves irrevocably, and espe-cially in its breaking, into the realm of the metaphoric, but the breakage of word into letter happens not at some conceptual remove but before our eyes, on the page. The signifier *IESU*, far from allowing transparent access to the identity of Christ, disintegrates into graphic units, signs that announce themselves as signs, parts that no longer function referentially. The term *IESU* is repositioned thus from signifier at the poem's beginning to opaque sign through its narrative of fragmentation. More to the point, the Word achieves material presence in "IESU" not by being named, for the name shows itself to be frangible, but in the physically perceptible artifacts of the word that persist whatever the semantic status of the name may be.

Similarly, the poem "Love-joy" engages the question of substantial tex-tuality both in the "hieroglyphic riddle" of its allegorical narrative and in the graphic signs of its poetic presence.[32] This poem foregrounds the ten-sion between representation and ground from its first line:

> As on a window late I cast mine eye,
> I saw a vine drop grapes with *J* and *C*
> Anneal'd on every bunch. One standing by
> Ask'd what it meant. I (who am never loth
> To spend my iudgement) said, It seem'd to me
> To be the bodie and the letters both
> Of *Joy* and *Charitie*. Sir, you have not miss'd,
> The man reply'd; It figures *JESUS CHRIST*.

The "window" upon which the speaker gazes advertises the interpretive dynamic of aesthetic media; as Herbert himself explains in "The Elixer,"

> A man that looks on glasse,
>   On it may stay his eye;
> Or if he pleaseth, through it passe,
>   And then the heav'n espie. (9–12)

In "Love-joy," the window becomes emblematic of the poem, which as it proceeds presents signs that the speaker must contemplate as objects. Whalen nicely summarizes what we might call, with a nod to Fish, the aesthetic catechism of the poem's narrative—the lesson in reading signs dramatized by the poem's dialogue:

> While the emphasis is on simply recognizing and accepting the presence of Christ, the speaker cannot resist offering an explanation, to wit, the letters J and C are "the bodie and the letters both / Of *Joy* and *Charitie*" (6–7). His interlocutor corroborates and adds "It figures *JESUS CHRIST*." The simultaneous presence of both body and sign is common to most sacramental formulae; here, however, the letters are "anneal'd on every bunch" thus suggesting an inscription that goes beyond the surface to share in a portion of the grapes' substance. The fruit is neither merely a vehicle for J and C, nor is it displaced by them. And because they do not simply reside on the surface, the letters are more than disembodied signs; rather, J and C do not cease to be signs even as they are inextricable from the matter to which they are joined.[33]

Whalen's insight about the annealing of letters into the substance of the grapes is a fine one, though the "matter" Whalen describes as manifesting "the simultaneous presence of both body and sign" is narrative rather than textual: the *grapes* are not materially present on the page, as they are present to the persons in the poem. Still, it is helpful to apply Whalen's impression to the way the poem's aesthetic catechism extends to the experience of the poem as a text that likewise manifests the presence of body and sign: for here, as in "IESU," the work of identifying appropriate signifieds for *J* and *C* (and the attendant allegorical claims about the way Christ and joy/charity figure one another) has not compromised their status as signs any more than the ontological identity of grapes is compromised by their typological association with the Eucharist. But unlike the visible sign of grapes, which is sensorily apprehensible to the persons in the poem but not to the reader of the poem, the letters *J* and *C* persist in their nontransparent textual substantiality beyond the resolution of the poem's interpretive drama. The poem sustains the artifacts of its own textuality, emphasizing their matter as distinct from the spiritual meanings generated by the poem's allegorical interpretations.

The poem's investment in the material of its own language redounds to its treatment of the figure of Christ (and by "figure" I mean to evoke both the physical and representational senses of that term). When the speaker reads the letters *J* and *C* as signifying "*Joy* and *Charitie*," his interlocutor both endorses and corrects that interpretation in his response: "It figures *JESUS CHRIST*." This statement simultaneously invites and frustrates a consideration of what "*JESUS CHRIST*," as a linguistic sign, means. Does the name of Christ reference the person of Christ? Or does it reference the principles of joy and charity? Or again, do we resolve the conundrum by concluding, with Fish, that "properly understood, they imply each other"?[34] And how exactly are we to read the verb "figures" here: with its corporeal echoes or as an act of metaphor? These perplexities foreground interpretation as the central action of the poem, and both the terms and the questions they provoke reveal the proximity of its hermeneutic concerns to the eucharistic debates, thematizing as they do the unstable referentiality of the visible sign. This sacramental crisis comes to a head in the last line of "Love-joy," where the figure of Christ is both referenced and supplanted by its own sign, a text the drama of whose interpretation constitutes the catechistic narrative of the poem. But even as that interpretive crisis reaches its uncertain resolution, the capitalized, italicized text "*JESUS CHRIST*" emphasizes the *wordiness* of the Word. The conclusion of "Love-joy" forces a confrontation with the Logos as a sign, one whose presence is ever more reified in the diminishing certainty of its signifieds. That is, as we grow more uncertain about how the words "*JESUS CHRIST*" mean, we grow more aware of their presence as words.

The incarnational underpinnings of such poetic strategies are made explicit in this short poem, in which Herbert engages in a series of incarnational puns:

$$Ana\text{-} \begin{Bmatrix} \text{MARY} \\ \text{ARMY} \end{Bmatrix} gram.$$

How well her name an *Army* doth present,
In whom the *Lord of Hosts* did pitch his tent!

In what continues to be after nearly fifty years the most attentive critical reading of this poem, Louis H. Leiter (who has a well-calibrated antenna for poetics) summarizes the overlapping vectors of typology and typography, noting that Christ's fleshly presence is anticipated in its title's graphic play. Here, the letters of Mary's name are braced on one side by the name of her mother (Anne, derived from Hebrew חנה [*Hannah*], or *divine grace*) and on the other by "gram," or *writing*, which points toward Christ as Logos. Mary is thus located physically between bodily generation and the Word, just as the phrase *"Lord of Hosts"* is tented typographically in the poem's final line, in the middle of two textual phrases. Noting that contemporary usages of the word "tent" included "pulpit" (specifically, a portable pulpit set up for administering the sacrament to overflow crowds) and "wine" (the *Oxford English Dictionary* describes it as "A Spanish wine of a deep red colour, and of low alcoholic content . . . Often used as a sacramental wine"),[35] Leiter ably delineates the poem's incarnational argument, beginning with the title anagram's rearranged *M*: " 'M' stands for Mary, Master, and Mass; 'Hosts' for eucharistic bread; 'tent' for red wine, a pulpit, and the means by which man is healed. The physical shape of the poem is then either an altar or a pulpit with the first line serving as the lectern on which the written word lies. . . . His presence is felt, implied, tucked away in words, buried in letters, before He is incarnated in the last line."[36] And with his use of the term "incarnated," Leiter suggests, though he does not articulate this point fully, that Christ is made present in the words of the poem, the words on the page, of whose material substance we have been made by the poem's title acutely aware. Far from being an interpretive transparency that gestures beyond itself to the idea of hypostasis, the text *is* the body in which the Lord of Hosts pitches his tent.[37] Moreover, the predominance of puns in this poem works to ensure that the text be encountered *as text*, as a set of signs whose sign-ness is reified by the uncertainty of their referents. The punning words resist determinate integration into a referential schema, instead announcing themselves as objects. Heather Asals has observed that Herbert's frequent punning, which she terms "equivocation" (in which "*one word* equals *two definitions*"), emphasizes "the surface of language";[38] and while Asals ultimately reads this focus on the discursive surfaces—or, to use the terminology of this present study, the *objecthood* of poetic artifacts—as aligning the creative work of poem-making with the creative character of divine making, unifying the poet with God, I wish to seize upon Asals's remark that in his language play "Herbert *breaks the host of language itself;* he *breaks* the Word itself."[39] With this rhetorical flourish, Asals identifies the fundamentally incarnational character of Herbert's writing and registers the crucial correspondence that Herbert perceives between the poetic text, Christ's Incarnation, and the physical event of eucharistic worship.

For Herbert does treat poetry as an incarnational mechanism, able to enflesh the abstract and make the absent literally present on the page. Throughout *The Temple*, the aesthetic is rendered as a site of immanence, an instrument by which presence is made possible. It is not, after all, by their referential transparency that "The Windows" in the poem of that title disclose God's "light and glorie," but rather by their resistance to referential transparency; like the *J* and *C* of "Love-joy," it is when divine principles are "anneal[ed]in glasse," made materially substantial objects of themselves, that they become apprehensible to man. The poem's conclusion meditates on the effects of incorporating such a material encounter into worship:

> Doctrine and life, colours and light, in one
> > When they combine and mingle, bring
> A strong regard and aw: but speech alone
> > Doth vanish like a flaring thing,
> > And in the eare, not conscience ring. (11–15)

Herbert's investment as a poet is not to produce "speech alone" but to produce the "aw" of presence, and in urging such veneration, Herbert's language echoes John Chrysostom's sentiments about the Eucharist: "Ὅπερ ἄγγελοι βλέποντες φρίττουσι, καὶ οὐδὲ ἀντιβλέψαι τολμῶσιν ἀδειῶς διὰ τὴν ἐκείθεν φερομένον ἀστραπὴν, τούτῳ ἡμεῖς τρεφόμεθα, τούτῳ ἀναφυρόμεθα, καὶ γεγόναμεν ἡμεῖς Χριστοῦ σῶμα ἕν καὶ σὰρξ μία" [That which when the Angels behold they tremble, and dare not even to look without awe because of the shining it bears, by that we are nourished, with that we are mingled, and we become one body and the one flesh with Christ].[40] Like Chrysostom's materially efficacious sacrament, Herbert's poetics seeks to acknowledge signs as effectual things, as becomes clear in the preponderance of his writing about the material efficacy of writing. In Herbert's aesthetic system, God may "Engrave" his "rev'rend law and fear" in the heart ("Nature," 14); the hungry man may "conceit a most delicious feast" and find that he has "had it straight, and did as truly eat, / As ever did a welcome guest" ("Faith," 6–7); the poet's rhymes may "Gladly engrave thy love in steel" ("The Temper," 2). The embodying effects of Herbert's immanent textuality offer an answer to the aesthetic complaint of "Jordan (I)": "Must all be vail'd, while he that reades, divines, / Catching the sense at two removes?" (9–10). Herbert's poetics collapses those "two removes" by asserting the substantial presence, the real presence of language in verse, and by registering writing as an incarnational act.

The notion that such incarnational power might be immanent in the textual finds authorization, of course, in the characterization of Christ as the Word, as Logos, an identification of which Herbert makes frequent use in *The Temple*. And it is precisely its status as an opaque set of signs on the page that makes the Word present to the senses in so many of Herbert's poems, as the poet invests this theological commonplace with all the material force he claims for the poetic text. This principle animates "The Sonne," a poem that celebrates not just the happy coincidence of meanings in a pun but also the way that the orthography and sound of a word intervenes in, even precedes, any engagement with its meaning. "A sonne is light and fruit" (6), Herbert explains, delighting (if not originally) that the sun/son homophone on which the poem turns encompasses both Christ's divinity and his humanity.[41] The poem's celebration of the ways in which the pun constitutes a kind of hypostatic union between two realms of christic signification leads Herbert to a consideration of the Word as a sign with sonic and graphic properties:

> So in one word our Lords humilitie
> We turn upon him in a sense most true:
> > For what Christ once in humblenesse began,
> > We him in glorie call, *The Sonne of Man*. (11–14)

As Elsky has shown, here "The Word as spoken sound thus becomes for Herbert the sounded encoding of a series of natural, historical, and spiritual truths," and these truths are revealed "as the sacred pun is vocalized when 'We him in glorie *call* [emphasis added] *The Sonne of Man*.'"[42] Elsky's remark recognizes the corporeal actualization of the Word's meaning in this poem; indeed, the central argument of "The Sonne" concerns the ways in which the word reifies the Word. It is "in one word," the poem argues, that we are able to grasp Christ's nature, but because the poem attends to the ways in which that word's referential function exhibits slippage—the same word has at least two different referents—the word as such is once again emphasized as distinct from its designative content. Rather than standing for a defined and stable signified, "*Sonne*" asserts itself as a sign; as we are conscious of engaging with it as a verbal artifact before we engage with its meaning, the referential function of "*Sonne*" is displaced by the idea that referentiality is one property of the word among many. As the word's referential function becomes distinct from its textual substance—one thing the word *does* rather than all that the word *is*—"*Sonne*" becomes apprehensible as an object, a perceptible and nontransparent textual presence. Moreover, the poem's title (which is consistently spelled "The Sonne" in both the Williams and Bodleian manuscripts as well as in the 1633 printing of *The Temple*) reinforces the presence of this word/Word by promoting the poem as a textual artifact even as it introduces the sun/son homophone: Matthias Bauer notes that "The form of this poem is actually announced by its title, to which one only has to add the sign of the son, the cruciform letter T," in order to spell *sonnet*.[43] This focus on the surfaces of language, on the sonic and graphic properties of words, makes the Word that is both representative and constitutive of Christ's presence in this poem ostentatiously available for sensory apprehension, an effect in strong contrast to the poem's thematic suggestion of referential or signifying instability. In other words, Christ is more present in this text as a sign than as a signified.

Poetry serves for Herbert, then, as an instrument for enfleshing Christ, for manifesting the divine as material presence. As in "Sepulchre," where the incarnate Christ appears as "the letter of the word," the graphic embodiment of divinity every bit as material as the engravings of the law on stone, the physical character of the Word achieves substantial expression in Herbert's antiabsorptive poetics. Exploiting the textual qualities of Christ as Logos, Herbert's formal extravagance promotes the incarnational capacities of language. The physical absence of the body of Christ, both from the world of flesh into which the Incarnation intervenes and from the experience of eucharistic observance across the confessional spectrum, provokes in Herbert's verse strategies that counter the troubling perceptual unavailability of divinity. It is worth recalling that the poem that concludes by identifying Christ as "the letter of the word" begins with the anxious exclamation: "O blessed bodie! Whither art thou thrown?" ("Sepulchre," 1). As the poet laments elsewhere, "thy absence doth excel / All distance known"

("The Search," 57–58). For Herbert, poetry itself begins to answer the terrifying proposition of Christ's absence, establishing the Word as an object that does not dissolve into the vapor of mere referentiality. Cognizant of the ways in which Christ as Logos is invested with textuality, Herbert makes deliberate use of the materializing valences of text to *present* Christ. To put it another way, Herbert's Christ is made present in the objecthood of text.

Given Herbert's investment in the capacities of text to make present what is perceptually absent, it is perhaps not surprising that the eucharistic poem "The Agonie" begins with an assertion of the epistemological obscurity of spiritual principles:

> Philosophers have measur'd mountains,
> Fathom'd the depths of seas, of states, and kings,
> Walk'd with a staffe to heav'n, and traced fountains:
>   But there are two vast, spacious things,
> The which to measure it doth more behove:
> Yet few there are that sound them; Sinne and Love. (1–6)

Though philosophers can "measure" geologies and geographies, the histories of nation and rule, sin and love resist this kind of empirical investigation. Vast and spacious in a way that physical things seem not to be, they exceed the senses. As Herbert's poem continues, it offers alternative means for understanding such spiritual matters:

> Who would know Sinne, let him repair
> Unto mount Olivet; there shall he see
> A man so wrung with pains, that all his hair,
>   His skinne, his garments, bloody be.
> Sinne is that presse and Vice, which forceth pain
> To hunt his cruell food through ev'ry vein. (7–12)

In order to understand sin, the poem instructs, we must "see" Jesus in Gethsemane, and Herbert's verse provides us with details from the scriptural record to compose a scene: Jesus's bloody garments, skin, and even hair so particularized as to conjure up the vision to our imaginations.[44] It is thus remarkable that the stanza begins by displacing these details out of the physical: the bloody skin and hair with all their physical vividness are explicitly identified as standing *not* for themselves but for something else—for "Sinne." Christ's corporeal particularities are offered here as a sign, whose presence in the poem delineates an abstraction too vast to be measured.

In the third and final stanza, the poem's eucharistic interests are made explicit, even as its language continues to redefine the visceral as significative:

> Who knows not Love, let him assay,
> And taste that juice, which on the crosse a pike
> Did set again abroach; then let him say
>   If ever he did taste the like.
> Love is that liquour sweet and most divine,
> Which my God feels as bloud; but I, as wine. (13–18)

Here, Christ's body is veiled, as it were, behind the rich language of religious emblem so thoroughly charted by Rosemond Tuve decades ago.[45] Christ's body, breached by a sword, spills forth the blood represented in eucharistic wine. And though Tuve finds Herbert's imagery perfectly "conventional,"[46] consistent with a long iconographic tradition, his handling of the vectors of referentiality is provocative both in the context of "The Agonie" and in consideration of the commitment to signs as such that pervades *The Temple*. For Herbert's poem does not make it easy to keep the figurative and literal registers separate. By inviting us to "taste that juice set abroach by the spear," he renders identical the figure and the ground—the blood that flows from the spear wound and the metaphoric juice by which it is represented to the eucharistic worshipper. Christ is in these lines the signified—as the body represented eucharistically in the wine. But Christ also serves here as the sign—the body whose "taste" prompts the figural leap into "juice" and "liquour." Yet after all, even these sign/signified complexes collapse into the sign position because the poem argues that they represent *something else*: the principle of Love. The body of Christ in agony, whether it is seen primarily as the emblematic subject or the emblematic object, is finally the word/Word that *means* love—just as in the previous stanza, it *means* sin. Helen Vendler has noted that though the qualities of sin and love stand in opposition to one another, the emblematic descriptions featured in stanzas two and three of "The Agonie" are "identical," both depicting "Christ shedding blood under torture."[47] Thus the suffering body of Christ signifies in multiple registers, meaning two distinct, even

opposite, ideas. The poem encourages us to stop on the surface of signification, on the Word which is Christ the Logos, and to register it as an artifact
whose referential transparency is prevented by its referential slippage. In
"The Agonie," the meaning of the Word becomes a pun of the same order
that Herbert explored in "The Sonne." Once again, Christ's body is offered
as a sign whose signified remains unfixed, a sign that therefore persists
untransparently, antiabsorptively, in the poem's system of signification.

In *Love Known*, Richard Strier asserts that the "knowledge" advocated
by these stanzas is "entirely a matter of immediate experience, not of conceptual formulation." Strier goes on to claim that what he calls "the essential terms of religion" gain priority over the sciences in Herbert's hierarchy
of knowledges because they are known by immediate experience. "For Herbert," Strier declares, "it is science that is abstract and religion that is concrete and empirical. The 'knowledge' described in stanza 3 is entirely a
matter of immediate experience, not of conceptual formulation." Strier
identifies the depictions of sin and love in "The Agonie" as exemplary of
the spiritual knowledge that comes by immediate experience. "Sin and
love," he claims, "cannot be fathomed in the way that seas can."[48] Strier is
absolutely correct in this last pronouncement, but I would argue that he is
absolutely wrong in his reasoning. For "The Agonie" takes pains *not* to
imagine "spiritual experience" as an event directly channeled into the worshipper's apprehension with epistemological immediacy. Mountains and
seas can be understood through the apprehension of the senses, but as
Herbert's poem presents it, the problem with spiritual knowledge is that it
must come through the mediation of terms whose objecthood is ultimately
more stable, more apprehensible, than the abstractions to which they refer.
In the case of "The Agonie," the spiritual meaning of Christ becomes available to our apprehension insofar as he is textualized: Christ is manifested
here not just *in* or *through* the eucharistic elements but as a text that by the
act of signifying maintains its own presence.

Herbert's sacramental stake in this dynamic is evident as the poem
moves toward its conclusion. The closing line posits two distinct versions
of the eucharistic element of wine: what "God feels as bloud" the communicant perceives "as wine." Interestingly, the poem does not privilege one
perception over the other, and there is little textual justification for R. V.
Young's brusque opinion that "what 'God feels' is surely more reliable than
what the poetic persona tastes."[49] Instead, the poem identifies two terms

that in the conditions of early modern sacramental worship come to stand, variably, for one another. The blood of Christ *means* nourishment and vitality, the kind of sustenance that is derived from the fruit of the vine; the wine *means* the atoning blood of Christ. The last line of "The Agonie" ingeniously propounds both terms as equivalently signifying and signified, and in the process foregrounds the act of perceiving the sign as an object, the event of sensory engagement with the thing itself. Herbert's final line refuses to subordinate, as signified to sign, either blood or wine, and so each term remains referentially present as a legitimate object of perception in the poem. This revaluing of sacramental symbols, a transformation that posits both wine and blood as signs, lends theological urgency to the poem's earlier demand, "let him say / If ever he did taste the like." The phrase "taste the like" rings a challenge with particular relevance to sacramental worship: can we apprehend the *like* that joins material and abstract? To do so is to prevent the dissolution of material into abstract, just as considering "like" as a substantial term makes the signifying operations of symbol the explicit thematic concern of the line rather than the transparent mechanism by which substitution is accomplished. Consistently offering conspicuously representational terms whose status as signs proves more durable than their uncertain signification, "The Agonie" encourages us to engage with the body whose symbolic function constitutes the poem's primary argument as a substantial thing in itself, its objecthood no less present that the perception of blood to God or wine to man.

This understanding illuminates a famously troubling passage in "Divinitie," in which Herbert mildly mocks religious converts who needlessly complicate doctrine, especially concerning the operation of the Eucharist. Herbert chides:

> But he doth bid us take his bloud for wine.
>   Bid what he please; yet I am sure,
> To take and taste what he doth there designe,
>   Is all that saves, and not obscure. (21–24)

Aside from the irony of Herbert's comment that the deliberately evasive phrase "what he doth there designe" is "not obscure," this stanza's first line has exercised critics for at least a couple of centuries. Samuel Taylor Coleridge objected, "Nay, the contrary; take the wine to be blood," and

Strier seizes upon the reversal as evidence that Herbert's poem "militates strongly against a specifically Eucharistic reading of the line," and shrugs, "Herbert frequently uses Eucharistic-sounding language—language of blood, wine, and tasting—metaphorically."[50] But the metaphor here is quite clearly about sacramental participation, and Herbert's sleight announces itself not as metaphor but as dissonance: the unmistakable eucharistic echo jars against the awareness voiced by Coleridge that the line has it backward. A sacramental gloss on Herbert's line is preempted by the need to stop and parse, to appreciate the distinction between what the words say and what they should mean. This is an encounter that is pointedly *not* "thicken'd . . . with definitions" (10), as the poem later muses, an encounter impervious to the action of reason; rather, it offers a different kind of "Gordian knot" (20), the knottiness of which is signaled by line 21's initial "But" and its departure from the interpretive simplicity of the poem's celebration of Christ's unclouded teachings:

> But all the doctrine, which he taught and gave,
> > Was cleare as heav'n, from whence it came.
> At least those beams of truth, which onely save,
> > Surpasse in brightnesse any flame. (13–16)

Departing in style from the commandments to *"Love God, and love your neighbor. Watch and pray. / Do as ye would be done unto"* (17–18), as Herbert's lines elaborate that sun-bright doctrine, the sacramental stanza deliberately complicates the language of instruction and obscures access to its content. At the very moment that Herbert discusses the mechanics of Communion, he severs sign from signified such that we become aware of the sign as an artifact interpretively prior to whatever content might be available from it. What seems to be offered to us to "take and taste" here again is a reified sign that constitutes the Logos against its interpretive vanishing.

Ryan Netzley has noted the tendency in recent criticism on Herbert to elide sacramental tasting into eating, and to privilege ingestion over the sensory encounter with the elements of bread and wine, and his critique of the seeming fetishization by modern critics of "the results, instead of the means of communion" in Herbert's eucharistic schema is acute. As Netzley rightly observes, Herbert's treatments of the Lord's Supper share "an insistence that one participates in communion via taste or smell, not consumption and digestion."[51] To put Netzley's argument in aesthetic as opposed to physiological terms, tasting privileges surfaces and promotes a mode of engagement with the sacrament that gives priority to a corporeal encounter with material objects over their dissolution, their digestion, their abstraction. This is the manner in which *The Temple* trains up its readers to participate in its own aesthetic and eucharistic program. "Taste and fear not," coaxes Herbert in his poem "The Invitation," "God is here / In this cheer" (16–17)—where the locating designations "here" and "In this cheer" indicate both Holy Communion and, reflexively, the incarnationally inflected text itself. And in "The Banquet," the sacramentally themed poem that immediately follows "The Invitation," Herbert exults that during Communion Christ sweetly "doth meet my taste" (39), even as the poet's language celebrates the hermeneutic overlap of text and altar, in each of which Christ "Here, as broken, is presented" (30). Once again, the aesthetic attentions of taste coincide with the sacramental presentation of Christ in both poem and ritual as an object for perception and appreciation, not diffusion into some abstract meaning elsewhere.

This final eucharistic series of poems culminates, of course, in the feast of "Love (III)," in which the anxious soul finally arrives at the Communion table presaged at the beginning of "The Church" by "The Altar." Here again, the instruction offered by Love in the poem's concluding exchange resists interpreting the Eucharist or explaining the mode of its operation: "You must sit down, sayes Love, and taste my meat" (17). The command to "taste" again presents the ritual as a sensory event, one whose somatic pleasures are signaled by the poem's sensual suggestiveness. Schoenfeldt's discussion of the poem's eroticism in *Prayer and Power* acknowledges the ways in which the corporeal intimacy suggested by the Lord's Supper is inseparable from human sexuality, and certainly the consummation offered by sacramental worship promises to bring the body of Christ into contact with the body of the communicant.[52] But it is striking that the poem's first moment of sensual contact between Love and the speaker leads into the poem's first instance of graphic play—its first overt pun: "Love took my hand, and smiling did reply, / Who made the eyes but I?" (11–12). Asals claims that the poem collapses "The subject who loves" into "the object who is loved" as the speaker "is gradually abstracted from himself as 'I' and recollected into himself as 'he'—'You shall be he,'" and Whalen follows Asals in arguing that "the graphic identification"—the *I* of the speaker and the *I* of Love—"suggest[s] a semantic one—'me' and 'Love.'"[53] By extension, these readings imply, although they do not actually get around to saying, that the *eye/I* pun creates a sonic identification between Love and the speaker, one that both reinforces the material exchange between speaker and Christ narrated by the poem and fuses it to the operation of language. Moreover, the pun on *host* as both Communion species and furnisher of the feast, which defines the two positions occupied by the Christ in the poem's drama but remains implicit throughout, replicates the perceptual absence of the hypostatic Logos whose material lineaments the poem provides. As the absent Word in its eucharistic function is made present in the text by language that points to but does not disclose it, the poem both reaffirms the objecthood of the Word as a sign and dramatizes the difficulty of maintaining a sacramental experience of that object—that is, the difficulty of tasting against the urge to abstract and digest, the challenge of perceiving the sign wherein Incarnation inheres against the desire to thicken with definitions. And though Netzley describes the last line of "Love (III)" as "the speaker's abrupt transgression" of Love's invitation to taste,[54] it seems more to the point that in stating "So I did sit and eat" (18), the speaker evidences the continuing precariousness of a hermeneutic stance that values the substance of texts, bodies, and objects as worthy of perception in their own right rather than as mere means to some deferred and imperceptible "real meaning." "Thy word is all," Herbert declares elsewhere, and then immediately qualifies the capacity of the human reader to comprehend the wordiness of the Word: "*if* we could spell" ("The Flower," 21, emphasis added).

Herbert's investment in an interpretive schema that mandates our awareness in the objecthood of signs is precisely that it reflects a brand of eucharistic worship deeply indebted to the Incarnation. Just as in the Incarnation the Word was made flesh, such that material and spiritual ontologies might be maintained simultaneously, Herbert poetics endorses a representational system wherein the material is not supplanted by spiritual significance but persists as a site of sensory participation, a program that aligns the poetic text with the incarnationalist potentialities of Communion. In Herbert's eucharistic poetics, signs become objects as such because he makes such zealous use of the antiabsorptive features of his own poetics. That Herbert's deployment of such a textually substantial poetics represents a self-conscious aesthetic strategy is borne out in his discussion of the material valences of poetry in his Latin poem "Ad Deum": "Sed faecunda poëseωs / Vis, & vena sacris regnat in artubus" [But in sanctified flesh, the vigorous force and vein of poetry reigns] (7–8).[55] Poetry, as Herbert recognizes, is an embodied art. It activates the flesh as a perceptual instrument and preserves in its nonreferential features the incarnational properties of language, and it is because of these qualities that poetry serves, for Herbert, a sacramental function. "A verse is not a crown," Herbert concedes in "The Quidditie," nor a "gay suit. . . . Nor a good sword, nor yet a lute" (1, 2, 4). A poem is also not a "banquet" (3), with its attendant digestion. Still, as Herbert triumphs at the poem's conclusion, "it is that which while I use / I am with thee, and *Most take all*" (11–12). It is through the formal assertions of poetry that Herbert as writer and as reader achieves communion with God. Poetry, in this formulation, manages a sense of presence, of *with*-ness, that the Eucharist cannot communicate. For where Herbert's first "H. Communion" questions "how shall I know / Whether in these gifts thou bee so," and the later "H. Communion" bemoans the separation of body and soul, the "Dispatches" of poetry throughout *The Temple* succeed in "Leaping the wall that parts / Our souls and fleshly hearts." Herbert's lyrics rely upon the objecthood of poetic language itself in order to recover the absent body of God.

In "Superliminare," the poem that introduces and induces the reader into the long central section of *The Temple* and serves as the lintel for the architectural organization of "The Church," Herbert invites his reader into the text using language that reinforces the material efficacy of the poetic event at hand. Asserting that the verse in *The Temple* is consequential, effecting manifest change in the reader who engages with it, the poem expands that consequentiality into an explicitly sacramental context:

> Thou, whom the former precepts have
> Sprinkled and taught, how to behave
> Thy self in church; approach, and taste
> The churches mysticall repast.

(1–5)

From this first entrance into "The Church," Herbert imagines the poetic text as a eucharistic encounter, an interpretive event in which the antiabsorptive experience of "taste" itself delineates and constitutes spiritual nourishment. Herbert's concern with the preservation of the substantial artifacts of worship upends the reading offered by Jonathan Goldberg, who

argues that the printed horizontal line dividing the stanzas of "Superliminare" enforces the materiality of the text with the result that the reader
encountering the first stanza, then the graphic line, then the second stanza
is "invited, barred, re-invited";[56] but given Herbert's stake in the incarnational expressivities of the Word/word, it is more accurate to read the textual bar of this threshold poem as its own invitation—a call to recognize
the importance of space, of form, of the physical presence of poetry on the
page to Herbert's project. For it is in our encounter with its antiabsorptive
artifact that poetry becomes most sacramental, indissolubly immanent in
its objecthood.

The immediacy of the textual encounter presented throughout *The
Temple* returns us again to the grievance Herbert gives voice to in "Jordan
(I)": "Must all be vail'd, while he that reades, divines, / Catching the sense
at two removes?" Critics are honest people; let them sing variations on
Fish's tune about this poem's indictment of art and artifice.[57] But in the
context of *The Temple*'s performance of artifice as a site of textual immanence, "Jordan (I)" reveals an objection not to poetic language per se but
to the view that would reduce poetic language to a mere referential vehicle,
valuable not for its own sake but for the "two removes" of mediation
between the object and its meaning. Herbert complains against an art that
would privilege the "fictions" (1) of content over the word which does
"plainly *say*" (15, emphasis added)—that is, the word that asserts itself as
bare utterance, as sign that refuses to be sublimated transparently into content. As both the structure and the argument of Herbert's poem on "Coloss.
3. 3" make clear, poetic utterance takes that which is "*Hid*" (4) and allows
it to be "wrapt *In* flesh" (5). By capitalizing on the ways in which Christ
the Logos can be made present in "the bodie and the letters both" of *The
Temple*, Herbert offers a corporeal encounter that circumvents theological
wranglings over eucharistic doctrine, and makes of poetry itself a ceremony
of immanence.

Edward Taylor's "Menstruous Cloth":
Structure as Seal in the *Preparatory Meditations*

George Herbert's influence on the poetry of Edward Taylor is readily apparent, sufficient to prompt Louis Martz to remark that "Edward Taylor appears to have had a mind saturated with Herbert's poetry." Martz's observation refers primarily to Taylor's devotional subject, numbering among the "thousand tantalizing echoes of Herbert" resonances of *The Temple* in the latter poet's lexicon along with a similar fear of inadequacy in attempting to praise God.[1] Taylor's great twentieth-century editor Donald Stanford expands the catalogue of Herbert's influence to include "An interest in typology, the frequent use of 'mixed' figures, a devout piety, and scores of verbal echoes and parallels."[2] And just as the pious content and the homespun posture of Herbert's poems undoubtedly authorize Taylor's own experiments in devotional verse, the earlier poet's formal innovations likewise provide for Taylor a sense of the kinds of communication that might be possible in the structures of poetic utterance. Taylor inherited from Herbert not merely the six-line stanza of *The Temple*'s long opening poem "The Church-Porch" but also a conception of poetic form's potential to produce immanent presence, to lineament that which is perceptually absent.

For Taylor as for Herbert, God's absence is a matter of urgent concern, but in Taylor's case, God's perceptual unavailability redounds to a corollary uncertainty about the status of one's own soul. In Taylor's religious observance, the occasion that precipitates the most harrowing awareness of these vacancies is the monthly event that he calls the Lord's Supper. Taylor, a nonconforming Calvinist who left England for the American wilderness, where he lived out his days as minister in the town of Westfield, Massachusetts, would have resisted any sacramental formulation that admitted the objective physical presence of the body of Christ in the ordinance. Nevertheless, he held the Supper to be a "seal" of God's covenant to save the elect. In a passage from one of his *Preparatory Meditations*, Taylor takes pains to distinguish his theology of that ordinance from the popish error of Christ's bodily presence:

> What feed on Humane Flesh and Blood? Strang mess!
>   Nature exclaims. What Barbarousness is here?
> And Lines Divine this sort of Food repress.
>   Christs Flesh and Blood how can they bee good Cheer?
>   If shread to atoms, would too few be known,
>   For ev'ry mouth to have a single one?

> This Sense of this blesst Phrase is nonsense thus.
>   Some other Sense makes this a metaphor.[3]

Taylor insists that rather than effecting any kind of essential transformation of the sacramental elements, the Lord's Supper is a ritual in which Christ communicates through a figure, using, as Taylor prayerfully describes it, "This Metaphor to make thyselfe appeare" (2.101.8). Here and elsewhere, Taylor stresses that the bread and wine must be understood as representational elements, not sites of miraculous action: "God Chose no Ceremonies for their sake / But for Signification did them take" (2.103.65–66).

Still, its status as a sign does not deprive the Lord's Supper of its spiritual significance. As a seal, the ritual manifests in the worshipper as a sign and assurance of God's covenant to redeem his elect. Taylor explains the sealing work accomplished by the ordinance as an instrument not for producing a regenerate spirit but for revealing the grace that inhabits the already regenerate worshipper:

> The Supper of the Lord (Choice Feast) to seale
> The Covenant of Grace thus, even so
>   The Ceremoniall Cleaness did reveale
>   A Spirituall Cleaness qualifying all
>   That have a Right to tend this Festivall. (2.103.44–48)

It is this capacity of the Lord's Supper to reveal the "Spirituall Cleaness" that proves the worshipper worthy to participate in the ordinance that is, for Taylor, its great blessing—and its great vexation. For as Taylor's homi-letic writings bear out, whether grace and true regeneracy are indeed pres-ent in a worshipper's soul proves maddeningly difficult to determine. And as Taylor wrestles in his lyrics with his own inconstant soul—a soul that sometimes glories and sometimes despairs, sometimes hopes and some-times rages—he must confront the unsettling puzzle of his own spiritual state and acknowledge that the matter of whether he has himself been quali-fied by right of grace to attend the Supper of the Lord, whether he is himself truly regenerate, remains just as indiscernible as it is in the secret souls of his congregants, opaque even to the most diligent self-scrutiny. Taylor's response to this crisis of unknowing is to perform the role of the regenerate in a stable and perceptible medium: lyric poetry.

Edward Taylor wrote one lyric poem each month to prepare himself spiritually both to administer the Lord's Supper to his small frontier con-gregation and to partake of the elements of that ritual himself. These poems express, with obsessive consistency over nearly fifty years, Taylor's com-pound anxiety about the perceptual elusiveness of the divine on the one hand and the doubtful condition of his own soul on the other, each of which flouts the confirmation of the senses. Without the assurance of sense-data, Taylor turns to poetic form in an effort to materialize that which cannot be perceived. Cognizant of a sacramental model in which God man-ifests his preexisting grace through the seal of a metaphor, Taylor employs the constancy of his poetic structure as a figure for demonstrating his own spiritual constancy, and performs poetically the kind of preparation that is necessary to receive the assuring seal of grace. In his long lyric cycle, collec-tively called the *Preparatory Meditations*, Taylor acknowledges explicitly the ways in which he is using poetic structures as a perceptible proxy, a kind of ideal and stable body for the erratic soul, a substantial form that will express him as a worthy recipient of Christ's redeeming grace. In the *Preparatory Meditations*, the poetic text comes to embody in a demonstrable and consis-tent form Taylor's own process of spiritual regeneration, and enacts struc-turally Taylor's effort to purge sin and to prove ready for Christ's grace.

In order to understand the crucial role that poetic structures play in Taylor's work, we must first establish his fervent, if complex, views on the sacrament that occupied so much of his attention both spiritual and tempo-ral, and come to understand the insurmountable hermeneutic problem his sacramental theology presented.

"The Soule's the Womb. Christ is the Spermodote / And saving grace the seed cast thereinto" (31–32). So writes Taylor in *Preparatory Meditation* 2.80, a poetic reflection on the sacramental transformations implied by John 6.53: "Except you eate the flesh of the Son of Man, etc., ye haue no life in you."[4] Taylor's rendering of soteriological doctrine in sexual and reproductive imagery is not particularly uncommon as a theological practice. Indeed, in addition to inheriting a long tradition of Judeo-Christian exegesis that recognized the human soul as properly feminine before God, Taylor was joined by his New England contemporaries in understanding themselves as, ideally, Brides of Christ.[5] Taylor's treatment of this spiritual commonplace, however, is deeply informed by what one critic has called his "peculiar fascination" with the "wedden garment," a sign of righteousness in the elect that is for Taylor a mandatory prerequisite for approaching the Lord's Supper.[6] As he, with striking regularity, engages in poetic meditations intended to prepare him spiritually to receive the Lord's Supper, Taylor must search himself for evidence that he possesses the wedden garment, that he is sufficiently converted to merit communion with Christ. The resulting *Preparatory Meditations*, so cyclical in their production, implement a poetics that contains Taylor's soteriological anxiety even as it articulates his fear and doubt regarding his own worthiness, enacting formally the conversion of which Taylor can never be completely assured in practice. In his meditative lyrics, Taylor performs periodic self-cleansing in preparation to receive the grace available through the Lord's Supper, using the very structure of his poems to accomplish a drama of self-feminization so that he can demonstrate his readiness for Christ's "Spermodote."[7]

Taylor's fascination with the wedden garment is given its most doctrinally explicit expression in his *Treatise Concerning the Lord's Supper*. A series of eight meticulously argued sermons delivered over a period of a little more than a year beginning in 1693, the *Treatise* was composed to counter the increasing popularity of ideas promoted by Solomon Stoddard, a minister from nearby Northampton, who argued for universal admission to the Lord's Supper. The controversy is worth summarizing in brief: the founders of the Massachusetts Bay colonies had become by the 1660s increasingly concerned about the unanticipated number of unregenerate souls in New England—church members who may have been baptized as children but who had never experienced a spiritual conversion (that is, an experience of assurance from God that they were among the elect) or were reluctant to make the required public confession that they had experienced such a conversion. Without a confession of spiritual conversion, these unregenerate persons were not eligible for full membership in the church and consequently not eligible to receive the sacrament of the Lord's Supper. The question arose concerning whether the children of these partial members could participate in the ordinances of worship, particularly baptism—a privilege traditionally reserved for the children of full, regenerate members. The clergy were forced either to accept an exponentially dwindling membership or to compromise the rules. In response to this imminent crisis, the Synod of 1662 devised the "Half-Way Covenant," which decreed that infants of parents who had been baptized could be themselves baptized, though partaking of the Lord's Supper would continue to be reserved for those who had made a full and public confession of their spiritual conversion experience. In 1667, Stoddard began to reject the decisions of the 1662 Synod as merciless and scripturally spurious, and called for open admission to the Lord's Supper to all who sought to partake of it, regardless of their formally regenerate or unregenerate status. But Taylor vehemently resisted Stoddard's attempt at sacramental reform because Stoddard's formulation implied that the Supper functioned as a channel of grace, capable of spurring conversion in the unregenerate, rather than as a seal of preexisting grace.[8]

In his *Treatise,* Taylor bases his extended defense of the ordinance's exclusivity on the text of the twenty-second chapter of Matthew, which relates the parable of the king's marriage feast. With its cast of characters including the invited and uninvited wedding guests, this parable not only provides Taylor with scriptural foundation for restricting the Lord's Supper to the fully converted but also supplies the terminology for defining the fundamental qualification for admission to the ordinance (as well as its central enigma): the worshipper's possession of the wedden garment. Taylor's extended exegesis on the wedden garment begins with an examination of the parable, in which Jesus teaches that "The kingdom of heaven is like unto a certain king, which made a marriage for his son." When the feast is prepared, the king's servants summon the guests to dinner: "And when the King came in to see the guests, hee sawe there a man, which had not on a wedding garment, And hee sayth vnto him, Friend, how camest thou in hither, not hauing a wedding garment? And hee was speechlesse."[9] Taylor's reading of this marriage supper as an allegory for the Lord's Supper has precedent both ancient and contemporaneous. From patristic times forward, theologians of all stripes had described the Lord's Supper as a marriage, a practice that flourished in the years immediately following the Reformation. The *Treatise* itself cites religious authorities from Augustine to James Ussher as "evidence proving the Lord's Supper to be this wedden supper."[10] In each of these sources, as Taylor reports, the communicant is charged to enter the feast preparedly, and is warned about the perils of arriving without the garment. "The wedden garment is such a thing that the soul in want thereof at the wedden feast is under the displeasure and wrath of the Almighty," Taylor intones, "such a thing the want whereof in the wedden guests is a damning sin."[11] But Taylor activates an additional allegorical register, and raises the stakes for participation in the Lord's Supper considerably, when he begins to discuss the purpose of the king's marriage feast. "Why is there a wedden feast to which all under the gospel are urged to come?" he asks, and he goes on to explain that the banquet's purpose is "To celebrate the soul's espousal unto Himself." Taylor's interpretation personalizes the marriage supper, declaring, "Now Christ hath His marriage unto the soul; He espouseth it, and promiseth it marriage, and God declares it that He is married unto His people. Hence the usual title he gives her is 'spouse' in the Canticles. Now He will have His marriage celebrated. It is a matter of the greatest concern. It is the result of all His gospel wooings; it is the efflux of the greatest love. . . . It is the constituting of [the] most happy relation which the soul can enter into, of the most intimate society with Christ."[12] Although the text in Matthew specifies that the wedden garment is required for the *guest* of the wedding, Taylor's explication of the wedden supper transforms the converted and appropriately clothed guest into the Bride of the divine Bridegroom, eligible for all the "intimate society" that marriage implies.

Taylor's personalization of the allegory reveals its embedded eroticism, an association that was not lost on earlier theologians.[13] While this interpretation of the marriage feast appears in the writings of Martin Luther and Huldreich Zwingli, as well as in some Catholic catechisms, anti-Roman reformer Cornelius Hoen was perhaps the most effusive on the subject:

> quemadmodum sponsus, qui cupit suam sponsam certam reddere ne quo modo dubitet, dat ei anulum dicens: Accipe, do me ipsum tibi, illa anulum accipiens, sponsum credit esse suum ac animum ab omnibus avertit amatoribus et suo ut placeat marito cogitat. Similiter sumens eucharistiam, pignus sponsi sui, qui seipsum dare testatur, firmiter credere debet Christum iam esse suum, pro se traditum

atque sanguinem eius pro se fusum, quare animum ab omnibus avertet quae prius amare solet et soli Christo inhaerebit, quaerens quae placita sunt ei semper.

[Just as a bridegroom, who desires to render his bride certain lest she doubt his intentions, gives her a ring, saying, "Take, I give myself to you"; she, accepting the ring, believes the bridegroom to be hers, and averts her passion from all lovers and considers how she might pleasure her husband. Likewise, when she takes the Eucharist—the pledge of her Bridegroom, who affirms He gives himself to her—she ought steadfastly to believe Christ now to be hers, for he surrendered himself and poured out his blood for her. Wherefore she averts her passion from all whom she loved before, and cleaves to Christ alone, seeking always that which is pleasing to Him.][14]

Authorized thus both by scripture and by theologians with certified Reformed credentials, Taylor does not shrink from borrowing amorous language from the Song of Songs to imagine the Bride's pleasures in the consummation of the banquet: "Now the Bridesgroom will welcome thee. He will lead thee by the right hand. He will bring thee into His banqueting house, and His banner over thee will be love. He will stay thee with flaggons. He will comfort thee with apples. His left hand will be under thy head and His right hand will embrace thee (Cant. 2:4, 5, 6)."[15] The unmistakably erotic posture of the Bride and Bridegroom makes overt and vivid, and astonishingly personal, the sexuality already implicit in the familiar metaphor of the Bride of Christ. In Taylor's imagination, this wedden feast is no dry ordinance but communion of the most intimate kind.

The wedden garment, then, qualifies the communicant not only to participate in the feast but also to enter into a marriage relationship with Christ. It stands as the mark of eligibility for bridehood, the sign of the soul's successful preparation for espousal to the divine Bridegroom. For Taylor, possession of the garment is absolutely necessary for admission to the Lord's Supper because it, like a betrothal, signals a preexisting, extraordinarily personal relationship to the Bridegroom, a relationship worthy of the sacrament's seal of God's loving grace. So vital is the wedden garment to Taylor's sacramental theology, in fact, that he devotes seven of the *Treatise*'s eight sermons to defining the garment, urging its cultivation, and warning those who lack it from the feast. Though the historical context of the *Treatise* involved the administration of a public ordinance, Taylor's central concern is a private one: to provoke the individual soul to examine itself, to determine whether it possesses the wedden garment.

In order to assist in this process of self-examination, Taylor painstakingly describes the garment. "I say," he proclaims, "it is the robe of evangelical righteousness constituting the soul complete in the sight of God," or, as Taylor explains it with a nod to Revelation 19.7–8, "the righteousness of the saints." This righteousness, he elaborates, "consists in: Imputed righteousness, i.e., the righteousness of Christ's active and passive obedience made ours by God's imputation, and our own . . . called the righteousness of God by faith," as well as "Implanted righteousness, the sanctifying graces of the Spirit communicated to the soul."[16] Evangelical righteousness, in other words, is a saving relation between man and God, a state of regeneracy, with all the reproductive associations of that word's etymology intact: "You have a new disposition. Your frame of spirit and constitution is changed. You are now run into a new mold. You have wedden affections. Your heart is as espoused to Christ. Oh! your love to Him is great; your joy in Him is sweet; your reverence of Him is high; your zeal for Him is hot." And in this "new disposition," Taylor explains, "You are savingly united to Christ."[17]

As Taylor's descriptions of the wedden garment accumulate, his insistence on the essential femininity of the converted remains unambiguous. He repeatedly sounds the theme of the marriage feast, quoting Paul's letter to the Corinthians for biblical precedent: "I have espoused you to one husband, that I may present you a chaste virgin to Christ."[18] He rehearses the amorous bliss of the lovers in the Song of Songs, traditionally read as an allegory of the relationship between the christic Bridegroom and the bridal soul: "Oh! what sweet, what heart-ravishing and soul-enlivening delight will here be unto thee? Christ will stay thee with flaggons, comfort thee with apples according to thy prayer (Cant. 2.5), and draw the canopy of love over thee."[19] And Taylor mines other biblical sources for the Bride trope, promising that "God will rejoice over" the soul dressed in the wedden garment, in echo of Isaiah's reassurance that "as the bridegroom rejoiceth over the bride, so shall thy God rejoice over thee."[20] "The queen (the emblem of the soul by conversion) shall be brought to the king in raiment of needlework (Psalm 45.14)," elaborates Taylor, his interpretation identifying the Bride with an explicitly gendered "emblem" for the devout worshipper.[21] "If the soul be espoused unto Christ, it hath the wedden garment. For none espoused to Him are without it," Taylor writes, again connecting the soul's regeneracy with sacramental bridehood, and he goes on to muse, "Something of this nature you have in Abraham's servant adorning Rebecca."[22] In his persistent presentation of gendered models for the converted, Taylor asserts that the "new disposition" he advocates has a specifically feminine character, and he represents regeneracy as the end of a process of self-feminization.

In his suggestion that conversion produces a new, and newly feminized, self, Taylor follows the pattern of his fellow Puritans, who regarded the submission of all trace of will and self that is required for conversion as a transformation from masculine to feminine. According to Calvinist doctrine, the Fall instituted a separation between the will of God and the will of man, and only man's voluntary abdication of the will, his submission and receptivity to the grace of God, offers the opportunity of redemption. Man is utterly dependent upon God, and all he can do is to empty out all aspects of selfhood in order to receive Christ's righteousness. In the Calvinist tradition, the irresistible grace of Christ is frequently figured as a physical and spiritual overwhelming, a ravishment, with all the erotic valences of that term fully activated—to the implications of which John Donne was certainly alert, as we shall see in the following chapter. This understanding of the force of grace in conjunction with the receptive posture of the worshipper posits a gendered relationship between the two parties, a dynamic that becomes formalized in long-standing ecclesiastical topoi like the Canticles-derived figure of the Bride of Christ, and finds abundant scriptural authorization in such passages as the famous counsel attributed to Paul: "Wiues, submit your selues vnto your own husbands, as vnto the Lord."[23] In accordance with such scriptural figures, worshippers who believed themselves to be regenerate were exhorted to behave like Brides toward their divine Bridegroom.[24]

In fact, as Margaret W. Masson has demonstrated, the language of self-feminization is uniformly encoded into the conversion experience for Puritan men. Masson (quoting Cotton Mather) explains that "the Christian who seeks the experience [of conversion] must wait passively for Christ's overtures and then reply, 'Lord, I am Thine, save me.' As Mather urged, 'in this Act of *Resignation* there must and will be nothing less than thy very *All* included. *Resign* thy *Spirit* unto Him, and say, *O my SAVIOUR. I desire that all the Faculties of my Soul may be filled with thee, and used for thee. Resign* thy *Body* unto Him . . .' In a total submission of body and will, the individual, like the church, was to have no reservations when accepting Christ as a lover."[25] As Mather extols what he calls the *"Glorious Espousal"* of the soul to Christ, he emphasizes most strongly the would-be Bride's *"Resignation,"* a term that links feminine passivity with a more global self-denial: the soul must be willing to relinquish everything to Christ, even its own being. Moreover, as Concord minister Peter Bulkeley explains, the soul must *"Resign* thy *Body* unto Him," just as wives were to surrender their bodies to husbands.[26] True regeneration—the weave of Taylor's wedden garment—involves, perhaps paradoxically, an active demonstration of feminine submission to the Bridegroom.

New England divines enthusiastically applied such gendered language as they admonished their congregants to submit to the will of God. Bulkeley advised that "It is a marriage-covenant that we make with God," and "therefore we must doe as the Spouse doth, resigne up our selves to be ruled and governed accordingly to his will."[27] So conventional is the figure, in fact, that John Winthrop relies upon it in a letter to his wife: "beinge thereby affected wth the remembrance of that entire & sweet love that had been sometymes betweene us, God brought me by that occasion in to suche a heavenly meditation of the love betweene Christ & me, as ravished my heart wth unspeakable ioye; methought my soule had as familiar and sensible society wth him, as my wife could have wth the kindest husbande; I desired no other happinesse but to be embraced of him; I held nothinge so deere that I was not willinge to parte wth for him."[28] Winthrop's willingness to part with everything he possesses, even his masculine selfhood, exemplifies the resignation of will that characterizes the soul espoused to Christ. The process of resignation and submission that empties out selfhood prepares the soul to be filled with Christ at the wedden feast, the Lord's Supper.[29]

If bridal self-resignation makes possible "intimate society" with Christ, it also promises the sequel of such a relationship. Taylor's contemporary Thomas Foxcroft preached ecstatically about the converted's consummation with God as a state in which "the Saints shall be impregnated."[30] Mather, too, in a pamphlet directed toward pregnant women, extends his sexualization of the soul's espousal to Christ to the marriage bed, advising that "The Voice of your Faith is, *O my Saviour, I am thine; Do thou Possess me; And by thee let me bring forth Fruit unto God*."[31] David Leverenz has explained that, as with marriage between a husband and a wife, the end of this spiritual marriage between the soul and Christ was expected to be progeny: "More crucial than the simile of intercourse in the marriage comparisons . . . is the fantasy of its fruition: the self's rebirth."[32] Such reproductive metaphors give voice to a hope that within the womb of the soul will grow a new version of the self wholly consonant with the divine, unblemished by the stain of sin—a regenerate selfhood characterized by its resemblance to Christ. As Mather exclaims to his expectant audience, "You have a *Child formed in* you. But, Oh! That you might have a CHRIST formed in you!"[33]

As Taylor understands it, possessing the wedden garment necessary for the local event of the Lord's Supper ultimately has eschatological consequences, for right attendance upon the wedden feast qualifies the communicant for all the fruits of marriage to Christ, including impregnation with his image. The wedden garment is fundamentally the sign of the elect. Throughout the *Treatise,* Taylor doggedly stresses the vital importance of having the wedden garment *before* approaching the marriage feast. Indeed, communicating this point is his primary concern over the eight sermons. As he repeatedly reminds his audience, the ill-clad wedding guest of the parable "was speechless" in the face of the king's rebuke. In Taylor's interpretation, there can be no excuse, no response, no justification for attending the Lord's Supper without the garment. In other words, regeneracy must precede participation in the ordinance: the soul must already display the signs of having become a Bride of Christ.

That the minister's exhortations continue so strenuously, even shrilly, over such a sustained interval suggests a profound anxiety about the process of discerning the garment. How, after all, can the communicant know whether his soul wears the wedden garment? In an effort to address this problem, Taylor goes to great lengths to classify the garment so that his congregation might more easily be able to discern it in themselves. He instructs all souls to examine themselves for signs of grace lest they approach the Supper unworthily and risk damnation. "Hence it behooves us, as we would secure ourselves from the peril of our souls, to try our souls whether they be arrayed in this wedden garment, that if we have the same we may have the comfort thereof, and if we have not the same, we might see our nakedness and seek for the wedden garment to be arrayed therewith."[34] Taylor counsels the listener at every turn to "examine himself," to "try by this," to "try thyself by the same," to "search after these properties in particular," to "put the case to the trial to see whether the wedden robe is ours."[35] But even as he enumerates the characteristics of the truly regenerate—"An humble frame of spirit," "A soul-trembling frame at the Word," and "An utter enmity against all sin," a "hunger and thirst after righteousness," and "A holy life and conversation"—Taylor recognizes that these signs of conversion remain at best indeterminate. "In general," these properties appear in the converted, he equivocates. That is, the presence of such characteristics indicates that "thou hast *a like spirit to such as have* this wedden garment." When it comes to describing how the signs of regeneracy may be discerned, Taylor makes no guarantees, but rather allows that humility and holy conversation *might* mean that the wedden garment is present. Likewise, the presence of sin, or "A multitude of carnal thoughts, or worldly ploddings about the things of this life" *might* indicate unregeneracy, but "though this darkens the evidence, thou art not to conclude hence that thou hast not the wedden garment." In short, he must resignedly conclude, "You may easier come to be sure that you have it not, if you have it not, than that you have it, if you have it."[36]

Despite his repeated clamor for self-examination, Taylor must concede that an individual's worthiness for admission to the Lord's Supper is finally unknowable, with the implication that no amount of clerical oversight and public confession can ascertain the wedden garment. For all his tenacity about restricting the Lord's Supper to the regenerate, Taylor must confront the fact that regeneracy is itself a matter impenetrable even to constant self-examination. Though like many of his Puritan contemporaries he regards righteous actions—such "outward fruits, as a holy life, and Conversation"—as likely indicators of conversion, he yet admits that some degree of doubt must persist in the conversion process.[37] In urging souls to try themselves for signs of salvation, he advises not to look for "A knowledge of assurance," but rather for "a *probable* knowledge that this wedden garment is ours."[38] It is significant that Taylor's discussion of the difficulty of proving conversion is delivered in the first-person plural; Taylor's hedging about assured signs of election, presented as encouragement to those who fear they are not worthy to approach the marriage feast, nevertheless acknowledges the principle of uncertainty that undergirds every soul's experience of saving grace, including his own. His public distress in the *Treatise* about the unworthy reception of the Supper articulates a private anxiety about the soul's inscrutable preparation for union with God, an anxiety that implicates his own indeterminable worthiness. When he cries out, in the midst of one of the *Treatise*'s sermons, "Oh! then try, try, Soul, whether this wedden garment is thine," it is to his own soul he cries.[39]

I do not mean to speculate that Taylor doubted that he had experienced God's saving grace. His own account of God's "gracious workings to me wards" was publicly related at the organization of the Westfield congregation.[40] Rather, I am arguing that despite such a conversion experience, Taylor continues to be alarmed by the persistence of sinfulness even after an apparent apprehension of God's grace. The *Treatise* preaches that fear of one's sinful unworthiness to approach the Lord's Supper need only be "equally balanced"[41] by a faithful hope in one's worthiness, which balance produces that "probable knowledge" of salvation. But even as Taylor offers this consolation, he darkens that "knowledge" with the specter of its mere probability, and remarks that "I may have a certainty of it, and may lose it again. For the apostle saith that where there is knowledge, it shall fail (1 Cor. 13.8), or vanish away."[42]

Against the difficulty of discerning the wedden garment with certainty, Taylor offers hope to "move affections, and bring over the soul to this wedden garment." He implores those who are in doubt to "Set upon a new life" purged of their sinful nature, and to "Endeavor with your heart and soul that they lay out their strong love and affections on God." And finally, in language that reaffirms the soul's absolute dependence on God to effect salvation, he presses, "Beg the Bridesgroom to give thee this wedden garment."[43] Taylor's counsel posits the solution to soteriological doubt in terms that continue the gendered drama of conversion. If true conversion is characterized by the soul's feminization, self-examination for signs of conversion reveals properly feminine traits, including submissiveness, receptivity, and "strong love and affections" toward the Bridegroom. But if self-examination does not reveal such signs, Taylor here urges those who doubt their possession of the wedden garment to put into play an early modern spiritualized ethic of *fake it till you make it*—that is, to act bridal, demonstrating to God a willingness to be the Bride by adopting her submissive, self-emptying posture.

If the *Treatise Concerning the Lord's Supper* is animated by Taylor's public concern about the wedden garment's undetectability, the *Preparatory Meditations* register the poet's private negotiation of his own soteriologically ambiguous status. In these lyric utterances, each composed as Taylor prepared himself both to administer and to participate in the Lord's Supper, we find Taylor confronting the condition of his own soul, conducting the self-examination he prescribes to his congregants in an effort to distinguish characteristics of the Bride. As Taylor readies himself for the marriage feast, he repeatedly expresses his fear that he is insufficiently converted, a fear that Taylor renders poetically, as in the *Treatise*, in gendered terms. Throughout the *Preparatory Meditations*, Taylor engages in the process of trying his own soul to discover evidence of the wedden garment, a process that with startling frequency finds the poet describing himself using feminine tropes. This pattern of self-feminization, as we shall see, is enacted not only in the recurrent bridal imagery of the *Preparatory Meditations* but in the lyrics' thematic concerns as well. Moreover, Taylor's investment in the cultivation of bridal readiness informs the poetic structure of the work as a whole.

Given Taylor's conventional reliance on the figure of the Bride of Canticles in the *Treatise*, it is not surprising to find such imagery recurring as he meditates in preparation for the wedden feast[44]—though the term "recurring" may be putting it mildly, for Canticles, as Barbara K. Lewalski has observed, "may fairly be said to encompass and dominate Taylor's poems."[45] To be sure, citations from and direct or indirect references to the Song of Songs permeate the *Meditations*: verses from the Song's eight short chapters make up nearly a third of the poems' source texts, and all but four of the poems from the last twelve years of composition are based on Canticles. Taylor borrows heavily from the Song's description of the Bridegroom, lauding Christ variously as "A Box of Ointments" (1.3.7), "Sharons Rose" (1.4.24), "Thou Lilly of the Vallys" (1.5.18), and, of course, "my Bridesgroom Deare Espousde" (1.23.48). His devotion to this trope persists over a remarkable stretch of time; it shows up in the first meditation of the series, composed in 1682, in which Taylor marvels at the power of divine love that "Marrie'de our Manhood, making it its Bride" (1.1.6), and reappears over and over again through the last meditation in 1725, in which he admits to being "Heart sick my Lord heart sick of Love to thee!" (2.165.1). As he appropriates the language of Canticles, Taylor reinscribes his position as the feminine, bridal "Spouse," preserving the gendered relationship between the self and God that he imagines throughout the *Treatise*.

Like his Puritan contemporaries, Taylor expands the spousal relationship from Canticles into the reproductive eventuality it implies, using language that emphasizes the self-emptying receptivity of the Bride. "Be thou my Flowers," he bargains, "I'le be thy Flower Pot" (1.5.6). "My Soul thy Violl make, and therewith fill," he petitions elsewhere, and later in the same poem, "Grace in thy Lips pourd out's as Liquid Gold. / Thy Bottle make my Soule, Lord, it to hold" (1.7.6, 17–18). And again, in a later meditation, "Lord, make me th'Vally where this Lilly grows. / Then I am thine, and thou art mine indeed" (1.69.37–38). In each of these instances and many others, the soul is offered up as the container, the vessel, the "Cabbinet" (2.6.40) ready for rifling, the "Pot" where flowers may be planted, the "Violl" for receiving Christ's liquid love, the visually suggestive "Vally" where Christ's "Lilly" can be implanted. These and a variety of other feminine images for the self thematize the change of form and constitution that Taylor's *Treatise* insists upon for the soul that would wear the "wedden garment." In assuming a female role, he shows himself to be quite literally willing to cast off the "old man" and to put on a "new mold."

Moreover, in his new, feminized conception of selfhood, Taylor demonstrates his resignation to Christ, offering up his sins, his body, and in Mather's words from *A Glorious Espousal*, "*all the Faculties of my Soul*" to be "*filled with thee.*" As I have already suggested, implicit in this abundant imagery of receptive femininity are not just the soul's bridal aspirations but also its readiness for the seed of grace. Taylor explicates the reproductive function of the marriage with startling lucidity in that striking passage from Meditation 2.80: "The Soul's the Womb. Christ is the Spermodote / And Saving Grace the seed cast thereinto." The end of Taylor's bridal self-feminization is to render the self a fruitful receptacle. "Lord make me Cask, and thy rich Love its Wine," Taylor prays, "Impregnate with its Spirits, Lord, my heart" (2.98.43–44). Nor does Taylor shrink from devising explicit representations of fruitful intercourse between God and himself. "Then let thy Sweetspike sweat its liquid Dew / Into my Chystall Viall," he writes, "and there swim" (2.62.19–20). And elsewhere:

> O let thy lovely streams of Love distill
> > Upon myselfe and spoute their spirits pure
> Into my Viall, and my Vessel fill
> > With liveliness. (2.32.49–52)

Taylor distinguished his interest from mere sexual consummation, stipulating that he seeks union not for its own sake but in order to become a legitimate vessel for reproduction. As he writes,

> Then, my Blesst Lord, let not the Bondmaids type
> > Take place in mee. But thy blesst Promisd Seed.
> Distill thy Spirit through thy royall Pipe
> > Into my Soule, and so my Spirits feed. (2.4.25–28)

In Taylor's schema, self-feminization leads to the possibility of occupying the position of the Bride, which leads in turn to a successful union with Christ, whose "royall Pipe" will "spoute" its seed into Taylor's receptive "Chrystall Viall." Having secured both wedlock and consummation, the Bride of Christ will "feed the Spouses infants in her womb" (2.149.36).

Taylor's reproductive tropes for regeneration articulate his conviction that within the womb of the converted soul a reformed and regenerate subjectivity will develop, a new self that is in harmony with the divine, undeformed by sin, and recognizable by its resemblance to Christ. Taylor wishes to *conceive* of Christ, in both senses of that term, and thereby to bring forth a self "new minted by thy Stamp indeed" (1.6.7), to "read / Thine image, and Inscription stampt on mee" (1.6.9–10). As the paternity of children was understood to be known by their resemblance to their father, so Taylor prays of the regenerate self he hopes to become: "My person make thy Lookinglass Lord, clear / And in my Looking Glass cast thou thine Eye. / Thy image view that standeth shining there" (2.92.38–40).[46] The conversion process, as Taylor's lyrics figure its drama of submission and surrender, is unavoidably sexualized, its sequencing suggests nothing so much as the logical progression from courtship to marriage to pregnancy and reproduction.

In a Meditation on Canticles 6.3, Taylor presents an idealized synopsis of this marriage narrative, again using language familiar from the Song of Songs:

> Lord, make my Heart the Vally, and plant there
> > Thyselfe the Lillie there to grow. No Scorns
> Shall me amuse, if I'me thy Lilly clear
> > *All though I be thy Lilly midst of thorns.*
> > *If I thy Lilly Fair and Sweet be thine*
> > *My heart shall be thy Harbor. Thou art mine.*

> If I thy Vally, thou its Lilly bee.
> > My Heart shall be thy Chrystall looking Glass
> Shewing thy Lillies Face most cleare in mee
> > In shape and beauty that doth brightly flash.
> > My Looking Glass shall weare thy Lillies Face
> > As tis thy Looking Glass of Every Grace. (2.132.25–36)

Taylor begins this passage with a plea for God to accept a feminized version of himself, a vaginal "Vally" ready for planting. In it, he hopes, God will plant himself, which seed will bloom into a perfect resemblance of the christic "Lillie." The "Lillies Face" overshadows the valley, supplanting the valley's own image with a new "shape and beauty." The now effaced speaker will be seen only as a reflection of Christ's qualities, transformed from "Vally" to "thy Lilly clear." Just as in the gendered paradigm of conversion the path to identity with Christ lies first through a feminine surrender of the self, so in Taylor's poetic fantasia on Canticles nothing short of the evacuation of selfhood removes all trace of will and sinfulness and results in successful insemination by the Bridegroom.

But even as Taylor implores that Christ's "royall Pipe" might discharge grace into his "Vessel," he recognizes that his own sinful nature stands as an obstacle to the viable implantation of evangelical righteousness. He understands his fallen, human state as "barren" and unfit for Christ's seed: "My barren heart thy Fruitfull Vally make" (1.5.7), he begs, wailing, "My barren Heart is such an hungry Soile / No Fruits it yields meet for thyselfe, my King" (2.123B.7). He wonders, "Shall this poore barren mould of mine e're bee / Planted with Spirituall Vines and pomegranates?" (2.144.31–32). In their frequent registering of the soul's infertility, Taylor's *Meditations* perform the same anxiety that fuels his ecclesiastical fervor in the *Treatise*. Taylor's lyrics personalize the concerns of the *Treatise*, communicating doubt that he is worthy to be the Bride and revealing a pervasive fear that his corrupt nature will bar him from intercourse with the Bridegroom and consign him forever to barrenness.

This is the crisis that animates Taylor's response to the Lord's Supper, and the solution he proposes entails its own problematics. From the pulpit, he preaches toward a cultivation of hope through self-examination to determine signs of the wedden garment, but if those signs prove too elusive to provide hope, he advises that the soul endeavor to act like the Bride, casting off the behaviors of the "old man" and begging the Bridegroom for full conversion. Taylor's enthusiastic appropriation of the feminine position in his meditative lyrics accomplishes a demonstration of his willingness to be the Bride, a performance that balances his fears of barrenness. This ostentatious show of receptive self-feminization saturates the devotional posture of the *Preparatory Meditations*. But the role of Bride, however vigorously undertaken, remains perceptually problematic for Taylor, in part because

of the impossibility of discerning true bridal regeneracy in the imperceptible soul and in part because of Taylor's own resolutely and perfectly perceptible masculine physicality. In order to secure the position he aspires to,
Taylor must experiment upon the model of the Lord's Supper, finding some
way to transform a metaphor into a seal, a reliable and effectual sign. The
cyclical structure of the *Preparatory Meditations* provides Taylor with the
stable, perceptible form he needs to perform the principles of constancy,
self-denial, and receptivity that characterize bridelike preparation for
Christ. As he returns each month to their composition, Taylor manifests
his readiness for Christ's gracious influence even as he laments his sinful
inadequacy. But against these myriad obstacles to his own bridehood, Taylor develops a poetic response: a cyclical poetics that rewrites failure as
success, each month's chastisements serving but to prove yet once more
that he has fashioned himself into the Bride.

The unvarying form of the *Meditations* has prompted some critics to
condemn Taylor as tedious, and to find in his lyrics what Karl Keller
describes as "a process of consecutive occurrences without climax, without
conclusion, without concern for time, without finish, without resolution."[47]
This sentiment is echoed by William Scheick, who announces with evident
disapproval that "when the reader realizes that Taylor wrote the *Preparatory
Meditations* over a span of forty-three years (1682–1725), he is struck by
their static quality. In spite of some thematic variety, there is, generally
speaking, no development, no divergence, no progress in the thought or
artistry of his verse."[48] The editor of Taylor's major prose, Norman Grabo,
likewise describes the narrative of the *Meditations* in less than flattering
terms as "repetitious and unending," which makes it all the less appealing
that "all the stages of it must be uttered throughout his entire life."[49] But
this same dramatic stasis in the lyric development of the series, which these
scholars consider to be a mark of Taylor's status as a minor and even a
"primitive" poet, contributes rather actively to Taylor's project of self-
feminization, ingeniously reenacting in the sequence's very structure the
poems' repeated concerns with emptying out the self to receive the Bridegroom's seed.[50] Taylor's lyrics, so regular in their production every four to
six weeks, enact a periodic self-cleansing in preparation for the wedden
feast, realizing a process of menstrual evacuation in preparation for the
possibility of receiving Christ's "Spermodote."

As we have seen, in order to receive Christ's seed, Taylor believes, the
self must be emptied out of its sinful nature. This principle obtains in the

mechanics of physical reproduction no less than in the soul's purgations. Accordingly, Taylor writes, "Empt me of Sin: Fill mee with Grace" (2.42.45), and repeats that plea in various terms throughout the *Meditations*. "Scoure thou my pipes then play thy tunes therein" (2.7.40), he petitions. "Cleanse, and enlarge my kask: It is too small" (1.49.19), he pleads. "I fain would purge the poison out" (2.67A.25), he frets, and prays that God will "purge away all Filth and Guilt" (2.14.11) and "get out my dross" (1.35.34). As he entreats God to effect an evacuation of his human sinfulness, Taylor employs language that emphasizes once again the gendered dynamic at work in his conception of salvation. Taylor's entreaties to be purged, emptied, scoured out, and cleansed of all sin articulate a fear that his womblike soul is not prepared for the Bridegroom's seed. In this formulation, sin becomes equivalent to the dross of the womb, the useless substance flushed out by menstruation as the uterus prepares itself for another cycle of fertility. Taylor's meditations repeat his homiletic observation that when we scrutinize our souls to find evidence of the wedden garment, the spectacle of our sin asserts itself, such that "our best service will appear unto us as an unclean thing, and all our righteousness as a filthy rag or a menstruous cloth."[51]

Taylor's recording of sin in language that recalls the female reproductive system's periodic cycle corresponds with the gynecological literature of the day, which was based as much on beliefs about women's inherent inferiority handed down from antiquity and in religious contexts as on scientific observation. The lengthy injunctions in Leviticus against the ceremonial and social participation of menstruating women explicitly defined the "issue" of the womb as "unclean."[52] This biblical proscription was sublimated in sixteenth- and seventeenth-century medical texts into more scientific discourse by way of Galen and Hippocrates, who had argued that women were of a colder and less active disposition than men: while constitutionally hot men could sweat out the impurities from their blood, constitutionally cold and sweatless women must purge their blood impurities another way. "Some call them purgations, because that by this fluxe all a womans body is purged of superfluous humours," explained one 1632 medical manual.[53] Nicholas Fontanus's popular handbook *The Womans Doctour* uses more explicitly moral terms to describe the physical effects of menstruation: "by benefit of those evacuations, the feculent and corrupt blood might be purified which otherwise as being the purest part of the blood, would liable to take poison should it remain in the body and putrefy."[54] In its identification of menstrual blood as the most "feculent and corrupt blood," this passage demonstrates the redaction of Levitican ritual uncleanness into gynecological axiom, and expresses a view widely disseminated in the medical literature of the late Renaissance that menstruation, in the words of a popular midwife's handbook from the 1700s, evacuates from the body its most "Excrementitious and Unprofitable Blood."[55]

Perhaps not surprisingly, given their frequent recourse to bodily terminology for spiritual concerns, Puritan preachers seized upon these gyneco-moral attitudes in their own writings, importing language familiar from medical writings on women's bodies to describe the soul's impurity. American minister Thomas Shepard warns that "the sin of thine heart or nature is the cause, the womb that contains, breeds, brings forth, suckels all the liter, all the troop of sins that are in thy life"; Shepard then graphically develops that trope to assert that the corrupted soul "is a menstruous cloth, polluted with sin."[56] Englishman Thomas Goodwin likewise declares that "all the righteousness that we could ever do, cannot make amends for one sin; for suppose it perfect, whenas yet it is but dung, Mal. ii. 3, and a menstruous cloth." Moreover, Goodwin asserts elsewhere, even "our best righteousness is but as a menstruous cloth."[57] The close association that Shepard and Goodwin (and ultimately Taylor) find between sin and gyne-cology can be traced to its scriptural sources in Isaiah 64.6, where Israel's uncleanness is described as "garments with menstrual filth" (וכבגד עדים), and Isaiah 30.22, where Israel is commanded to cast away its sinful idolatry like a "menstruous cloth" (דוה).[58]

Taylor's own homiletic concern with the "menstruous cloth" of sin works within the already active trope of self-feminization to indicate that sinfulness prevents the desired union with Christ the Bridegroom—and, by extension, that it will block the implantation of Christ's seed. Menstruation becomes, in Taylor's reproductive drama, a sign of the sinful soul's failure to conceive of Christ. "Cleanse mee thus with thy Rich Bloods Sweet Shower," Taylor begs, invoking Christ again in seminal imagery and pleading for the suspension of the cycle in fertility: "My Issue stop" (2.27.61–62).[59] However, Taylor's lyrics also acknowledge menstruation as a means of self-cleansing. In all his desire for scouring, emptying, and purging of the soul, Taylor implicitly acknowledges that menstruation serves to "get out my dross" and prepares the soul to receive Christ's Spermodote. Menstruation thus becomes a model for spiritual self-examination and purification; after all, as Taylor teaches in the *Treatise*, "We are always to be purifying ourselves from all filthiness both of flesh and spirit."[60] In the context of Taylor's own self-examination and preparation for the Lord's Supper, the *Preparatory Meditations* document the poet's efforts to purify himself from all filthiness before he enters the marriage supper, and thus to gain "probable knowledge" that he possesses the required wedden garment. Taylor's lyrics demonstrate his willingness to perform the necessary self-feminization of conversion not only in their proliferation of feminine images for the self and figurative dependence upon the Canticles allegory but even in the cyclical, menstrual schedule of Taylor's self-purging. This appropriation of the feminine position into the poetic structure of the *Preparatory Meditations* fortifies the lyrics' more overt imagistic and thematic projects of self-feminization, coding Taylor's "new disposition" into the very form of his poetic self-representation.

This structural expression of femininity affirms Taylor's bridal posture even in the absence of assurance—and what is more, even as a function of doubt. The integration of a feminine program into the *Meditations*' recurrent poetic structure arises, after all, in response to the wedden garment's perpetual elusiveness. For the *Meditations* continue to register an awareness of Taylor's sinful unworthiness to be the Bride, and continue to communicate doubt in both content and form, throughout the period of their composition. Meditation 1.1, written in July 1682, concludes with Taylor's conviction that he is frigid in response to the ardent grace of God:

> Oh! my streight'ned Breast! my Lifeless Sparke!
>> My Fireless Flame! What Chilly Love, and Cold?
>> In measure small! In Manner Chilly! See.
>> Lord blow the Coal: Thy Love Enflame in mee. (15–18)

Meditation 2.161B, composed over forty years later, finds Taylor worrying still that he does not merit the Bridegroom's affections:

> My Love alas is a small shrivled thing
>> A little Crickling a blasted bud . . .
>> And shall I then presume therewith to greet
>> The precious jewels that adorn thy feet? (7–8, 11–12)

The lyrics continue to express doubt about the soul's worthiness to occupy the Bride position, as Taylor's self-examination reveals to him a heart hobbled by the "carnal thoughts, or worldly ploddings" characteristic of the unregenerate. "Oh! woe is me!" he complains in one poem,

> Was ever Heart like mine?
> A Sty of Filth, a Trough of Washing-Swill
> A Dunghill Pit, a Puddle of mere Slime.
> A Nest of Vipers, Hive of Hornets; Stings.
> A Bag of Poyson, Civit-Box of Sins. (1.40.2–6)

But the structure of Taylor's *Meditations* provides that balance of hope against the poet's doubt which is necessary in his view for probable knowledge of one's conversion. Taylor's cyclical practice of self-examination does not usher in a full assurance that he has attained a feminized, regenerate state but rather points up his "shrivled" love and "Chilly Heart," his unaffectionate and unresponsive unworthiness to occupy the bridal role. However, in the absence of certainty, Taylor returns each Supper day to his lyric process of self-examination, representing himself in terms that display his preexisting femininity, his qualification to be the Bride, before approaching the marriage feast. Taylor's poetic process of purgation and preparation, conducted with menstrual regularity, achieves a structural femininity that persists despite the poems' thematic uncertainty about conversion. In fact, it is precisely this uncertainty that prompts further cycles of purgation and preparation, such that Taylor's soteriological doubt produces regularly recurrent periods of formal self-feminization. By incorporating the reproductive drama of conversion into their lyric calendar, the *Preparatory Meditations* inscribe femininity onto the whole of Taylor's poetic self-representation. This self-feminizing poetics accomplishes a structural expression of the gendered process of conversion, allowing Taylor to exhibit bridal characteristics even as his lines communicate despair at his unworthiness to be the Bride. By periodically emptying out sin, purging the dross of his nature as if it were a "menstruous cloth," Taylor displays his persistent hope that he is prepared for Christ's Spermodote, dressed in the wedden robes of a converted selfhood and qualified to enter into the wedden supper's glorious espousals.

This gynecological model of self-emptying and preparation, so crucial to Taylor's scheme of salvation, is effected in Taylor's *Preparatory Meditations* by the unvarying poetic structure of the series. It's not sufficient to say that poetic structure here serves to reinforce the content of the poems; rather, the structural organization of the series—the regular intervals of its composition, the remarkable stanzaic consistency over nearly five fertile decades—makes its own set of claims that both complements and contradicts the thematic drama of the poems. Indeed, the success of the structural argument of the *Preparatory Meditations* depends upon the failure of their thematic argument, for it is Taylor's continued apprehension about his own base unworthiness that prompts the next poem, and the next, and the next, his anxiety presenting finally as another sign of feminized submission in the menstrual dynamic of the poetic cycle.[61] Even as Taylor's self-scrutinizing verse agonizes repeatedly and regularly over his apparent lack of qualification to fulfill the Bride position, the menstrual poetics of the *Preparatory Meditations* affirm that he has already managed to do just that.

It is no coincidence that this contrapuntal argument is made by means of a conspicuously fixed stanzaic form, a form that aggregates into a display of astonishing constancy over the *Preparatory Meditations'* long composition. The cyclical structure of Taylor's meditations comes to stand as a sensorily perceptible expression of the argument he hopes to make about his own submission. The structural method of the series is striking on its own, and especially given the temporal span of the project, but it becomes even more noteworthy when one takes into account the obvious influence of Herbert on Taylor. Herbert's devotional priorities and tortuous self-examination clearly inform Taylor's work, and Taylor freely adopts many stylistic qualities from the earlier poet, including the colloquial register of his self-interrogation as well as his domestic imagery and quotidian language. But Herbert's most distinguishing poetic feature—the astonishing and ostentatious formal innovation discussed in the last chapter—Taylor passes by, in part because the incarnational program of Herbert's verse is less theologically relevant to the Calvinist minister and in part because Taylor seeks to marshal the expressivities of form to a different end than Herbert required, one that advertises a version of selfhood based on steadfastness and continuity.

Moreover, where Herbert's form is calculated to produce a kind of eucharistic immanence in the materiality of the poem, Taylor seeks to replicate another kind of sacramental ordinance, one that conforms to his anti-Stoddardean view that the Lord's Supper is not a channel of grace but a seal. The Lord's Supper reveals, according to Taylor's formulation, the preexisting reality of the presence of grace in the worshipper. It renders grace, an intangible and imperceptible phenomenon, visible as a ritual of bread and wine. This ordinance does not, in Taylor's conviction, bring the body of Christ into objective presence on the altar; rather, it is a perceptible

sign of God's covenanted redemption made apprehensible to the regenerate. The Lord's Supper constitutes the wedden feast, the physicalized and
tangible cognate for the already accomplished spiritual communion
between the bridal soul and God.[62] The ordinance offers a sort of incarnation, finally—not by substantiating Christ's material presence in the elements of bread and wine but by confirming and enfleshing the indiscernible
operation of grace, sealing it into perceptibility. Taylor's own poetic writing
on the institution of the sacrament bears out this function; in one of the
preparatory lyrics, Taylor delineates the representational valences of Jesus's
actions at "his Supper last" (2.105.30):

> To shew that he our nature took, he then
>   Tooke breade, and wine best Elementall trade,
> Designed as the Sign thereof. Which when
>   He had his blessing over it display'de
>   To shew his Consecration, then it brake,
>   To signify his Sufferings for our sake. (2.105.31–36)

In Taylor's formulation, the bread and the wine manifest not Jesus's body
but his nature and his actions, the operations he undertakes in his christic
role. As these lines describe this first iteration of the Lord's Supper, the
elements in the context of their sacramental institution serve as a seal, or a
visible sign, of Jesus's present but imperceptible consecrated and redemptive nature. In their continual application in the ritual, which repeats that
paschal feast of bread and wine, the elements likewise stand as a visible sign
for the mysterious presence of imperceptible grace.

Taylor's lyric cycle functions in much the same way as does his sacrament of the Lord's Supper—that is, as a seal that makes perceptible a preexisting but intangible condition. Taylor's menstrual poetics actualizes the
spiritual principle of bridal preparation it suggests, and serves as a poetic
seal of Taylor's devotion, his self-denial, his purgative self-emptying and
perpetual readiness for the seed of Christ. The cyclical and persistent structure of the *Preparatory Meditations* embodies Taylor's process of bridelike
submission, manifesting the imperceptible qualities that may demonstrate
his regeneracy in a fully apprehensible poetic body. This body is not suscep-
tible to the transparency of referential semantics—not defined by all those
content-based declarations with which Taylor's lyrics always end in a conviction of the failure of his devotional project. Rather, this poetic body

refuses to be absorbed into the thematic failures of Taylor's preparatory lyrics. In the context of Taylor's long meditative project, the structure's consistency and cyclical regularity assert themselves antiabsorptively against Taylor's recurrent lamentations about the failures of his own righteousness and his corresponding despair about the capacity of God's mysterious grace to form in him a "new mold." The uncertainties of Taylor's spiritual state, so constantly the desolate theme of his self-exploratory poems, are answered by an unyielding structural certainty that manifests the character-istics of regeneracy in an assured poetic form, fully available to sense per-ception. Taylor's reformed and regenerate selfhood is sealed thus not in the semantic content of his protestations but in his menstrual poetics, the poetic cycle itself serving as a reformed lyric body. And this lyric reforma-tion of the self posits an alternate corporeality in which the gendered valences of both spiritual conversation and sacramental worship, so objec-tively insurmountable for Taylor, might be satisfied.

Like Herbert, Taylor avails himself of the communicative properties of structure itself. In his *Preparatory Meditations* the expressivities of poetic form are marshaled as a means of securing the lyric event to its material expression. Taylor's use of form-in-time, embodied in the structure of his lyric series as a seal of regeneracy, makes use of the poem's status as a sensorily apprehensible matrix of signs that materialize that which is per-ceptually absent. Taylor exploits the structure of his *Preparatory Meditation* as a communicative end in itself—that is, as an object whose signification is self-contained. In so doing, Taylor is able to construct a drama of regen-eracy that develops alongside and distinct from the narrative of self-doubt and failure thematized in his poems, and stands as an *a priori* seal of the bridal position for which he aspires to qualify. Taylor capitalizes on the embodied qualities of poetic structure to substantiate his refractory and barren self into the assurance of grace.

The ways in which poetics are necessarily bound up with embodiment are not limited to poetic form. I have to this point been discussing devo-tional strategies that rely upon the capacities of structure and form to serve as instruments for producing an antiabsorptive textual substantiality, but the commitment we see in post-Reformation devotional verse to an antiab-sorptive poetics informs all aspects of poetic production and ramifies into the symbolic system itself, producing surprising and at times disorienting effects. Though its materialist registers are often overlooked, symbol is deeply invested in the relationship between the apprehensible and the abstract, and this feature is amplified in the incarnationally invested context of the sacrament of the Lord's Supper. Like both Herbert and Taylor, John Donne is concerned with the role of the body in sacramental worship—Christ's body as well as his own. For Donne, the most plangent site of bodily significance is not poetic structure but rather the symbolic functionalities of metaphor. Rendering comprehensible and familiar terms that elude apprehension by their abstraction or absence, symbol summons the material as a site of presence. For Donne, the materialist valences of symbol are central to its potential to realize presence. And just as Taylor's poems employ structure to construct a corporeal argument that supplements his inconsolable lyric thematics, Donne's extravagant metaphors, as we shall see, answer his own uncertain spiritual position with the assurance of a persistent materiality. Like Taylor's menstrual poetics, Donne's metaphors relocate significance to the fleshly, in order to claim the poetic sign as an efficacious and substantive object and a communicative end in itself.

Chapter 3

Embracing the Medium: Metaphor and Resistance in John Donne

The practices that we have seen in the poems of George Herbert and Edward Taylor call attention to the way that poetic form and structure refuse to be sublimated into the transparency of semantic content. In the work of those poets, the material and substantial valences of the poetic text are themselves significant, objectively present and full of the substance of meaning in themselves. As the architectural elements of poetry constitute the site in which meaning inheres, they serve as organizing principles of perception, propounding, to return again to Allen Grossman's phrase, "the presence of presence."[1] In this capacity, poetic form is not unlike metaphor, which, as Renaissance rhetoricians were aware, presented "the formes of knowen things . . . to mans use"—or, to put this description by Henry Peacham another way, metaphor serves as an apprehensible object of knowledge, neither incidental nor merely ornamental but operative and substantially constitutive.[2] For John Donne, it is the very apprehensibility of metaphor that makes of it such an optimal presencing engine, a feature that God uses to fullest advantage in biblical text. Donne singles out the "livelier" effects of figurative language in a 1623 sermon, noting that metaphor "may work *greater impressions* upon the Readers."[3] Donne's homiletic description of the palpable force brought to bear by metaphor helps illuminate the poet's energetic experiments upon figuration. As Taylor does, Donne leaves in his sermons a healthy metacommentary on the concerns that animate his poetry; not surprisingly, over the course of his numerous extant sermons, Donne turns frequently to the subject of figuration, its operation, its use, and its effects. In his sermons, Donne both explains and enacts his tropic poetics. As he says in a 1620 sermon, "It is true that S. *Augustine* sayes, *Figura nihil probat*, A figure, an Allegory proves nothing; yet, sayes he, *addit lucem, & ornat*, It makes that which is true in it selfe, more evident and more acceptable."[4] Donne's formulation here, based on his reading of Augustine, is that metaphor works to manifest, to make "acceptable"—by which he means *receivable*—that which is. Trope is, in Donne's symbolic metaphysics, not a referential tool but a presencing machine, working to accomplish a pleroma of substance in itself. The relationship between the perceptible and substantial impression available in metaphor and Donne's investment in the singular significance of materiality, so crucial to his poetics, is most explicitly theorized in his prose, to which we must first turn.

Perhaps the best place to begin an examination of Donne's interest in material substance is with its disintegration. The fate of the body after death is the subject of repeated rumination throughout Donne's work, and the topic becomes the center of gravity in the last sermon that Donne preached, a few weeks before his death. This final performance from the pulpit, preached at Whitehall before the king at the beginning of Lent in 1631, was published after Donne's death as *Deaths Duell, or A Consolation to the Soule, against the dying Life, and living Death of the Body*. Though the title is not Donne's own invention, its paradoxes capture well the sermon's themes of mortification and redemption, death and resurrection, and hint at Donne's sometimes disorienting method of collapsing those terms together. As Donne considers the "dying Life" of the mortal body, doomed to death even from the moment of its birth, and the "living Death" of the resurrected body, recompacted by God's power out of decomposition and dispersal, he reveals a deep concern with what happens to the body, in life and in death. The frail and fragile flesh, whose susceptibility to disease and infirmity Donne had chronicled and spiritualized in his *Devotions upon Emergent Occasions*, is for Donne ever in peril of corruption and vulnerable to the depredations of mortality; and when death finally does overtake the body, as it must sooner or later, the repugnance of its decay exceeds Donne's imaginings. "Painters have presented to us with some horrour, the *sceleton*, the frame of the bones of a mans body," Donne says in a 1620 sermon on Job 19.26, "but the state of a body, in the dissolution of the grave, no pencil can present to us. Between that excrementall jelly that thy body is made of at first, and that jelly which the body dissolves to at last; there is not so noisome, so putrid a thing in nature."[5]

The state of that body in dissolution is the animating theme of Donne's final sermon. In *Death's Duell*, the propensity of the mortal body to death is vividly and assiduously considered, from the "winding sheet in our Mother's womb," in which "we are dead so, as that wee doe not know wee live," to the "final dissolution of body and soule" in the grave.[6] Indeed, the subject of death frames the sermon, in which Donne offers a three-fold explication of his scriptural source text in Psalm 68, "Unto this God the Lord belong the issues of death." Against the awful mortality of the body, Donne argues that God has custodianship over this "*exitus mortis*, this *issue of death*": "*First*, as the *God* of *power*, the *Almighty Father* rescues his servants from the jawes of death: *And then*, as the *God* of *mercy*, the glorious *Sonne* rescued us, by taking upon himself this *issue of death*: *And then* betweene these two, as the *God* of *comfort*, the *holy Ghost* rescues us from all discomfort by his blessed impressions beforehand, that what manner of death soever be ordeined for us, yet this *exitus mortis* shall bee *introitus in vitam*, our *issue in death*, shall be an *entrance into everlasting life.*"[7] Thus, Donne's sermon promises to sift the details of bodily death in order to affirm what he calls "our deliverance *à morte, in morte, per mortem*,"—that is, "*from death, in death*, and *by death.*"[8] Donne's argumentative conclusion, that Christ redeems men from both the spiritual corruptions of sin and the physical corruptions of the decaying body, seeks to offer a consoling vision of the miracle of resurrection and its power to undo the horrors of the grave, to restore the body to perfection. It is the persistence of the body in the divine scheme of redemption to which Donne repeatedly appeals, the noxious jelly of its decomposed flesh mysteriously reconstituted into one frame by the power of that God who saves *in* death, as well as *from* and *by* death.

Still, his homiletic appeal to the doctrine of resurrection does not seem to convince Donne himself out of his unease about the fate of the body. Ramie Targoff has written recently of Donne, "however much he claims to trust in the promise of resurrection, he is still fraught with anxiety about the logistics of his material reassemblage."[9] Targoff delves further into this anxiety as she examines the 1620 sermon on Job, paying particular attention to a passage in which Donne asks, "Shall I imagine a difficulty in my body, because I have lost an Arme in the East, and a leg in the West? because I have left some bloud in the North, and some bones in the South?" Donne's answer to these questions again seeks to dispel worry: "Consider how much lesse, all this earth is to him, that sits in heaven, and spans all this world, and reunites in an instant armes, and legs, bloud, and bones, in what corners so ever they be scattered."[10] But Targoff's assessment of this sermon, and of *Death's Duell* as well, is that their images of the extremity of bodily dissolution lay the foundation for Donne's affirmation of the miraculous resurrection of the body, occasioning a declaration of his faith that, as Targoff puts it, "However debilitating the effects of death may seem to be, God will effortlessly overcome them."[11] Targoff's reading provides a good summary of the arguments of Donne's sermons, but in her intent to prove that Donne's primary stake is in the integrity of body and soul through the eternities—that is, that man is made up of both body and soul, mutually dependent in mortality and beyond—Targoff fails to register the dissonances that each of these sermons sounds against the consolations of its own argument. For Donne's rhetoric throughout *Death's Duell* reveals that his anxiety about the fate of the body persists beyond his declarations of faith in God's threefold dominion over "the issues of death." Donne's final sermon is remarkable less for the confidence of its eschatology than for its vivid insistence on the body's materiality. The physical presence of the body in *Death's Duell* overshadows the sermon's narrative of spiritual redemption and bodily resurrection, and the privileging of the body as a material artifact in Donne's text offers one response to the problem of the body's fate in the eternities.

This phenomenon is strikingly apparent in Donne's treatment of the resurrection. In the central section of *Death's Duell*, as Donne turns his attention to man's deliverance *from* death, he explains that one effect of the resurrection of Christ was that his body did "not see corruption."[12] This piece of doctrine leads Donne into an extended fantasia on the death of the mortal body, that slow, unsavory process that Donne calls "*death* after *death*, nay this death after burial, this *dissolution* after *dissolution*, this *death* of *corruption* and *putrifaction*, of *vermiculation* and *incineration*, of *dissolution* and *dispersion* in and *from* the grave."[13] Donne's Christian hope may look toward the resurrection, but his imagination is lodged fully in the flesh, for his commentary on its decay gives rise to a grotesque descant on the body as he continues to imagine the process of decomposition: "When those bodies that have beene the *children* of *royall parents*, and the *parents* of *royall children*, must say with *Iob, to corruption thou art my father*, and *to the Worme thou art my mother and my sister. Miserable riddle*, when the *same worme* must bee *my mother* and *my sister* and *my selfe. Miserable incest,* when I must be *maried* to my *mother* and my *sister, beget,* and bee both *father* and *mother* to my *owne mother* and *sister, beget,* and *beare* that *worme* which is all that *miserable penury;* when my *mouth* shall be *filled* with *dust,* and the *worme* shall *feed,* and *feed sweetely* upon me."[14]

This passage churns with the implications of its own initial conceit and makes its associative leaps one point to the next with an increasing intensity of horror. Donne's scriptural sources here are Job 17.14—"I haue said to corruption, Thou art my father: to the worme, Thou art my mother, and my sister"—and, once again, Job 19.26, the very text upon which Donne had produced his earlier sermon on the body's fate after death: "And though after my skin, wormes destroy this body, yet in my flesh shall I see God."[15] But Donne extends these commonplaces beyond their scriptural familiarity, exposing the logical ends of their conceits. The *"Miserable incest"* Donne here describes is clearly embedded in the lamentations of Job, but Donne elaborates that figure into such vividness that it is barely recognizable—and barely tolerable. And as if to ensure revulsion, the passage ends with an explicit turn to the senses as Donne imagines the process of dissolution not just figuratively but physically. Here, the *"sweetely"* in *"feed sweetely"* introduces an entirely new dimension of disgust to an already grotesque meditation, in the way it provokes a specifically sensual apprehension of this worm's diet. For the word *"sweetely"* ensures that the decomposing body is registered as a material artifact, fully available to the suite of perceptual senses, including taste. Inviting his audience to reflect on the flavor of a corpse, Donne exceeds the scriptural commonplace that served as ground for his comments, overwriting it with the vivid sense-data of vermiculation.

The extent to which such a focus subverts the stated spiritual ends of the sermon can be better appreciated if we compare the vermiculation passage with its immediate sequel: Donne's praise for the resurrection, which glorious event promises to undo the shocking ignominies of the grave. But Donne concludes his long and flamboyant cataloguing of the body's disintegration with a surprising anticlimax: "This death of *incineration* and dispersion, is, to naturall *reason,* the most *irrecoverable death* of all, and yet *Domini Domini sunt exitus mortis, unto God the Lord belong the issues of death,* and by *recompacting* this *dust* into the *same body,* and *reanimating* the *same body* with the *same soule,* he shall in a blessed and glorious *resurrection* give mee such an *issue from* this *death,* as shal never passe into any other death, but establish me into a life that shall last as long as the *Lord of life* himselfe."[16] After the breathless exorbitance of Donne's depiction of bodily decay, this affirmation of the very doctrine that should negate all the deaths of the flesh falls rather flat. Its brief explanations, lacking in imaginative embroidery or elaboration, its programmatic and even redundant rhetoric—these qualities stand in sharp relief to the more extravagant stylings of the vermiculation riff. That is to say, the treatment of the resurrection here is merely conventional, lacking the aesthetic force of the earlier passage. The discrepancy between these two registers of expression suggests that although Donne's theology may look toward the resurrection as the lodestar of Christian striving, Donne's own interest lies a little nearer than eschatology. In this central movement of *Death's Duell*, the vibrant and sense-able substance of the material rhetorically supplants the redemptive aims of the homiletic argument. The image that lingers at the conclusion of this section of the sermon is not the vaguely imagined "blessed and glorious resurrection" but the dissolution and putrefaction, the *"Miserable riddle"* of incest, the sweet devourings of the worm. The material aspects of mortality remain far more vivid than any redemptive doctrine such imagery might be used to illuminate. That is to say, the body is most present in the text in its decomposing, most persistent as a material article whose spectacular decay prevents us from reading through it to appreciate the spiritual ends of death.

Just as the decaying body in *Death's Duell* flouts a transparent symbolic function, Donne's description of the crucified Christ at the sermon's conclusion retreats from spiritual referentiality into materiality for its own sake. Thoughout the final movement of the sermon, Donne leads his congregation through a comprehensive meditation on the hours leading up to the passion, urging his auditory to absorb the details of Christ's final hours as tropes that communicate imitable principles, following the *imitatio Christi* model of contemplation. "Make *this* present *day* that *day* in thy *devotion*," Donne instructs, "and consider what *hee did*, and remember what *you have done*." As he moves through the events of the Last Supper, the prayer in Gethsemane, the betrayal by Judas, Donne encourages the internalization of symbolic cognates: Christ prayed in *"agony* and *bloody sweat*"*; therefore, Donne counsels, *"prayer actually* accompanied with *shedding of teares*, and *dispositively* in a readines to *shed blood* for *his glory* in *necessary cases*, puts thee into a *conformity* with him." The literal details of Christ's prayer are sublimated here into a figurative application to the self. Similarly, the crucifixion offers a model for repentance, for *"wee presse* an utter *Crucifying* of that *sinne* that governs thee; and that *conformes* thee to *Christ.*" But such figural uses of the Passion fail as Donne lingers over the details of Christ's crucified body. Shifting abruptly into the present tense, Donne constructs the scene of the crucifixion:

> There now hangs that *sacred Body* upon the *Crosse, rebaptized* in his owne *teares* and *sweat,* and *embalmed* in his *owne blood alive.* There are those *bowels of compassion,* which are so conspicuous, so manifested, as that you may *see them through his wounds.* There those *glorious eyes* grew faint in their light: so as the *Sun ashamed* to survive them, *departed with his light too.* . . . There we leave you in that *blessed dependancy,* to *hang* upon *him* that *hangs* upon the *Crosse,* there *bath* in this *teares,* there *suck* at his *woundes,* and *lye downe in peace* in his *grave,* till he vouchsafe you a *resurrection,* and an *ascension* into that *Kingdome,* which hee *hath purchas'd for you,* with the *inestimable price* of his *incorruptible blood.* Amen.[17]

Given Donne's explicit intent to provoke his listeners into a figurative appropriation of Jesus's acts into their own lives, the abandonment of that program in the sermon's final gesture is especially notable. Gone are the parallels to the worshipper's spiritual life; gone is the symbolic repackaging of these events into portable spiritual principles. Instead, the body of Christ hangs in the attention, stark in its physicality. The familiar biblical phrase "*bowels of compassion*" is reclaimed from trope to material as those bowels are "conspicuous," manifested through his wounds. They are, in other words, actual bowels—intestines, rather than metaphorical sites of empathy. The physicality of Christ ultimately resists figural identification, and Donne's last gesture leaves his congregation not in the midst of a meditative application to themselves but confronting the unassimilable body of Christ on the cross. And though he may reference Christ's eucharistic function at that moment in enjoining worshippers to "*suck* at his *woundes,*" the specificity with which Donne has described those wounds and the bowels they reveal repels rather than invites. At the climactic moment of this *imitatio,* Donne effectively refuses the possibility of imitation, offering a Christ whose body is just too *bodily* to be sublimated into generally appropriable symbolism.

Indeed, in its resistance to a transparently symbolic reading, the description of Christ's body in *Death's Duell* resembles the "picture of Christ crucified" in the sonnet that begins "What if this present were the worlds last night?"[18] The sestet of that sonnet invokes a symbolic scheme in which visible signs correspond legibly to unseen qualities of the heart. "Beauty of pity, foulness only is / A sign of rigor," Donne simpers, sweet-talking God as he would any profane mistress. "To wicked spirits are horrid shapes assigned, / This beauteous form assures a piteous mind" (11–12, 13–14). As readers long have noted, the image he describes as a "beauteous form" is difficult to conceive as beautiful: "Teares in his eyes quench the amasing light, / Blood fills his frownes, which from his pierc'd head fell" (5–6).[19] The picture is a gruesome one, to be sure, but again its ghastliness arises from its unsublimable particularity: the "Teares" and the "Blood" that falls from wounds "pierc'd" in the flesh are details redeemed by their inclusion in the sacramental symbolary, which transfers the liquid effusions of the crucifixion into the cup of the altar. However, the "frownes" suggest not the body of Christ in its sacrificial, sacramental function but the human visage, the features of the physical face contorted in agony. Like the bowels of *Death's Duell*, these "frownes" particularize a familiar conceit into discomfiture—or rather, familiar *conceits*, for the poem makes use of the courtly motif of the beloved's portrait in miniature engraved into the heart of the lover as well as invoking the "beauteous" salvific function of the "picture of Christ crucified." But Christ's "frownes" lodge themselves stubbornly outside of both the courtly and sacramental symbolic systems, and in their resistance suggest the physicality of Christ's flesh, the body as body.

Such resistances to a spiritualized experience of the body of Christ are consonant with the way that the vermiculation passage asserts the substantive reality of the body over its spiritual meaning. Donne's practice, in "What if this present" and in the rebarbative sections from *Death's Duell*, is to seize upon a perfectly conventional figure and to elaborate that trope until it reveals the strangeness it contains. In the process of that elaboration into strangeness, Donne's tropes cease to function referentially, the figurative term's substance interposing itself into any symbolic transparency. In his now classic essay on Donne's disquieting metaphors, William Kerrigan begins to grasp this very quality of Donne's writing, identifying it as an almost inevitable consequence of the human tendency to represent divine things by way of human terms—to anthropomorphize the holy so that it is accommodated to mortal understanding. Donne "reinvigorated the dead trope," Kerrigan observes—the familiar, tired poetic or religious conceit—by "assuming its literal truth and proceeding to complicate the tenor . . . to fit the extended vehicle."[20] In Kerrigan's view, Donne's figural complications, which seem bewilderingly or shockingly inapplicable to spiritual concerns, serve to highlight the differences between man's fallen perception and the sublime unknowability of God, and so to produce "a reverentiall feare" of God's superhumanity—that is, to reinforce the ontological gulf between God and man.[21] Though he perceptively identifies a pattern in Donne's methods of figuration, Kerrigan becomes an apologist when it comes to postulating a rationale for such discomfitingly elaborated tropes. By explaining that Donne's disjunctive tropes are meant to produce that "reverentiall feare" and awe of God's difference from man, Kerrigan normalizes the strangeness of Donne's metaphors, explaining soothingly that they are finally in the service of dogma.

But to argue that strange or discomfiting tropes serve dogmatic ends does not actually cancel their strangeness. After all, the symbol at the heart of sacramental worship is an institutionalized trope whose explicit end is to communicate the divine to man, and we need only recall the recurrent anxieties about cannibalism and eroticism that resurface over the centuries in writings on the sacrament, whether those writings seek to condemn or to explain away such associations, to recognize the interpretive difficulty presented by the ritual, despite its dogmatic justification.[22] In *Death's Duell*, the Eucharist is never far from Donne's mind. He begins his extended meditation on Christ's final day with the Last Supper, when Jesus "*instituted and celebrated the Sacrament.*"[23] Donne uses that biblical moment to remind his congregants that they must prepare themselves to participate in that ceremony—again, each worshipper must "consider what *hee did*, and remember what *you have done*" in order to bring the self "into a *conformity with him*"—and he offers the *imitatio* that follows as a model for sacramental preparation. Donne's symbolic application of Christ's last actions to devotional practice in his final sermon is thus generated by the Eucharist, and it culminates in a depiction of Christ's eucharistic function that turns upon a conventional trope for the nourishment of grace in the sacrament, as he enjoins his congregants to "*suck* at his *woundes.*"[24] In light of the central role that the Eucharist plays in *Death's Duell*, it is telling that as Donne turns his descriptive attentions to the sacrificial moment that gives rise to the ritual, symbol fails to be sublimable: the bowels are simply bowels, and the blood is simply blood. There is, it seems, no generally applicable symbolic valence to the crucifixion. In his final sermon, Donne acknowledges the proximity between the eucharistic figure and poetic trope, but Donne's treatment of trope does not serve merely to reinforce dogma or to demonstrate the awful unknowability of God. Instead, Donne's strategies of elaborative figuration interrogate the very assumptions that underlie the eucharistic figure, registering both its strangeness and its symbolic limits.

That Donne views the sacrament as an interpretively problematic event is indicated in part by the inconsistencies in his homiletic commentary on the rite.[25] Donne's sacramental theology is famously difficulty to fix, and the debate over whether his confessional identity is influenced primarily by Rome or by Geneva has been the subject of critical controversy for the last few decades.[26] Seeking to moderate between these binary positions, Robert Whalen has suggested that Donne's eucharistic theology occupies its own kind of *via media*, which attempts to "reconcile the ceremonial and sacramental impulses of the 'old religion' with the predominantly introspective, word-centred, and predestinarian pieties of English Calvinism."[27] In Whalen's view, Donne balances ritual worship with a sacramentalized view of the word in which sermons are conceived as "a means of grace," a channel for communicating the Word to man, for "Hearing the word in a ceremonial, sacramental, and public context involves a spiritual ingestion."[28] One consequence of such a sacralization of rhetoric is that it raises the question of the suitability of language to content, of sign to signified; Whalen points to a passage in the sermon that Donne delivered on Christmas 1626 that would seem to reflect on this very consideration. Here, Donne distinguishes between "the Logique, or the Retorique, or the Ethique, or the poetry of the Sermon" and "the Sermon of the Sermon," acknowledging that the allurements of eloquence and style may work to obstruct the substance of whatever spiritual truth is intended to be communicated by such rhetorical flourishes.[29] Whalen rightly recognizes that the distinction Donne makes between "the poetry of the Sermon" and "the Sermon of the Sermon" is analogous to the relationship between the elements of the Eucharist and Christ's body, in which "the rhetorical dress of homily, with its images, figures, and conceits, corresponds to the material aspects of sacrament." Having made this connection, Whalen concludes that "The danger . . . as Donne well knew, is that the 'Logick' or 'Retorick' or 'poetry of the Sermon' may somehow contaminate, render less pure, the eternal verities that are the 'Sermon of the Sermon,'" and in order to counter that "danger," Whalen argues, Donne uses the homiletic word to excite "a vivid apprehension of the truths he imparts."[30]

But in his assumption that Donne's priority is to achieve un-dangerous poetic transparency, to communicate spiritual truths by evading the contaminants of style, Whalen portrays Donne as hostile to the rhetorical extravagance that is a signature of his style in both prose and poetry. In fact, Donne everywhere foregrounds such contaminants; it is precisely this stylistic ornamentation that prompted Samuel Johnson's notorious complaint about the seventeenth-century lyric's "*discordia concors*," in Johnson's view a perversion of style characterized by "a combination of dissimilar images" where "The most heterogenous ideas are yoked by violence together."[31] Donne certainly is aware of the ways in which style obtrudes into the apprehension of substance; as he explains in an early sermon, rhetoric works "first to trouble the understanding, to displace, and to discompose, and disorder the judgement, to smother and bury in it, or to empty it of former apprehensions and opinions, and to shake that beliefe, with which it has possessed it self before, and then when it is thus melted, to power it into new molds, when it is thus mollified, to stamp, and imprint new formes, new images, new opinions in it."[32] Donne's language here bears more than a passing resemblance, in content and in style, to the way the Christmas 1626 sermon describes the operation of the sacrament, in which the "internall form, which is the very essence and nature of the bread, so it is transformed, so the bread hath received a new form, a new essence, a new nature, because whereas the nature of bread is but to nourish the body, the nature of this bread now, is to nourish the soule."[33] While other critics have worked to extrapolate Donne's sacramental theology from this and other such passages, what is particularly germane to my interests here is not fixing the poet's doctrinal view of eucharistic operation but rather teasing out the implications of Donne's describing the sacrament as working like a piece of rhetoric.[34] Donne expands this point in a sermon preached on Trinity Sunday of 1621, which frames the rhetorical valences of the Lord's Supper as a function of Christ's status as the Word: "The Son of God, is Λόγοσ [sic], *verbum, The word;* God made us with his word, and with our words me make God so farre, as that we make up the mysticall body of Christ Jesus with our prayers, with our whole liturgie, and we make the naturall body of Christ Jesus appliable to our soules, by the words of Consecration in the Sacrament."[35] In Donne's formulation here, both language and sacrament serve complementary incarnational purposes. Even as it may "displace," "discompose," and "disorder" perception, "Yet Rhetorique will make absent and remote things present to your understanding"— just as the sacraments make Christ apprehensible "in visible and sensible things."[36] Indeed, I argue that for Donne the aesthetic extravagances of rhetoric and poetics accomplish this metaphysical feat precisely because, like the sacramental trope itself, they discompose and disorder perception.

Certainly, the Eucharist as Donne describes it is an experience that requires a profound disordering of perception. As Donne labors in the Christmas 1626 sermon to explain the mechanics of the sacrament, his fits and starts suggest the difficulty that comes of parsing out the interpretive demands of a change that does not present itself to any perceptual faculty as a change. "Beloved, in the blessed, and glorious, and mysterious Sacrament of the Body and Blood of Christ Jesus, thou seest *Christum Domini*, the Lords Salvation, and thy Salvation, and that, thus far with bodily eyes; That Bread which thou seest after the Consecration, is not the same bread, which was presented before; not that it is Transubstantiated to another substance, for it is bread still . . . but that it is severed, and appropriated by God, in that Ordinance to another use; it is other Bread, so, as a Judge is another man, upon the bench, then he is at home, in his owne house."[37] This affirmation of eucharistic efficacy is freighted with the tensions the ritual imports into interpretation: Christ's body and blood are seen and yet not seen; the bread is bread, but "not the same bread." The change that Donne ascribes to the sacramental act defies sense-data even as he explicitly invokes sense-perception. While according to Donne's rhetorical logic, the sacramental trope should make the absent and remote body of Christ more present—that is to say, more visible, more sensible/*sense-able*—to the communicant, as Donne is only too aware, the eucharistic trope confronts the communicant with an interpretive object more akin to the "poetry of the Sermon" than to the "Sermon of the Sermon." The figural scheme of sacramental worship discomposes and disorders perception, the symbolic function of the bread and wine at odds with their manifest presence to the "bodily eyes" of the worshipper. What the communicant sees "with bodily eyes" is not "the Lords Salvation," but a sign whose signification contravenes the "visible and sensible things" of eucharistic observance.

The eucharistic trope is, as Donne defines it in his Easter 1628 sermon, a "*Medium*," one that "may prepare you to see him then in his Essence," but not finally an instrument for making God present to perception: "here we see God *In speculo, in a glass*, that is, by reflexion, And here we know God *In aenigmate*, says our Text, *Darkly*, (so we translate it) that is, by obscure representations, and therefore it is called a *Knowledge but in part*."[38] But Donne's surprising response to the representational inadequacies of the sacramental trope is to encourage his auditory to "embrace the *Medium*."[39]

He explains that in eucharistic worship "our *Medium*" serves, by its very resistance to sublimation, as a site of immanence: "our way to see him is *Patefactio sui*, Gods laying himself open, his manifestation, his revelation, his evisceration, his embowelling of himselfe to us, there."[40] As Donne seizes upon the basic tenets of the sacramental trope—that it re-presents Christ in the salvific moment of the crucifixion—he elaborates the body of Christ out of spiritual principle and into corporeality: the sacramental medium points not toward some transcendent drama of salvation but rather toward evisceration and disembowelment, the body of Christ made apprehensible through its particularization. This vivid treatment of a eucharistic commonplace displaces the sacramental transparency of the ritual, replacing its symbolic principles of communion and redemption with the piecemealed body of Christ. In other words, Donne's description offers not spiritual "meaning" but a physicalized depiction of butchery, whose corporeal valences irrupt into the disembodied hermeneutics of doctrine. By activating the material registers of eucharistic participation, in which the sign obtrudes into the symbolic, the trope may effect a visceral, and thus apprehensible, manifestation.

In an earlier sermon, from Easter 1624, Donne articulates a kind of statement of poetics based on precisely this model of holy figuration: "The literall sense is always to be preserved; but the literall sense is not always to be discerned: for the literall sense is not alwayes that, which the very Letter and Grammar of the place presents, as where it is literally said, *That Christ is a vine,* and literally, *That his flesh is bread.* . . . But the literall sense of every place, is the principall intention of the Holy Ghost, in that place: And his principall intention in many places, is to expresse things by allegories, by figures; so that in many places of Scripture, a figurative sense is the literall sense."[41] Here, the tension between the inapprehensible sacred tenor and the apprehensible figure is resolved as Donne outlines a sacred aesthetic in which the "figurative sense" becomes identical with the "literall sense," the tenor not separable from the vehicle that represents it but rather inherent in that vehicle. Such a view of the figurative *as literal* establishes the trope itself as a site of spiritual immanence. As Donne continues in the same sermon, in engaging in such figurative expansion and elaboration, "neither do those Expositors ill" who "do propose another and another such sense."[42] If the literal resides in the figurative, Donne seems to argue, then the proliferation of tropes serves to manifest the literal more abundantly. This conclusion justifies the poet's tropic method because, by his own formulation, Donne's practice of extending metaphors becomes a strategy for realizing what he calls here the literal, the tenor of the figure, the imperceptible signified. The medium of metaphor, that dangerous contaminant that "troubles the understanding" and disorders perception by interposing itself into the relationship between sign and signified, becomes by that very troubling and disordering an apparatus for expressing, rather than merely referencing, the literal. By amplifying a readerly sense of symbolic disorientation, metaphor promotes the figurative surface, reinscribing the vehicle as a thing in itself, and provides a model of tropic immanence as it gestures not beyond but toward itself. The elaborated figure serves for Donne as an incarnational machine, exemplifying the capacity of the medium to embody as it asserts the persistence of the trope for its own sake: indissoluble, antiabsorptive, present.[43]

In his poems, as in his prose, Donne exhibits an alarming tendency to embrace the medium of his tropes, trafficking in metaphors that interfere in their own referentiality. In the devotional poems, this effect is never more apparent than when his figures import erotic desire into the spiritual relationship between man and God. And, as in the sermons, the most indecorous tropes in the Holy Sonnets build upon conventional metaphors, familiar from religious discourse. The sonnet that begins "Show me deare Christ, thy spouse, so bright and cleare" engages a theological commonplace that identifies the church as the mystical Bride of Christ. The poem's dramatized quest for the true church begins with a set of droll personifications of the candidates. In language that contrasts the sumptuous spectacle of the Roman church with the stern, embattled piety of continental Protestantism, Donne wonders, "What, is it she, which on the other shore / Goes richly painted? or which rob'd and tore / Laments and mournes in Germany and here?" (2–4). These characterizations—or rather caricatures, for they rely on the broad strokes of familiar stereotypes—present the Catholic and Reformed churches as similarly dissatisfying representations of Christ's bridal church, each one "distinctly unbridelike and very different from Christ's spouse as described in either Song of Songs or Revelation," as Claude J. Summers remarks.[44] But when Donne turns from these unsatisfying versions of Christ's mystical spouse to plead for a vision of the true Bride, his terms become even more "unbridelike" as he introduces into the characterization a strain of erotic deviance that resists assimilation into the traditional symbolic scheme of Bride and Bridegroom:

Betray, kind husband thy spouse to our sights,
And let myne amorous soule court thy mild Dove,
Who is most trew, and pleasing to thee, then
When she'is embrac'd and open to most men. (11–14)

Though the central conceit in these lines is derived from the perfectly conventional identification of the church as Bride of Christ, Donne's unfolding of that marital conceit to reveal its embedded implications renders it unfamiliar. As Donne formulates it here, in its most ideal form, God's marriage culminates in adultery—indeed, in many adulteries, since this spouse is "most pleasing" when she is most profligate, making herself sexually available to any suitor while God procures his own cuckolding, a generous wittol. Though critics have attempted to offer theologically safe readings aimed at neutralizing the disturbing turn at this poem's conclusion, it remains baldly, boldly, and bawdily resistant to rationalization.[45]

"Show me deare Christ" deforms conventional figuration not by blasphemously importing eroticism into the relationship between God and man; eroticism is already firmly encoded into biblical depictions of that relationship, as when Isaiah writes that "as the bridegrome reioyceth ouer the bride, so shall thy God reioyce ouer thee" and admonishes Israel to remember that "thy maker is thine husband." The Christian tradition appropriates the marriage trope from the Hebrew Bible, and Paul does not scruple to acknowledge its erotic vectors when he writes to the Corinthians, "I have espoused you to one husband, that I may present you as a chaste virgin to Christ."[46] The logic that the poem derives from this allegory is clear enough: if the church is understood as the mystical Bride of Christ, then participation in the church enfolds the worshipper into the erotic drama that is contained within the originary conceit. But by plumbing that convention and extending the relationship it describes to its logical conclusions, Donne reifies the figure and impedes access to the poem's putative narrative of spiritual seeking. In the sonnet, eroticism ceases to be symbolic, the details of the marriage trope actualized into a particularity that cannot be sublimated into allegory. The figurative topos of erotic devotion is familiar enough from scripture, but when the conceit encompasses the specter of a God who is more than pleased to be cuckolded, it jars, and resists allegorization. God's willing cuckoldry has no spiritual cognate, and so the figure is displaced from allegory into opaque sexuality. Kerrigan views this displacement as a poetic failure, alleging that as the metaphor "crumbles . . . Donne almost loses control of his reader's imagination and therefore of his intentional meaning."[47] But Kerrigan's verdict presumes that the poem's "intentional meaning" is to narrate the search for truth, as if it were a simple dramatization of Donne's imperative in "Satire 3": "Seeke true religion."[48] Donne's conceit argues against such a presumption, for it develops into such deliberate extremity that it must impede the narrative of the poem. The poem's final lines swerve attention away from any spiritual drama and onto the metaphor itself as a performance in figuration. By announcing itself as an outrageous metaphor, the concluding conceit of "Show me deare Christ" surveys the figurative limits of figuration itself. The sluttish dove and the happy cuckold do not yield to a set of abstract spiritual referents; they assert themselves, such that what endures interpretively of the poem's final lines is their distasteful tropings, and not the tropes' corresponding principles of devotion or incorporation or seeking or spiritual calling (it's difficult even to identify what the tenors for such vehicles might be). What we must perceive in Donne's poem, in other words, is the metaphor as an object, not as a referential ephemeron. We might describe this phenomenon, to borrow Donne's own terms, as a shift from the "sermon of the poem" to the "poetry of the poem."

This priority on trope as end in itself over trope as conduit to meaning underwrites Donne's progress through a radically divergent series of metaphors in the sonnet that begins "Batter my heart." Critics have attempted to impose order on the poem's figurative swings from metalwork to militarism to marriage, suggesting that the three image families correspond to the Trinitarian God of its opening line or that the poem does not actually present discrete metaphors but multiple, even interinforming, figures referencing the same principle.[49] More than establishing any secure interpretation of the poem's metaphors, this critical wrangling points up the recalcitrance and elusiveness of metaphoric referentiality in Donne's sonnet, an effect compounded as the poem moves through each succeeding tropic scheme.

> Batter my heart, three-person'd God; for, you
> As yet but knocke, breathe, shine, and seeke to mend;
> That I may rise, and stand, o'erthrow mee,'and bend
> Your force, to breake, blower, burn and make me new.
> I, like an usurpt towne, to'another due,

Labour to'admit you, but Oh, to no end,
Reason your viceroy in mee, mee should defend,
But is captiv'd, and proves weake or untrue,
Yet dearely'I love you, and would be lov'd faine,
But am betroth'd unto your enemie,
Divorce mee,'untie, or breake that knot againe,
Take mee to you, imprison mee, for I
Except you'enthrall mee, never shall be free,
Nor ever chast, except you ravish mee.

That Donne once again constructs his metaphoric rococo on the foundation of established scriptural tropes indicates how self-conscious is his engagement with figuration. Indeed, the accumulation of alternating metaphors foregrounds the very act of figuration and calls into scrutiny the capacity of these figures to serve as vehicles for *any* identifiable tenor, much less to express in concert a single idea. The first quatrain's tinker God is implored to intensify his exertions upon the heart, to replace the relatively gentle amendments of "knocke, breathe, shine" to the severe re-making accomplished in "breake, blowe, burn." While this argument gestures toward a narrative of spiritual regeneration, the unrelenting physical force of the lines, their plosives alliterating powerfully from the trochaic opening command "Batter," insists upon the clenched physicality of the scene. Such a focus prevents, or at the very least discourages, the dissolution of metaphor into abstraction, keeps the terms of the metaphor substantially present. This tension between literal and figurative is reinforced by the third line's expressed desire to "rise, and stand," which would seem to describe a spiritual aspiration until its remedy lurches back into the loudly visceral language of the foundry. Such jockeying back and forth over the threshold of literal and metaphorical, disembodied and corporeal, preempts the identification of a stable tenor and maintains interpretive focus on the surfaces of the trope.

The second stanza's abrupt shift into the military siege of a "usurpt towne" continues to foreground the mediating device of the conceit, not least by demanding that its terms be reconciled to those of the previous figure. The significative ground bucks as this new set of terms usurps the figurative scheme established in the first four lines of the poem, presenting a trope whose referential meaning is destabilized by its uncertain relationship to the preceding quatrain. Does it refer to the same tenor as the tinker trope does, or to a new tenor altogether? Does it describe a physical encounter or a spiritual one? The indeterminacy of such questions emphasizes the operation of the figure as a medium, and this change of focus blocks the mediated term from view. The occlusion of the tropic signified is of sufficient import to the poem that it is enacted in the siege figure itself, when Reason, we are told, "is captiv'd, and proves weake or untrue." But which is it: weakness or betrayal? Was the viceroy a stalwartly faithful but inadequate guard for a vulnerable town, or did he collude with the enemy? These two potential causes for the failure of reason each have radically different spiritual implications, but even as the poem moves to explain its drama, it obscures that explanation behind the elaborations of its metaphor.[50] The trope's inconclusive gloss on its own terms obstructs its application to a spiritual narrative and compounds the sense of interpretive impenetrability that has already been produced by the lack of referential correspondence between the first and second figures.

The final movement of the poem presents yet another vertiginous shift, into the language first of betrothal and then of physical intimacy. The pleadings to "be loved faine" reach their climax in a final figure that intensifies into the extremities of desire.[51] Turning to this the call for ravishment in the last line, Kerrigan once again runs into trouble in his effort to synthesize a coherent orthodoxy from the centrifugal energies of the poem's proliferating metaphors. He resolves the conflicting tropes by arguing that rather than reeling disjunctively from image set to image set, "really the poem evolves from and toward a single metaphor"—that is, intercourse, which is itself a figure for "the forcible entry of deity into an otherwise impenetrable soul." Though Kerrigan is alive to the poem's vacillations between vehicles and tenors, his teleological handling of the poem's several tropes deafens him to their fundamental dissonance with one another, and to their evasion—individually and especially in proximity to one another—of stable referentiality. He registers only in passing a sense of the indissolubility of Donne's final trope when he observes, of the sexual event depicted in the poem's last lines, that it "acquires the force of a tenor. The intercourse of the speaker and God becomes virtually a 'real' presence in the poem, a final repository of reference."[52] Kerrigan's recognition that the metaphoric vehicle becomes a referential terminus speaks to the dazzling endurance of the sign in Donne's trope. The shock of holy rape in the last line is produced at least in part because of its absolute resistance to sublimation, its amorous terms extended into raw and obstinate corporeality. The figurative details, here as elsewhere in the poem, are far more thoroughly worked out than the still-nebulous ideas they signify, but here the disjunction between tropic sign and signified is amplified because the erotic strains, as its elaboration grows more particular, against a spiritual reading. Thus, when Targoff remarks that "Donne seems to insist that we read his requests literally and not metaphorically," she recognizes that the trope asserts itself so aggressively that it short-circuits interpretive absorption, presents itself as the referential end, as substantial in and of itself.[53]

Both Targoff and Kerrigan use language that draws upon a discourse of sacramental operation, but neither critic acknowledges any connection between the substantiating effects of Donne's figures and the presencing potentialities of the sacramental trope. For when Donne insists in the Christmas 1626 sermon that the bread of the Eucharist is "bread still" though changed in use, "other Bread" though altered in signification, he refuses to allow the perceptible object of the bread to be subsumed into irrelevance. Indeed, the objection he levies in that sermon against the doctrine of transubstantiation is that it obviates perception by severing sign and signified: "since there is no bread, there might be no dimensions, no colour, no nourishing, no other qualities of bread neither; for, these remaining, there is rather an annihilation of God."[54] But neither does Donne express sympathy for the disembodied abstractions of memorialism; as he instructs, the sacramental elements are themselves the sites of meaning: "This Sacrament of the Body and Blood of our Saviour, *Luther* calls safely, *Venerabile & adorabile;* for certainly, whatsoever that is which we see, that which we receive, is to be adored."[55] Between what he views as the perceptual absurdity of transubstantiation and the perceptual indifference of memorialism—where on the one hand the material medium is obliterated and on the other hand the medium is merely referential, transparent—Donne's figurative strategies suggest a middle path, a *via media* whose *media* is the *medium* of metaphor. As his tropes particularize and elaborate the metaphorical into presence, they assert the significance of the sign as a perceptible object. In Donne's metaphors, the figurative becomes "the literall sense," perceptibly embodied precisely because it disrupts its own referentiality. This strategy preserves significance in the discursive surface of the metaphor, creating a sense of presence that endures in the trope as such. The effect is incarnational, to be sure, but that effect is not achieved because the trope points away from itself to make present some other term, annihilating itself as it invokes an absent tenor.[56] Rather, the trope incarnates *itself*, the word fleshing itself out, intruding substantially into the referential and replacing signification with immanence: being in itself. Insisting on rape as rape and cuckolding as cuckolding, Donne's sonnets approach the logic of the sacramental elements, which, as Donne describes them, maintain robustly their status as artifacts (witness the almost fetishistic repetition of the word *bread* as Donne explains the operation of the Eucharist: "That Bread . . . is not the same bread . . . it is bread still . . . it is other Bread") that are venerable *in*, not *despite*, their materiality.

The sacramental value of indissoluble signs sanctions Donne's production of referentially opaque poetic tropes. The eucharistic intersection of substance and sign is both the thematic focus and the method of Donne's poem "The Crosse," which begins by suggesting the identity of representational ground and figure: "Since Christ embraced the Crosse it selfe, dare I / His image, th'image of the Crosse deny?" (1–2). By making "His image" equivalent to "th'image of the Crosse," Donne suggests a tropic scheme that recalls his homiletic description of the operation of sacred language, in which the "figurative sense is the literall sense." The "picture" (7) of the cross is worthy of veneration, the poem argues, because it cannot be distinguished from Christ himself; as Donne explains, the cross is "his image, or not his, but hee" (36). Such a formulation sacralizes the sign, reimagining the referential medium as an end in itself, a site of immanence. Accordingly, Donne's poem proceeds ingeniously to locate the cross in virtually all points of material experience:

> Swimme, and at every stroake, thou art thy Cross,
> The Mast and yard make one, where seas do tosse.
> Looke downe, thou spiest out Crosses in small things;
> Looke up, thou seest birds rais'd on crossed wings;
> All the Globes frame, and spheares, is nothing else
> But the Meridians crossing Parallels. (19–24)

As cruciform things and actions accumulate, the cross comes to be more and more present in the poem not in its symbolic function as a sign for Christ but as an artifact whose meaningfulness the world at large communicates. The sign of the cross becomes the signified, literalized into referential objecthood. Finally, it is the cross itself in which significance inheres, with an unassailability that withstands the vicissitudes of confessional squabbling:

From mee, no Pulpit, nor misgrounded law,
Nor scandal taken, shall this Crosse withdraw,
It shall not, for it cannot; for, the losse
Of this Crosse, were to mee another Crosse. (9–12)

Donne's cross persists beyond its symbolic value so steadfastly that even its removal merely generates a reassertion of its presence.

The pervasive material presence of the cross is amplified by the poem's almost obsessive, incantatory repetition of the word *crosse*, which recurs as noun and as verb a full thirty-one times over the course of this sixty-four-line poem. Theresa DiPasquale describes the poem as "a cross-filled universe" populated by "the individual cruciform letters x (which appears at the poem's center—line 32—in the word 'Crucifixe') and t (which appears either in lower case or, as a Tau cross—uppercase T—at least one in every line of the poem). Donne ensures that readers' eyes will gaze continually on crosses as they scan the lines of his poem."[57] DiPasquale makes these astute observations in order to argue that the poem urges in its readers a particularly visual embrace of visible signs of the cross, as one instance of which the poem offers itself, visibly inked on the page. Though DiPasquale concludes that the poem, because of its attentiveness to its own textual visibility, serves as a channel of grace for those who are prepared to "read it reverently,"[58] the sacramentality of the poem has more objectively to do with the opacity of its central conceit than with some unmeasurable and subjective transmission of spiritual strength. Indeed, DiPasquale's take on the poem promotes a kind of literary receptionism, wherein the reader is charged with making the poem into a sacramental experience. But such a poetic doctrine is weakened by the prospect of uncooperative readers, people who just do not respond to its spiritual lessons, as DiPasquale must concede.[59] The multiplying of graphic crosses throughout the poem certainly does affirm the text as a perceptible object on the page, and this sense is amplified as the word *crosse* repeats again and again. The proliferation of verbal crosses on the page announces that term as a sign, particularly as the term's many figurative referents shift so frequently as to become interchangeable. What endures to the apprehension is not whatever the cross may figure, but the sign of "crosse" itself—an effect available not only to "reverent" readers but to all who perceive the poem. The sacramentality of this "crosse" is contingent on its achievement of poetic presence, as medium becomes manifestation. Donne's 1628 Easter sermon explains the operation of the divinely invested medium, the sign in which presence inheres: "God himself is All; God himself is the place, we see Him, in Him; God is our *medium*, we see Him by him; God is our light; not a light which is His, but a light which is He; not a light which flowes from him, no, nor a light which is in him, but that light which is He himself."[60] The cross, which is "his image, or not his, but hee," presences God by being itself most present, the figure of the cross surrendering referentiality, upon which the conceit of the cross-filled world would seem to be dependent, for opacity. The cross, both as trope and as word, remains perceptibly and unsublimatedly substantial, on the page and in the poem.

The notion that God is the medium by which he is known provides Donne not only with a cosmology but with a representational system in which language—the surface of it, the object of language—becomes sanctified. Language is an instrument worthy of celebration in itself, because rather than offering a sense of *difference* (or perhaps *différance*) between sign and signified that reproduces the ontological gulf between the material world and the sublime, it demonstrates the potential for being-in-itself, exemplified by the Incarnation.[61] Donne himself makes this connection between the linguistic medium and presence when he contemplates the name of God. "*Verum nomen Dei, Semper esse,*" Donne quotes Ambrose in a 1627 sermon, "*Gods* proper name is *Always Being.*"[62] He visits this point in an earlier sermon as well, where he considers the name "*Jehovah;* his radicall, his fundamentall, his primarie, his essentiall name, the name of *being, Jehovah,*" and explains further that in the name of Jesus is contained the force of the Incarnation: "It is the name that cost God most, and therefore he loves it best; it cost him his life to be a *Jesus,* a Saviour. The name of Christ, which is Anointed, he had by office; he was anointed as King, as Priest, as Prophet. All those names which he had in *Isaiah, The Counsellor, The Wonderfull, The Prince of Peace,* and the name of *Jehovah* it self, which the Jews deny ever to be given to him and is evidently given to him in that place, Christ had by nature; But his name of *Jesus,* a Saviour, he had by purchase, and that purchase cost him his bloud."[63] Donne identifies the name of Jesus with his incarnated body, and with the salvific actions accomplished in that body. The name is inextricable from the material being of Jesus: just as *Jehovah* is identical with being, so *Jesus* is identical with enfleshed being. When Donne quotes Philippians 2.10 to proclaim that "every knee bow . . . at the name of Jesus,"[64] he performs the same reverence for the sign as a site of presence that elsewhere governs his description of the sacramental elements as "*Venerabile & adorabile.*" Like the name of Christ itself, the sacramental elements embody Christ, the eucharistic trope explicitly incarnational in its operation: still bread, as Donne insists, but bread suffused with the presence of God, holy because it is an object of being, not because it points away from itself toward some distant or disembodied sphere. The theology of language that Donne articulates describes a system of sanctified signification in which the figurative is literal, substantial because it stands as a referential end in itself. For Donne, the sacramental trope serves as an incarnational event because it preserves its objective status—which is to say, it preserves being-in-itself. Such sanctified signs as we find in the name of God and in the Eucharist supersede their symbolic function; in these holy figurations, signs are privileged as plenitude, as copia of being, because they are themselves referential ends.

Certainly, the copious elaboration of Donne's metaphors is a defining hallmark of his verse, and his lyrics are lavished with figures that expand to an impenetrable extremity, with the effect that we remain dazzled by the figurative surface rather than confident in what they indicate referentially. Such a theology of language does not merely apply when addressing sacred subjects but necessarily penetrates to the heart of Donne's treatment of figuration in all contexts. Accordingly, such emphatic troping strategies are not by any means limited to Donne's devotional poems, as is evidenced by the famous compass metaphor that concludes "A Valediction: forbidding Mourning." Even as the conceit figures "Our two souls" as inextricably bound, such that "they are two so / As stiffe twin compasses are two," the figure veers out of any heartening correspondence to a love relationship.[65] "Thy soul the fixt foot," the trope designates, while "the other far doth rome" (27, 30). This conceit seems to offer a sweepingly romantic image of fidelity, as the fixed foot, swiveling dependably with the movements of the roaming point, "leans, and hearkens after it, / And growes erect, as it comes home" (31–32). But the last stanza lingers over the compass figure, expanding it until it reveals its own problematics:

> Such wilt thou be to mee, who must
> > Like th'other foot, obliquely runne;
> Thy firmnes makes my circle just,
> > And makes me end, where I begunne. (33–36)

To put it plainly, the compass cannot work as Donne describes. If the roaming foot is to "come home," as the poem's penultimate stanza promises it will, it cannot make "my circle just" because by definition all points of a circle are equidistant from its center. Either the perfection of the circle must be dented by affection and reunion or the permanent separation of the stiff twin compasses must preserve it. Donne's figure emphasizes its own logical contradictions, which keeps focus not on the love relationship but on the compass itself and on its operational dynamics. The lovers fade into referential obscurity as the trope calls attention to itself: what we remember about this poem is its audacious conceit, not the love relationship, which is effectively beat to an aery thinness by the poem's powerful figuration.

So charged a mechanism does metaphor provide for experimenting on its own capacity to assert presence that Donne thematizes this very experiment in a number of poems. Readers have noted the echoes of sacramental language in "A Valediction, of my Name in the Window," in which the speaker considers whether his name, engraved on his beloved's window, might keep him present to her thoughts in his physical absence. Clearly, the poem's situation invites comparison to Communion, that ritual of absent presence, but in arguing variously that the poem's terminology serves a Counter-Reformation agenda, or a counter-Counter-Reformation agenda, recent critics seem willfully determined to look through the poem's ostentatiously opaque figure.[66] Indeed, the central conceit of the poem revolves around an ostentatiously opaque figure, a sign whose objecthood supersedes its meaning. The opening stanzas of the poem offer up a number of signifieds for the sign of the name: it is "all confessing, and through-shine as I"; "it shews thee to thee"; and then again it is a metonymy for the speaker, so that when the beloved's image reflects back to her with the name etched across its surface, "Here you see mee, and I am you" (8, 9, 12). Finally, Donne more powerfully suggests the similarities between the name in the window and the sacramental elements: "thinke this ragged bony name to bee / My ruinous Anatomie" (23–24). Or, as Jesus puts it in Matthew 26.26, *Hoc est corpus meum.* But more than concerning itself with the manner and mode by which the speaker's presence might be actualized by the sign of the name on the glass, the poem takes greatest pains to assert the presence of the sign, which endures as an object: "no one point, nor dash, / Which are but accessarie to this name, / The showers and tempests can outwash" (13–15). The lines and grooves of the etched name, which are but "accessarie to," or signs of the name, are themselves solidly present, resistant to erasure. The trope for the lover supplants the lover as a real presence in the poem, persistent precisely because it flouts transparency both literally (because its textual scoring interrupts the window's glassy clarity) and figuratively (because the speaker never quite decides what his figure represents). In the absence of such certainty, the etched name is offered as a talisman, a sign whose power derives from its being rather than from its meaning.

That the poem settles on the sign's being as the locus of its meaningfulness offers an alternative to an approach motivated by a need to believe, as the lover in Donne's poem ceases to do, that the function of the sign is to point beyond itself. James Baumlin concludes that the poem "describes the poet's loss of the power of naming (or rather of self-presencing and self-preservation *through* naming)" because the engraved name does not perish even when the lover's remembrance erodes, through time or rivalry. "The poet of 'A Valediction: of my Name in the Window,'" Baumlin flatly states, "is unable to claim for his language the power . . . of sacramental presence."[67] But it seems to me that Baumlin has it exactly backward, for while the lover whose uncertain departure is represented in the poem may be left to suspect his "idle talke" (65) to be idol talk—that is, to suspect that his conceit aggrandizes a sign that has no substantial referent to secure it—the poet, by contrast, claims for his figure profound sacramental presence, representing not the body of the speaker but the "scratch'd name" (20) sharply "cut" (37) into glass, the solidly embodied "bone / Being still with you" (28–29) as an object of contemplation both within the poem's narrative and in the reader's hermeneutic engagement with the poem's text. As the poem's opening lines declare, the figure of the name "engrav'd herein" makes the surface of the window (and the surface of the poem) a perceptible object, giving "firmnesse to this glasse" (1–2).[68] The poem makes of its central conceit a substantial event, a symbol that dramatizes the durability of its own surface even as the poem shrugs off its utility as an efficacious sign: "But glasse, and lines must bee, / No meanes our firme substantiall love to keepe," the lover complains in the poem's last stanza (61–62). And yet, as the line break slyly emphasizes, those surfaces "must bee"—that is, they achieve a state of *being* in the poem that is not subject to the vicissitudes of love and leaving. The figure of the name, we might say, is the only reliable presence in the poem.

Perhaps the most dramatic interrogation of metaphor and its potential to resist transparency is performed in the strange seduction attempted in "The Flea." Again, the eucharistic echoes of this poem are well established,

and, as with many poems in which Donne makes use of religious terminology, critics have leveraged those echoes into assertions of one distinct doctrinal position or another. M. Thomas Hester traces the poem's many
allusions to eucharistic liturgy and exegesis to show that the poem "appropriates the precise lexicon and paradigms of the current theological debate"
over sacramental operation, pitting what Hester cleverly calls a "Protesting"
lady who "deny'st" the mystery of real sacrifice in the speaker's central
conceit against a speaker whose Recusant point is that the Real Presence of
Christ's blood in the sacrifice of the sacrament "does not 'take life' from
me, nor him, nor 'thee,'" any more than the flea's blood does when it is
shed by the lady.[69] Taking the doctrinally opposite view, DiPasquale reads
the speaker as instructing the lady toward what she broadly calls a "Protestant" understanding "that the reality is a thing separate from the sign"; the
lady's act of violence in killing the flea "destroyed only the signifier, not the
thing it represented," just as the yielding of her "maidenhead" does not
mean that she likewise yields the thing it represents, her "honor."[70] It is not
surprising that both Hester's Catholic take on the poem and DiPasquale's
"Protestant" reading acknowledge that the poem's central drama turns
upon the success or failure of a metaphoric figure, the titular flea, since the
poem's concern with the operation of signs evokes rather flagrantly the
eucharistic controversies of the period. To be sure, the poem is shot
through with sacramentally loaded language, from the first word's "Marke"
or sign of union, to the flea's "blood of innocence" in the last stanza, to
the striking repetition of unmodified pronouns throughout the poem,
which Hester ingeniously links with Jesus's words of institution at the Last
Supper: "it is significant to see how the poem moves through a series of
befuddling grammatical and figurative twists on the indefinite pronouns
'this' and 'that'—in serio-ridiculous affectation of the controversialists lexical and grammatical disputations about the syntax, grammar, typology, and
Greek and Hebrew sources for the (Counter)Reformation debate about the
referends for Christ's 'Hoc.'"[71] But what Hester dismisses in the poem as a
"serio-ridiculous affectation" is fully in keeping with the poem's sacramental strategies of figuration, which invite attempts to fix referents—for "this"
and "that," for "Christ's Hoc," and for the flea itself, only to undermine all
such attempts. "The Flea," like the flea it incarnates, enacts the disintegration of symbol into unsublimably perceptible object.

Even before the poem's second stanza imports the explicitly religious
language of the "mariage temple" (13) and the "cloyster" (15), the poem's

first stanza is crowded with pronomial allusions to Reformation debates over *Hoc*. "Marke but this flea," the poem begins, "and marke in this, / How little that which thou deny'st me is" (1–2). But to what does the first line's concluding "this" refer, exactly? The flea? The "Marke" it leaves when it bites? The "Marke" of attention commanded as an opening imperative? The poem in which "this" elaborate metaphor will unfold? The polyvalence of the word *this*, which serves as the crux for the metaphor of flea-as-sex (because it is "in this" that the comparison is effected), emphasizes by its evasion of interpretive certainty its own status as a thing, a sign in itself. This focus on the significative surface of the language continues in the second line, where "that" suggests intercourse *and* the lady's physical "maidenhead" (6) *and* the abstract "honour" (26) equated with that tangible sign of chastity. In each case, the opaque and confused referentiality of these often overlooked parts of speech ensures that the pronoun be confronted in itself: in the absence of any indicative stability the pronoun is reified as an object.[72] This pattern is repeated throughout Donne's short lyric, which contains no less than seven indefinite pronouns—five of those in the first stanza alone: pointers with nothing clear to point to, so that what is finally communicated is the gesture of pointing. Such sustained emphasis on referentially resistant signs does not merely accomplish a satiric appropriation of the controverted terminology of eucharistic exegesis; it replicates the very ground of that controversy. The reader of "The Flea" must, like the Reformers and their Counter-Reformist counterparts, address the operation of the *Hoc* directly and grapple with the referential gesture it both performs and frustrates.

Moreover, the poem's seduction drama hinges upon conflicting interpretations of such cunning indeterminacies. Both Hester's and DiPasquale's readings chart (albeit from opposite perspectives) the tug of war that unfolds between the speaker and the lady, the poem's dramatized argument turning upon the question of whether the figure of the flea corresponds to an objective truth, mingling their bloods to the detriment of nobody's virtue, or whether it is a mere empty sign, an inconsequential and inefficacious metaphor. Certainly, the speaker seems to manipulate the lady toward a denial that the flea is an effectual sign for erotic mingling, so that when she, with a triumphant flourish, squashes both the flea and the speaker's intricate figuration, he celebrates with her the apparent disseveration of tropic sign from the abstract idea it represents. "'Tis true" (25), he exults, and barrels onward to declare that because she admits that metaphoric terms are distinct from the principles they figure, she should not therefore fixate overly on the "little that" which she continues to deny him, since by her own admission her "maidenhead" is not identical with her virtue; rather, it is as dispensable a symbol as the flea.

But to rest on this conclusion (as both DiPasquale and, to a lesser degree, Hester do)—that is, that its romantic narrative makes the poem's strongest case for the emptiness of the metaphoric sign—is only satisfying if we as readers put ourselves in the position of the wooed, as if we were to be seduced by the poem into entertaining the notion that the flea *might* signify "Our mariage bed, and mariage temple" (13) and that the success of that figure is ours to ratify or decline.[73] However, the poem does not encourage such gullibility where figuration is concerned. Blatant in its self-awareness, it presents its series of increasingly magnificent metaphoric claims as patently, unapologetically outrageous: the flea's vehicle shifts and amplifies from blood-mingling, to "mariage bed," to temple, to a Trinity whose squashing would constitute "three sinnes in killing three" (18), to Christ himself, whose "blood of innocence" purples the "naile" of the blaspheming lady who dispatches it (20). It is a ridiculous progression, a high-wire act of ever-intensifying figurative bravado, and the concluding twist ("'Tis true"!) testifies that the ridiculousness is calculated, deliberately fashioned to provoke a firm—not to say violent—rejection of the poem's tropic program. It's not just that "The Flea" dares us to resist the referential function of its central metaphor; it's that "The Flea" is gleefully ostentatious in assembling metaphors so tenuous, so extreme in their yoking of heterogenous terms, that they can only be resisted. And while its referential quantum does not stabilize on the bed or temple or Christ, the figure of the flea stubbornly and flamboyantly does indicate, consistently throughout its many changes, its own status as a metaphoric sign. Nor can it be said to be an "empty sign," for the metaphoric operation of the flea is the central concern of the poem, the matter (in both senses of the term) that generates both its erotic drama and its semiotic debate, commanding the attention of interpreters both in the poem and of the poem. And in its metaphoric function, the flea keeps asserting its presence precisely because of its discord with any of the poem's tenors, obtruding preposterously into the provinces of the cloister and the cross, leaving its marks on the skin of the poem. Just as the flea's corpse remains after it has served its argumentative purposes, the flea-figure endures as a hermeneutic artifact, a significative remainder amid the poem's rhapsodically compounding tropic signifieds.[74] Donne's most extravagant trope proves to be a most indispensable object, though the lady, and critics, grudge.

The figure of the flea, the ever-splayed compasses, the holy rape of God: each of these tropes remains unresolvable into the principle of a perceptually absent tenor. By exceeding their own referentiality, such figures achieve the status of objects in themselves, fully present to the apprehension. Donne's extravagant tropes exert figuration as a substantial force, expressing in their symbolic indissolubility the presencing capacity of language. This strategy reflects Donne's sense of the incarnational effects of divine language, especially in its deployment of tropes. In a powerful passage from his *Devotions upon Emergent Occasions*, Donne praises God's use of metaphor as an incarnational device:

> My *God*, my *God*, Thou art a *direct God*, may I not say, a *literall God*, a *God* that wouldst be understood *literally*, and according to the *plaine sense* of all that thou saiest? But thou art also (*Lord* I intend it to thy *glory*, and let no *prophane mis-interpreter* abuse it to thy *diminution*) though art a *figurative*, a *metaphoricall God* too: A *God* in whose words there is such a height of *figures*, such *voyages*, such *peregrinations* to fetch remote and precious *metaphors*, such *extentions*, such *spreadings*, such *Curtaines* of *Allegories*, such *third Heavens* of *Hyperboles*, so *harmonious eloquutions*, so *retired* and so *reserved expressions*, so *commanding perswasions*, so *perswading commandements*, such *sinewes* even in thy *milke*, and such *things* in thy *words*, as all *prophane Authors*, seeme of the seed of the *Serpent*, that *creepes*; thou art the *dove*, that flies.[75]

God's language incorporates the material, the objective: it is fleshed out with "sinewes" and substance; it has, wonderfully, "*things in thy words.*" The language that Donne so admires here is explicitly praised for having achieved a distinct and consequential objecthood. And it is central to an understanding of Donne's figurative elaborations to recognize that Donne locates the objective substantiality of God's words, its very *thinginess*, in metaphor. Donne's rapturous aria on his "*metaphoricall God*," itself sumptuous with figurative language in a proliferation that mimics the ostentatious poeticism of the discourse he extols, situates the incarnational power of God's language in its expressive tropes.

Moreover, as he winds himself up to the passage's climactic approval of the "*things* in thy *words*," Donne's own words evoke the *res* and *verba* of sacramental signification, the substance and the sign, in order to collapse them together.[76] In God's metaphors, the referential function of the *verba* is made obsolete by its being inseparable from the *res*, just as the Incarnation effects the hypostatic union of the material sign of flesh with the transcendent spirit. Christ is *Logos*, and for Donne that means that Christ is also the preeminent metaphoric term, the figure that authorizes all figuration as an incarnational act. "Thou spokest in thy *Son*," he continues in the same expostulation, and goes on to identify Christ as both an incarnate trope and the underwriter of all tropes: "How often, how much more often doth thy *Sonne* call himself a *way*, and a *light*, and a *gate*, and a *Vine*, and *bread*, than the *Sonne of God*, or of *Man*?" This "*Metaphoricall Christ*," as Donne styles him, the express substance of God, is apprehensible not *through* trope but *as* trope.[77] In Christ, and in the sacrament that repeats his holy semiotics and presents him to the communicant, the figurative is itself literal. For Donne, the figure of the sacramental word/Word doesn't *mean* presence; it *is* presence.

Donne's metaphoric strategies emulate the sacrament's poetics of figuration as Donne describes it, a radical literalization of the figurative that effects the stable, perceptible presence of being-in-itself. By constructing metaphors whose symbolic function is interrupted by their own elaboration, Donne asserts figures as objects that must be confronted in themselves, not as mere vehicles to be absented into referentiality. As trope gets extended and unfolded into particularity, it becomes a thing whose terms are apprehensible, present, and significant. The figurative is made substantive, the word enfleshed as a referential end. In the 1626 Christmas sermon, Donne chides doctrinal disputants for abstracting presence away from sacramental worship: "the Roman Church hath catched a *Trans*, and others a *Con*, and a *Sub*, and an *In*, and varied their poetry into a Transubstantiation, and a Consubstantiation, and the rest, and rymed themselves beyond reason, into absurdities, and heresies."[78] Donne's figures reject formulations that would understand being to be disjointed by the ontological divides of a representational system; disposing of distracting prefixes, of the Roman "*trans*" and the Lutheran "*con*" and all the others, Donne offers a system that stands on substance alone. Donne's metaphors substantiate, intransitively. His sacramental poetics, flush with extreme tropes and enthusiastic in its disruptions of interpretive clarity, posits the metaphoric sign as an object in itself, as durable and present as a name carved into a window.

Chapter 4

Richard Crashaw's Indigestible Poetics

Suppose he had been Tabled at thy Teates.
　　Thy hunger feeles not what he eates:
Hee'l have his Teat e're long (a bloody one)
　　The Mother than must suck the Son.
　　　　—Richard Crashaw,
　　　　"Luke 11. Blessed be the paps which Thou hast sucked"

In his editorial headnote to Crashaw's epigram on Luke 11, George Walton Williams notes mildly that "This little poem has provoked extravagant comment."[1] Williams then goes on to catalogue examples of what he views as a troubling critical focus on the poem's physicalized terminology, including Robert Adams's infamous opinion that the epigram imparts "a nasty twist to the spiritual-carnal relation" and William Empson's remark that it encompasses "a wide variety of sexual perversions."[2] Williams springs to Crashaw's supposed defense, insisting that the poem's shocking imagery merely represents a spiritual principle and is therefore not really shocking at all. "The bloody teat is the spear-wound in Christ's side, imaged here as near the breast," he instructs, and points out that "The image of the nourishing breast of God is a devotional metaphor found in the Scriptures" and elsewhere in the exegetical tradition.[3] Williams's headnote goes some way toward explaining by example the "extravagant comment" surrounding this poem, positing as it does a divide between interpretations that trouble themselves about the poem's rebarbative physical details on the one hand and interpretations that seek to dissolve those physical details into metaphysical precepts on the other.

The problem with each of these approaches—a problem to which Emp-son's commentary on the poem is attuned—is that they binarize the inter-pretive possibilities of a text whose argument turns precisely on collapsing binaries, on bringing into proximity terms that would seem to be in opposi-tion to one another. As R. V. Young notes, reinforcing Empson's response to the poem, "Crashaw was certainly not unaware of the overtones of sexual perversion, incest, and cannibalism that might be evoked in this epigram by modern critics." Indeed, continues Young, these elements are far from accidental, for "it is evident that Crashaw is attempting to impart some sense of the truly shocking implications of Holy Communion. But it is truly shocking only for a man with a belief not merely in a vague 'real presence,' but in the actuality of Christ's Body and Blood under the outward forms of the sacrament."[4] Young's argument recognizes that the carnal elements of Crashaw's epigram exist simultaneously with its spiritual concerns, that they even work to illuminate those spiritual concerns. Yet Young takes the "shocking implications" he observes to reaffirm a doctrinally orthodox reading of the poem, identifying the epigram's shock value as a reflection of the physics of a thoroughly unreformed Eucharist, in which the body of Christ actually enters into the body of the communicant.

I would like to suggest that Crashaw's epigram communicates the prob-lematics of the Eucharist not only by acknowledging the indecorous "over-tones of sexual perversion, incest, and cannibalism" intimated by sacramental contact with the body of Christ but also in the hermeneutic challenge it thrusts before its reader. For Crashaw, I propose, the most shocking aspect of the Eucharist is not precipitated by the possibility of physical intimacy between the worshipper and the body of Christ; like many of his contempo-raries—including, as we have seen, George Herbert, Edward Taylor, and John Donne—not to mention the centuries of exegetical commentary that pre-ceded them, Crashaw seems to proceed from the premise that the achieve-ment of intimacy with the divine is rather the point of the sacrament.[5] Rather than whatever carnal implications may follow from the presence of the body of Christ in the Eucharist, what seems to exercise Crashaw most strenuously is the bald imperceptibility of Christ's body in the consecrated elements. In acknowledging the necessity of faith to recognize the substantial presence of Christ's flesh beneath the accidents of bread and wine, Crashaw does not depart from the explanation of transubstantiation that had served as Catholic institutional orthodoxy since the Fourth Lateran Council in 1215 and was later explicated so clearly by Thomas Aquinas in his *Summa Theologiae*. But

Crashaw sounds the tension between sensory and spiritual modes of perception with a telling consistency, thematizing over and again in his poems the difficulty of interpreting by faith, and against the evidence of the body. This difficulty finds articulation especially in Crashaw's poems concerning the Eucharist, which express the hermeneutic obscurity of sacramental worship in the very terms they use to commemorate the rite. The reader of Crashaw's eucharistic poems must confront language whose irreducible physicality works to veil the spiritual principle it represents, a poetic strategy that replicates the challenge of discerning Christ's body through the representational veils of bread and wine.

Crashaw's engagement with this perceptual challenge leads him to employ poetic strategies that strain the symbolic function of language itself. Like Donne, Crashaw is cognizant of the capacity of symbol to be significatively substantial in and of itself, and both poets employ symbols that foreground their corporeal valences in order to emphasize the resolute superficiality of poetic language. That is, both Crashaw and Donne trouble what we would think of as the symbolic function of their symbols, reifying figures into antiabsorptive signs that prevent their own interpretive transparency. But where I have described Donne's conceits as interrupting referentiality, disorienting the correspondence between a metaphoric vehicle and its tenor with the result that the vehicle endures indissolubly to the perception, unmoored from any symbolic gesture, Crashaw's method of figuration seems to deny such a dualistic notion of representation, in which symbols and their referents occupy different categories of perception. Crashaw's use of symbols destabilizes their referential efficacy. To put it in more direct (if somewhat reductive) terms, if Donne does not let us see through to the referential field "behind" his figures, Crashaw seems motivated by his doubt that such a "behind" can ever be available to the apprehension by any means. For Crashaw, the symbolic system is itself fully manifest in its corporeality, and that corporeality must constitute our experience of the divine, however incomplete. By substantiating his language into antiabsorptive symbol, Crashaw adopts a poetics that reflects the experiential, sense-able dynamics of sacramental worship even as it exposes the consequences of a theology that would locate meaningfulness beyond the apprehension of the senses. This tension is nowhere more apparent than in Crashaw's brief eucharistic poem on Luke 11.

Originally composed in Latin while Crashaw was a student at Cambridge, over a decade before he converted to Catholicism, the epigram on Luke 11 bespeaks both in its first version and in Crashaw's later English translation (published the same year as his formal conversion) an aesthetic sympathy for the materially inscribed operation of the transubstantial rite. Crashaw's earlier Latin epigram makes its eucharistic interests overt, describing man's spiritual nourishment by Christ in language lifted directly from the Roman liturgy:

> Et quid si biberet Jesus vel ab ubere vestro?
> > Quid facit ad vestram, quòd bibit ille, sitim?
> Ubera mox sua & Hic (ô quàm non lactea!) pandet:
> > E nato *Mater* tum bibet ipsa suo.
> [And what if Jesus should indeed drink from your breast?
> > what does it do to your thirst because he drinks?
> And soon He will lay bare his breast—alas, not milky!—
> > from her son then the *mother* will drink.][6]

Three times in four lines appears some form of the verb *bibere,* "to drink," a clear echo of the Latin missal's exhortation to the celebrant: "Accepite, et bibite," or "Take, and drink."[7] This reference to sacramental speech encodes the act of drinking as a ritual performance, sublimating its physicality and rendering typological the interaction between mother and son.

But the liturgical echo of the Latin epigram disappears in Crashaw's own English version. Here, the word "suck" dispels the Latin poem's direct allusions to the sacrament and emphasizes instead the physical activity of nursing. Although medieval and Renaissance representations of Christ as a nursing mother abound, Crashaw's transition from "bibet" to "suck" creates an interpretive disjunction in the English epigram that the Latin version lacks.[8] As Thomas Healy puts it, "An understanding of the imagery's origins . . . does not stop a reader's response to the very physical 'teat' and 'suck' giving rise to collocations which are not only grotesque but vulgar." In contrast to the conflation of physical and sacramental concerns that occurs in the word "bibet," "suck" operates outside the sacramental system, its associations restricted to extra-ritual forms of bodily nourishment and erotic activity. But where Healy would conclude that "It is difficult to compose a visual emblem of the scene as suggested by the epigram," I suggest that the epigram's images are so resolutely physical that it is perhaps *only* possible to imagine the scene visually.[9] There is no sacramental echo to mitigate the image of Mary suckling at Jesus's breast/wound, and we are left to contemplate the unsublimated corporeality of "suck."

If anything, the ritual transgressiveness of "suck" is amplified by Crashaw's use of "Teat," a term that refers specifically to the nipple—or, more commonly, to the udder—in the context of lactation. While the sacramental force of "bibet" works to allay the physicality of the Latin "ubere" (as do the more abstract connotations of richness and fertility suggested by "ubere"), "Teat" again permits no such sublimation. Like "suck," and especially in conjunction with "suck," "Teat" is a term inescapably tied to the body, not easily assimilable into the sacramental system. Moreover, Christ's teat in Crashaw's English is "a bloody one," a vivid and startling revision of the more conceptually associational and indirect Latin lamentation "ô quàm non lactea!" For while the Latin offers the locally nondisjunctive "lactea," the English "bloody" makes intolerable the already unsettling image of Christ giving suck to Mary. This ornate grotesquerie may work, in Young's words, "to impart some sense of the truly shocking implications of Holy Communion," but perhaps more forcefully, and more surprisingly, it effectively expels the reader from the scheme of sacramental reference constructed so carefully in Crashaw's Latin version. In the English poem, interpretive access to the eucharistic principle signified by Mary's sucking Christ's bloody "Teat" is impeded by the insurmountably extra-ritual physicality of the image.

It is worth noting that all the major English Bibles in circulation during the sixteenth and early seventeenth centuries—the Wycliffe and Tyndale translations, as well as the Geneva, Douay-Rheims, and King James versions—translate the source passage in Luke 11.27 using "suck," a natural choice considering that the Greek verse's ἐθήλασας does indeed denote suckling. Likewise, Wycliffe translates μαστοί (which indicates the female breasts) as "tetis," and the others settle upon the no less bodily "pappes." The difficulty of Crashaw's English epigram comes not from its importation of physical terms into a holy context, as is evidenced by the unremarkable use of "Teates" in the poem's first line, in which it indicates the infant Jesus in the act of nursing. "Teat" only becomes impertinent in the third line, when Christ's fully adult male body grows a bloody teat for suckling. When they are applied to Christ's body, "Teat" and "suck" beg to be read in the context of the eucharistic mystery, of Christ's nourishing the communicant, but the exclusively physical sense of these terms obstructs such a reading. In other words, though the sacramental scheme of the poem would sublimate the physical body into ritual significance, "suck" and "Teat" assert themselves outside the sacramental system; too real in their presence, they refuse to give way to spiritual analogues.[10] Alerting the reader to what is, for Crashaw, perhaps the most shocking implication of eucharistic worship, the poet problematizes our reading of Christ's body by making it ritually unrecognizable, undiscernible beneath the manifest distractions of the physical.

Healy acknowledges the aversive nature of Crashaw's imagery, but nevertheless insists that the poet's perceived vulgarity should be understood within the context of Laud's English Church, which endorsed the use of "physically exaggerated and explicit imagery in describing sacred events."[11] Citing the Laudian reformer John Cosin's admonition that the communicant ought "not to look barely on the outward Elements" but "with their hearts lift up to feed on that heavenly meat," Healy goes on to argue that Crashaw's epigram on Luke 11 "causes the reader not to 'rest in the outward Elements' through the sheer indecorousness of the image."[12] For Healy, the "indecorousness" of Crashaw's imagery works instructively, to prompt the reader to bypass a literal interpretation in order to discern the doctrine it implies. The epigram, he claims, "will not strictly bear a 'literal sense' (there is no scriptural authority for the Virgin sucking, or even sharing, Christ's wounds). This directs the reader to consider the figurative uses of the expression."[13] But Healy's conclusion echoes Williams's editorial defenses of Crashaw even as it acknowledges that the imagery may in fact be objectionable. The hermeneutic test proposed by Healy's explanation mandates that Crashaw's ideal reader must learn to *read through* the carnal details in order to access the epigram's divine argument, an approach that Healy rightly links to conventional explanations of sacramental worship. But, as Gary Kuchar is forced to admit even as he supports and expands Healy's argument, "most readers, even those contemporary to Crashaw, are not as ideal as the one Healy presumes."[14] Perhaps the documented failure of so many of Crashaw's readers to spiritualize the physical (their failures left as trace suspicions of Crashaw's poetic maturity throughout the critical tradition) is a consequence not of their ritual unpreparedness but rather of the poem's insistence on language that refuses to give way to the spiritual. Indeed, as we have seen, Crashaw's epigram requires that the reader confront the irreducible corporeality of Mary's discomfiting "suck" at Christ's "Teat."[15] This poetic strategy, whereby the sacramental is interrupted by terms whose physicality defies symbolic assimilation, manifests itself whenever Crashaw turns his poetic attention to the Eucharist.

In the English epigram "Our Lord in his Circumcision, to his Father," Crashaw's insistence on extra-ritual somatic details again introduces interpretive insolubility into the symbolic system of eucharistic worship. Like

"Blessed be the paps," Crashaw's epigram on the circumcision explores the eucharistic significance of Christ's body in terms that stymie a sacramental reading. Again, the poem offers a familiar symbolic argument, finding an early parallel for Christ's blood sacrifice in the event of the infant ritual:

> To thee these first fruits of my growing death
> (For what else is my life?) lo I bequeath.
> Tast this, and as thou lik'st this lesser flood
> Expect a Sea, my heart shall make it good.
> Thy wrath that wades heere now, e're long shall swim
> The flood-gate shall be set wide ope for him.
> Then let him drinke, and drinke, and doe his worst,
> To drowne the wantonnesse of his wild thirst . . .
> These purple buds of blooming death may bee,
> Erst the full stature of a fatall tree.
> And till my riper woes to age are come.
> This knife may be the speares *Praeludium.* (1–8, 15–18)

As in "Blessed be the paps," Crashaw's eucharistic intentions here are unavoidable. The promise that the small trickle of blood from the wound of circumcision will become a "Sea" of gore refers beyond this infant moment to the offering of Christ's body on the cross as the "first fruits"—a sacrifice repeated at the altar during the Mass. The "fatall tree," the spear, the bloom of death, all mark the occasion commemorated by the sacrament, in which wrath (both man's and God's) can "drinke, and drinke" itself to propitiation. Crashaw's treatment of Jesus's circumcision as a harbinger of the crucifixion is typologically conventional, but when the poem seeks to underscore the relationship between this small blood offering and the greater offering to come, Crashaw's language pushes beyond convention yet again, into terms that exceed sacramental orthodoxy. The third line demands that its audience "Tast this," the first drop of Christ's shed blood, a gesture that stands in direct contradiction to eucharistic doctrine. As Thomas Aquinas explains in his *Summa Theologiae,*

> Dicendum quod sensu apparet, facta consecratione, omnia accidentia panis et vini remanere. Quod quidem rationabiliter per divinam providentiam fit. Primo quidem, quia non est consuetum hominibus, sed horribile, carnem hominis comedere et sanguinem bibere.

[It is obvious to our senses that, after the consecration, all the accidents of the bread and wine remain. Divine providence very wisely arranged for this. First of all, men have not the custom of eating human flesh and drinking human blood; indeed, the thought revolts them.][16]

The species of bread and wine, says Thomas, were divinely (and shrewdly) instituted so that communicants might avoid experiencing the disquieting taste of blood in the sacrament. In Crashaw's epigram, then, Christ's invitation to "Tast" explicitly transgresses doctrinal formulations of the rite.

Moreover, in Crashaw's epigram, the Eucharist is not the immediate context of all this blood drinking. Rather, the context here is the explicitly nonsacramental event of circumcision, a shift that intensifies the discomfort of the epigram by demanding that its audience—God and the reader simultaneously—"Tast" the offering of specifically penile blood. Because the circumcision in its function as a foreshadowing of the crucifixion is not therefore intrinsic to the event venerated in the eucharistic rite, the charge to "Tast" the blood of Christ's circumcision refuses a sacramental reading. We are left with yet another indecorous image, another set of terms whose troubling and intractable materiality inhibits hermeneutic access to the eucharistic principle the epigram invokes.

That the sacramental insolubility of "Tast" in the English epigram on the circumcision serves deliberate antiabsorptive ends is borne out, once again, by a glance at Crashaw's two Latin epigrams on the same subject. The epigram "In sanguinem circumcisionis Dominicae. Ad convivas, quod haec dies apud nos solennes habet" [On the blood of the Lord's circumcision. To the guests who celebrate this day with us], uses the verb *bibere* in various conjugations and grammatical moods a full eleven times over the course of ten lines. The poem virtually drowns in drinking. "O bibite & bibite," it invites, "& restat tamen usquè bibendum" [O drink and drink; still there remains more to be drunk] (7). The profusion of potable substance in this poem, however, hovers in the symbolic, transcending the physical both by virtue of its supernatural overabundance and, as in the Latin epigram on Luke 11, by its repeated echo of the Roman rite.

We can compare the self-consciously sacramental language of these lines with the poet's other Latin epigram on the subject, "Christus circumcisus ad Patrem" [Christ, circumcised, to the Father], Crashaw's first working of what would later become his English poem:

Has en primitias nostrae (Pater) accipe mortis;
  (Vitam ex quo sumpsi, vivere dedidici)

Ira (Pater) tua de pluviâ gustaverit istâ:
  Olim ibit fluviis hoc latus omne suis.

Tunc sitiat licèt & sitiat, bibet & bibet usqué:
  Tunc poterit toto fonte superba frui.

Nunc hastae interea possit praeludere culter:
  Indolis in pœnas spes erit ista meae.
[Lo, receive these first fruits of our death, Father, (to you)
  from whom I have received life, I have dedicated my life;

your wrath, Father, will have tasted of this shower:
  at a later time this whole side will flow forth in its own
  streams.

Then let (your wrath) thirst and thirst, let it drink and drink forever:
  Then it will be able to enjoy the whole splendid spring.

Meanwhile now let the *knife* foreshadow the *spear*:
  the hope of my (whole) being will be in the torments (that
  are to come).]

As in Crashaw's English version of this epigram, when the poem anticipates the moment of Christ's sacrificial piercing on the cross, its language duly echoes the Communion rite, both with "bibet & bibet" and by indicating the infinite satiation available through the sacramental elements. But the poem's third line, as in the English rendering, presents not an echo of sacramental language but "gustaverit," a verb that denotes the physical faculty of taste, and the relish thereof. Both English and Latin versions, rather than resonating with the terms of the Mass, unfold in territory that doubly transgresses the possibilities of eucharistic interpretation, imagining the blood of Christ's extra-ritual penis as having an appetizing flavor.

This pattern in which physicality disrupts sacramentalism recurs in "In die Passionis Dominicae" [On the day of the Master's Passion], where Crashaw contemplates the crucifixion through its traditional association with the winepress (because that machine metaphorically brings forth the eucharistic wine of Christ's sacrificial blood).[17] After imagining the "vinum . . . dulce," the "sweet wine" issuing forth from the side of Christ at the spear's thrust (1–2), Crashaw turns his praise once again to a theologically impossible effect of sacramental contact with Christ:

Jámque it; & ô quanto calet actus aromate torrens!
　　Acer ut hinc aurâ divite currit odor!

Quae rosa per cyathos volitat tam viva Falernos? . . .
Vincor: & ô istis totus propè misceor auris:
　　Non ego sum tantis, non ego par cyathis.
[Now it goes, and oh with what fragrance does that burning torrent
　　stream!
　　　　as hence a stinging odor rushes out like a heavenly breeze!

What rose so fresh flutters through Falernian glasses? . . .
I am overcome; oh I am almost completely mingled with these
　　aromas:
　　　　I am not, I am not equal to such glasses.] (7–9, 13–14)

Here, as in the circumcision epigram, Crashaw records the eucharistic experience of Christ in sensual terms that defy orthodoxy. It is not the sacramental element of wine but rather the "burning torrent" of Christ's blood
whose odor intoxicates like the famed vintage of Falernus. The aroma of
Christ's blood, like the "Tast" of Jesus's penile blood and his bloody "Teat"
in the epigram on Luke 11, refuses hermeneutic absorption into the sacramental. In each case, the sensorily charged, bluntly somatic terms assert
their ritual indigestibility, and obtrude into the overtly eucharistic project
of their respective epigrams. In these verses, Crashaw's integration of sacramentally unassimilable details into conventional typologies reifies those
figures out of symbolic significance and into a distracting corporeality.

　　Recently, Richard Rambuss has contributed to Crashavian scholarship
a welcome perspective, one that acknowledges the coincidence of Crashaw's
spiritual ecstasies and corporeal focus. Rambuss observes that "Crashaw's
devotional verse displays little propensity to leave the body behind, to
recuse the flesh from the operations of redemption." Instead, Rambuss
continues, Crashaw's poetry "insists upon the corporeal, intent on exploring its many expressive possibilities."[18] And indeed, Rambuss's focus on the
physically inscribed nature of Crashaw's imagery, especially as it displays
Christ's body as an erotically spectacularized site of penetrable wounds and
penetrating fluids, provokes renewed appreciation of Crashaw's profound
investment in the material particulars of divine corporeality. Rambuss
makes an important point when he argues that to relegate the off-putting
elements of Crashaw's imagery (not to mention the similarly off-putting
elements of much of Renaissance poetry and art) to the bounds of what he
calls "the 'merely' metaphorical" is to ignore the ways in which devotion

enlists the body as a mechanism for encountering the divine.[19] Still, although Rambuss's critical identification of Crashaw's investment in "Incarnational Christianity" goes a long way toward contextualizing the poet's corporealist poetics, Rambuss mistakes Crashaw's anxious fixation on the body for enthusiasm, largely because he overlooks the ways in which Crashaw's handling of the corporeal is illuminated by the poet's own commentary on the central sacrament of Christian worship, a sacrament that simultaneously activates and denies the body as a site of devotion. Through the vigorous accumulation of details that both excite and block a material experience of ritual spirituality, Crashaw's epigrams on Luke 11 and on Jesus's circumcision offer a sharp and uneasy commentary on the hermeneutic experience—and more important, on Crashaw's experience, as he himself describes it—of the Eucharist.

In the Sacrament of the Altar, as Catholic doctrine came to define it, the body of Christ, while substantively present under the accidents of bread and wine, cannot be detected by the senses.[20] The accidents constitute, or rather substitute for, the communicant's material experience of Christ. The challenge facing the worshipper, as Thomas Aquinas himself was believed to have delineated it in the eucharistic hymn "Adoro Te Devote," is that the material substance of bread and wine is uncompromisingly apparent, available to the senses in a way that Christ's body is not.[21] Given Crashaw's long fascination with Christ's corporeal presence in the Eucharist, it is not surprising that he should have turned his poetic attention to translating Thomas's hymn. Rather than providing a direct translation, however, Crashaw enlarges and complicates the argument of his Latin source text, turning out a poem twice the length of Thomas's original. Crashaw's augmentations should not be dismissed as baroque ornament, for they signal the poet's sustained consideration of the burden of faith in light of both the allurements of the senses and Christ's material inapprehensibility.[22] These elaborations indicate Crashaw's particular concern with the perceptual persistence of sense-data, an anxiety that strains beyond the formal and imagistic bounds of the Latin hymn.

In the early lines of Crashaw's "Hymn in Adoration of the Blessed Sacrament," we find the poet engaged in an inventory of self-instruction, whose corporealized terms alert us to the translation's attentiveness to the distractions of the body:

> Down down, proud sense. Discourses dy.
> Keep close, my soul's inquiring ey!

Nor touch nor tast must look for more
But each sitt still in his own Dore.
Your ports are all superfluous here. (5–9)

These lines expand a single line by Aquinas, "Visus, tactus, gustus in te fallitur" [Sight, touch, taste are in you deceived] (5).[23] The very amplification of one line into five indicates Crashaw's persistent concern with the impediment presented by the senses. Thomas's line recognizes the misleading character of sense-data during the Eucharist, when the perceptible accidents of the sacrament conceal the imperceptible essence of Christ's body. But where the original hymn remarks on sensory deception, Crashaw declares that the senses are "superfluous," a term that hints at the excesses of perception, not its delusion. And where the theologian addresses his "latens Deitas," or "hidden God," directly, Crashaw instead admonishes the recalcitrant flesh itself, commanding the organs of "proud sense" to "sitt still" with an insistence that suggests the senses' unwillingness to comply.

Indeed, the unrelenting activity of the senses penetrates even to the soul, which in these lines gains an "inquiring ey" to interfere with its spiritual discernment of Christ's body in the consecrated bread. This rhetorical gesture, which works to substantiate the spiritual matter of the soul, recurs when Crashaw turns his attention to the Eucharist itself, rhapsodizing,

Rich, Royall food! Bountyfull BREAD!
Whose use denyes us to the dead;
Whose vitall gust alone can give
The same leave both to eat and live. (39–42)

In triumphant apostrophe, Crashaw praises Christ through his expression in the sacramental element of bread, alluding to Jesus's familiar figure from John 6.35 ("I am the bread of life: hee that commeth to me shall neuer hunger"). But just as Crashaw activates the trope's spiritual associations, he arrests our capacity to read the figure spiritually by commending the "gust" of the bread. Its Latin root in the verb *gustare* is absent from Thomas's Latin. Calling Christ "Panis vivus, vitam praestans homini" [Living bread, which gives life to men], Aquinas prays, "Praesta meae menti de te vivere / Et te illi semper dulce sapere" [Grant that my mind may live by you / And ever taste your sweetness] (18–20). In developing his figure, Thomas uses terminology that abstracts the sense of taste away from the mouth. The agent of "sapere," the verb for *taste* found in line 20, is not the tongue but the mind. Such a determined denial of physicality in the line's grammar subordinates the sensually inflected meanings of "dulce" and "sapere" to their more immaterial designations (*delightful* or *pleasant* for "dulce," and *to understand* for "sapere"—as in the modern *sapience*). In Thomas's lines, the sense of taste is disembodied, a shift away from the physical in keeping with the Latin hymn's argument for the necessity of faith and the denial of the body. But in Crashaw's reimagining, taste permeates the celebrant's relationship to the Bread of Life: the "vitall gust" of this "Bountyfull Bread" imposes an explicitly corporeal mode of perception onto an operation of the spirit and postulates, as in the circumcision epigram, that the doctrinally untastable body of Christ can be discerned by the mouth. Even as he translates a hymn whose very purpose is to declare the vanity of sense-perception, Crashaw persistently asserts his senses, importing terms that emphasize their operation where, according to doctrine, they can have no efficacy.[24]

The motive for Crashaw's poetic practice, especially in those poems offering emblematic renderings of the Eucharist, is illuminated by his handling of the central confessional passage from the "Adoro Te Devote," where Crashaw's declaration of his own faith collides with his depiction of a God whose physical presence remains maddeningly unavailable to the senses. Though Crashaw never deviates from Thomas's view that the sacrament is a mystery of faith, his translation's plea for increased faith follows from a series of objections regarding the perceptual difficulties of sacramental interpretation. In the Latin hymn's confessional section, we find Thomas musing:

> In cruce latebat sola Deitas,
> At hic latet simul et humanitas;
> Ambo tamen credens atque confitiens . . .
> Plagas, sicut Thomas, non intueor
> Deum tamen meum te confiteor:
> Fac me tibi semper magis credere.
> [On the cross, only your divinity was hidden,
> but here your humanity too is hidden;
> both alike I believe and confess . . .
> Though I do not gaze upon your wounds, as Thomas did,

yet I confess you my God:
make me always to believe more in you.] (9–11, 13–15)

Aquinas here contrasts his own corporeal remove from Christ's "Deitas" and "humanitas" with that of another Thomas, the doubting disciple who required sensory confirmation of Jesus's resurrection. Aquinas makes this distinction in order to assert that faith provides a witness of Christ's body despite its concealment beneath the sacramental elements, a degree of heightened assurance that the Latin hymn pleads to achieve. Crashaw's translation prefaces this recognition of the need for faith with a complaint "That faith has farther, here, to goe / And lesse to lean on." He continues,

Because than
Though hidd as GOD, wounds writt thee man,
Thomas might touch; None but might see
At least the suffring side of thee;
And that too was thy self which thee did cover
But here ev'n That's hid too which hides the other. (20–26)

Documenting Christ's retreat behind a compounding series of representational dislocations, Crashaw emphasizes his own interpretive distance from Christ's body. In Crashaw's lines, Doubting Thomas is able not only to "gaze upon" Christ's wounds but intimately to "touch" them, and the disciple's privileged vision of Christ's "suffring side" is extended to a generalized audience, follower and faithless alike ("*None but* might see"!)— an audience of visual immediacy that pointedly excludes Crashaw, who remains removed from all perceptual access to Christ's body.

So acute is the English poem's consciousness of hermeneutic separation from the substantial presence of Christ that in its translation of Latin lines 9 to 10, it elides even Aquinas's signifiers for divinity and Incarnation, veiling the nouns "Deitas" and "humanitas" behind the unmodified demonstrative pronouns of lines 25 and 26: "that . . . That . . . the other." This scheme of concealing Christ representationally persists throughout Crashaw's hymn, its very language shrinking from unmediated apprehension of Christ. The poet goes so far as to eliminate the name of Christ from his translation. When Thomas affirms "Credo quidquid dixit Dei Filius" [I believe whatever the Son of God has said] (7), Crashaw replaces the christic designation with an abstract epithet: "Faith can beleive / As fast as love new lawes can give" (11–12). When Thomas salutes "Pie pellicane, Jesu Domine" [Holy pelican, Lord Jesus] (21), Crashaw retains only the symbol, leaving out the direct appellation: "O soft self-wounding pelican!" (45). Even the translation's title reflects the poet's reluctance to approach God directly: Thomas's "Adoro Te Devote" addresses its adoration to the "latens Dietas" of line 1, but the 1652 printing of Crashaw's translation directs its adoration to another object, "The Blessed Sacrament"—a set of symbols instituted to mediate between the perceptual faculties of man and the substance of Christ's body.

This attention to the sign without reference to a signified finds an effusive cognate in Crashaw's original hymn "To the Name above Every Name, the Name of Iesus," another poem whose title focuses its praise on the mediating symbol. But where Crashaw's translation of the Thomist hymn admonishes the senses to "sitt still" so as not to scrabble after access to the divine where none is available, the poet's own hymn marshals all the senses to the praise of the linguistic sign for divinity. And where his "Adoro Te Devote" chastens, "Keep close, my soul's inquiring ey," "To the Name above Every Name" urges rather, "Goe, Soul, out of thy Self, and seek for More" (27), and the resulting traverse through the material world's aids to devotion soon enlivens all the senses, each in turn: Crashaw invites "Lute and Harp / And every sweet-lipp't Thing / That talkes with tunefull string" (46–48), and "All the store" (66) of music into "This unbounded All-imbracing Song" (91).[25] This grand and universal "Fitt-tuned Harmony" (50) is not limited to hearing: Crashaw welcomes as a sunrise the coming Name, in language that suggests nothing if not ocular immediacy, as the veils of mediation (eyelids and window shades) are flung wide to this arising vision:

> The'attending World, to wait thy Rise,
>   First turn'd to eyes . . .
> O see, The Weary liddes of wakefull Hope
> (Love's Eastern windowes) All wide ope
>   With Curtains drawn,
> O To catch the Day-break of Thy Dawn.
> O dawn, at last, long look't for Day! (135–136, 145–149)

Finally, Crashaw's raptures expand to encompass the whole of sensory experience, in a passage so suffused with synesthetic sensuality that it merits quoting here at some length:

> O fill our senses, And take from us
> All force of so Prophane a Fallacy
> To think ought sweet but that which smells of Thee.
> Fair, flowry Name, In none but Thee
> And Thy Nectareall Fragrancy,
>   Hourly there meetes
> An universall SYNOD of All sweets;
> By whom it is defined Thus
>   That no Perfume
>   For ever shall presume
> To passe for Odoriferous,
> But such alone whose sacred Pedigree
> Can prove it Self some kin (sweet name) to Thee.
> SWEET NAME, in Thy each Syllable
> A Thousand Blest ARABIAS dwell;
> A Thousand Hills of Frankincense
> Mountains of myrrh, and Beds of spices,
> And ten Thousand PARADISES
> The soul that tasts thee takes from thence. (170–188)

Especially in light of Crashaw's denial of sensory efficacy in his translation of the "Adoro Te Devote," it may seem strange that this poem finds him so vigorously rousing hearing, sight, smell and taste into this sensual synod of devotion. But it is important to recognize that the object of praise in Crashaw's hymn never extends past the Name to its referent. It is the Name itself that rises like dawn, the Name itself whose flowery fragrance ravishes the nose, the very syllables of the Name whose taste is Arabia and Paradise all in one. Crashaw's poem enacts an elaborate and fully embodied devotion to a sign as a perceptible object, without regard to its significative function. The metonymic associations of that Name dissipate in the face of its sensorily robust presence in the poem, immanent and fully available to perception. Yet even as it celebrates the sign itself in a lavish sensuality that eclipses whatever divine principle might have been signified, the poem does register an alternate response to the Name. As the poem reaches its conclusion, Crashaw articulates the consequences of not venerating the Name:

> They that by Love's mild Dictate now
>> Will not adore thee,
> Shall Then with Just Confusion, bow
>> And break before thee. (236–239)

As Crashaw imagines it here, those who attempt to do otherwise than adore the Name itself face "Confusion" and will end up submitting uncomfortably to the sign's dominion. This threat gives voice to the same difficulty that Crashaw enacts in his translation of "Adoro Te Devote." In the Thomist hymn, Crashaw orders the senses to be subdued because they impede spiritual discernment, only to find that they are enduringly present and insistent.[26] In this poem, Crashaw likewise suggests that if devotion attempts to disregard the sign, to look through it to some transcendent object, it will find itself flummoxed as perceptual access to the signified remains occluded by the intervening veils of signification. The Name that yields to no signified in Crashaw's original hymn mirrors the circumlocutions that veil the "Deitas" and "humanitas" of Christ in his translation of the Latin hymn, each set of unyielding signs suggesting Crashaw's thoroughgoing suspicion about the capacity of signs to communicate anything other than themselves.

Indeed, the retreat of divinity from interpretive accessibility in Crashaw's translation enacts in verse an argument that is implicit even before the poem's text begins, in its accompanying illustration (Figure 1). In the 1652 volume *Carmen Deo Nostro*, and in all subsequent editions, Crashaw's translation is printed with this emblem—a rendering of the ciborium, the vessel that holds the consecrated elements of the Eucharist. The text beneath the ciborium's figure reads "*Ecce panis Angelorum*," or "Behold the bread of Angels." The image, however, does not represent bread but rather the *container* of bread, the receptacle into which the sanctified (that is, transubstantiated) host is placed after the celebration of the Mass. "*Ecce*," the emblem exhorts us: *behold* the miraculous bread of life, the nourishing body of Christ. But the exhortation is delivered even as it points up the impossibility of such a task, given the mediating materiality of the ciborium.[27]

Figure 1: Emblematic depiction of the ciborium, printed at the head of Crashaw's "Adoro Te Devote" translation, *Carmen Deo Nostro, te decet hymnus, sacred poems* (1652). Photo courtesy of the Newberry Library, Chicago; call number Case Y 185. C8528, p. 67.

The tension expressed in this emblem, which simultaneously invites an encounter with the divine and physically contravenes its own invitation, reflects Crashaw's sensitivity to the opposing demands of eucharistic worship. The communicant is adjured to understand that Christ is really, objectively present under the species of bread and wine, and exhorted to chew and digest his body: "Accipite, et manducate."[28] At the same time, the communicant is cautioned against seeking to perceive that body, though the encounter with it is framed, by Aquinas's own admission, in disquietingly somatic terms. The ciborium emblem, like its pronomial and sacramental counterparts in Crashaw's hymn translation, points toward the sensorily apprehensible presence of the divine even as it declares the sensory inaccessibility of that presence, interjecting veils of mediation between the perceiver and the holy object of desired perception.

In the last stanza of his hymn, Crashaw gives voice to the frustration he feels concerning the hermeneutic contradictions of eucharistic worship, pleading for the obviation of the perceptual mediations that interpose themselves between communicant and Christ. The sentiment certainly echoes his source text; Thomas's "Adoro Te Devote" draws to a close with an expression of longing for contact with Christ "unveiled" by the sacramental elements:

> Iesum quem velatum nunc aspicio
> Oro: fiat illud quod tam sitio,
> Ut te revelata cernens facie,
> Visu sim beatus tuae gloriae.
> [Jesus, whom I now discern veiled
> I pray: let that for which I so thirst come to pass,
> That, seeing you with your face unveiled,
> I may be happy in the vision of your glory.] (25–28)

In Crashaw's translation, however, the soul does not merely yearn to be "Visu . . . beatus tuae gloriae"—blessed by a vision of Christ, in Thomas's petition—but demands a more direct and unmediated form of contact with the holy body:

> Come love! Come LORD, and that long day
> For which I languish, come away.
> When this dry soul those eyes shall see,

And drink the unseal'd sourse of thee.
When Glory's sun faith's shades shall chase,
And for thy veil give me thy FACE. (51–56)

Thomas's thirst for a vision of Christ's face becomes in Crashaw's hands a languishing desire to "drink the unseal'd sourse" of Christ's substance, a literalized accomplishment of the eucharistic *bibite* that replaces the mediation of accidents with a direct and sensory experience of Christ's substance. Pleading for a form of contact with Christ that retains the manner of sacramental contact but dispenses with the distracting veils of bread and wine, Crashaw seeks an unmediated physical manifestation of Christ's body in its eucharistic function. He cries out for an experience of sacramental union with the divine that preserves the rite's somatic apprehensibility yet is uncomplicated by the interpretive digressions of the accidents, whose insignificant materials render the body's ports superfluous.

This realization prompts us to revisit Rambuss's assessment of Crashaw's exuberant physicality. As Rambuss remarks, Crashaw's work articulates "a devotion that is profoundly attuned to the Christian doctrine of the Incarnation, of God becoming flesh." This theological system, Rambuss continues, exhibits "surprisingly little inclination to efface the corporeal"; rather, it proffers "a spirituality that paradoxically bespeaks embodiment, doing so in ways that often enhance or extend the expressive possibilities of bodies and desires."[29] Rambuss, like Caroline Walker Bynum and Leo Steinberg before him, provides ample evidence that, especially for enthusiastic participants in incarnational Christianity, the body presents a site of intensified spirituality: having been valorized by Christ's becoming human, the body offers a point of identification between man and God.[30] For Rambuss, the hallmark of Crashaw's poetic corpus is that it so enthusiastically "aligns religious devotion and its affects with the body and its most visceral operations."[31]

But what becomes apparent in surveying Crashaw's corpus of eucharistic verse is that it is simply not the case that, as Rambuss and other critics have alleged, Crashaw's sensualism flaunts itself in blissful profligacy.[32] As these poems make clear, Crashaw's participation in the corporeal expressivities of incarnational Christianity is not enthusiastic but fretful, undertaken with an ambivalence that communicates, as Empson rightly recognizes, both adoration and horror—the horror in this case arising directly out of the blunt sensuality of a practice of adoration that denies the legitimacy of the sensual. For Crashaw, the body, which in eucharistic worship becomes an active channel for experiencing the divine, also impedes access to that experience by asserting its perceptual primacy, its interpretive durability. Thus the authorizing principles of eucharistic theology become, in Crashaw's work, most horrifying when they appear as concretized forms of conventional devotional topoi—that is, when the body intrudes into the symbolary of the sacrament: Christ's nourishing and self-sacrificing bosom becomes a grotesquely bleeding and elongated "Teat" for us to suckle, the typological penile blood of the circumcision ends up on our tongue, and by such aggressively physicalized figures we as readers are ejected from the symbolic system even as it is invoked. This pattern, it seems, does not prove Crashaw's "bad taste" so much as it indicates the profound discomfort that the devotional body presents for the poet.[33]

As Crashaw records his experience of sacramental worship in his translation of the Thomist hymn, the body perseveres in its perceptual excesses despite its being chastened ("Down down, proud sense"), the senses sticking at the substantiated figure of "Bountyfull BREAD" even though faith yearns to find the "unsealed source." The concluding entreaty of Crashaw's "Hymn in Adoration of the Blessed Sacrament" dramatizes, finally, the soul's desire to partake of Christ's sacramental offering without the impediments of the flesh and its perceptual faculties. Indeed, throughout his eucharistic verse particularly (and arguably in his larger poetic canon as well), Crashaw continually exposes his apprehension about the body's tendency to distract from the operations of the spirit, a concern expressed in the very effrontery of his poetry's obdurate physicality. To paraphrase Young, Crashaw is certainly not unaware of the discomfiting effects of his somatized devotions, and it is no accident that Crashaw's extreme physical imagery provokes revulsion perhaps more frequently than it inspires admiration. Crashaw's imagery works precisely to prevent the referential transparency of symbolic language and foregrounds the unhappy effects of a symbolic system that does not yield to an ameliorating spiritual reading.

Revulsion is certainly the effect in the epigram "On the wounds of our crucified Lord," which effectively thematizes the failure of symbolic language to function symbolically. In this poem, Crashaw inhabits a scene in which Mary of Magdala weeps over the crucified body of Jesus, her clear tears mixing with the blood that runs from Jesus's wounds as she kisses his feet and hands. Crashaw begins by imagining the wounds as reciprocating Mary's devotional actions, but the conceit quickly breaks down under the force of its own physical details. Crashaw begins by asking, "O these wake-full wounds of thine! / Are they Mouthes? or are they eyes?" (1–2). In describing the wounds as mouths or eyes, the poem attempts to articulate a meaning for Christ's injuries beyond the cruel fact of them. As mouths, the wounds might be understood as emblems of Christ's love, "a Mouth and lippes / To pay the sweet summe of thy kisses" (13–14). As eyes, they might express the same care and adoration in return that Mary displays in her mourning, or serve as a signal of Christ's compassion: "To pay thy Teares, an Eye that weeps" (15). As Christ's flesh returns Mary's gestures, the poem's symbolic argument seems to suggest, it transcends the corpore-ality of the crucifixion, the wounds becoming significant of divine love and sacrifice.

Yet once more the insurmountably extra-ritual physicality of Crashaw's language obtrudes into the operation of the symbol he endeavors. As he elaborates on the associational alternatives the poem presents, they become increasingly less palatable:

> Lo! a mouth, whose full-bloom'd lips
>> At too deare a rate are roses.
> Lo! a blood-shot eye! that weepes
>> And many a cruell teare discloses. (5–8)

As the wounds multiply into mouths, or eyes, or mouths and eyes together, their capacity to act as symbols for spiritual principles diminishes. The mouth with "full-bloom'd lips" blurs into a rose by virtue of its bloody suffusion. The eye that weeps is "blood-shot," reifying the bloody hole that it stands for rather than translating perception to another term. Both the mouth and the eye remain hostage to the bloody wound, and the persis-tence of that originary image into the symbolic arrests its signification in the corporeal. The sanguinary excesses of the wounds stain the mouths and eyes, with the effect that they begin to overlap uncomfortably: the wounds are also bloody mouths that are also bleeding eyes. And as the qualities of the wound are transferred to the mouths and eyes, they obstruct the princi-ples of divine compassion that those terms might wish to activate. It's not that the idea of Mary's kissing Christ's wounds is "unlovely and perverse,"[34] for that tableau reflects a common enough devotional impulse in the Chris-tian tradition, but rather that the unyielding corporeality of Crashaw's sym-bolically arrested language prevents Christ's body from meaning anything beyond its wounds.

The poem registers this difficulty even as it casts around for an appropriate cognate for Christ's wounds. After wondering at the poem's outset in what metaphor best to communicate the meaning of those wounds, Crashaw muses, "Be they Mouthes, or be they eyne, / Each bleeding part some one supplies" (3–4). The indeterminacy of the wounds' symbolism indicates that it is their function rather than their form that takes precedence for Crashaw. These lines seem to decide that it is finally irrelevant whether the wounds more aptly resemble mouths or eyes; the bleeding itself is of greater consequence than whatever symbol he chooses. But it is precisely this focus on the bleeding itself that makes impossible the comparison, for the emphasis on bleeding compromises the suitability of either mouth or eye to the poem's symbolic system. Instead, Crashaw's attention to the action of bleeding interrupts its eucharistically symbolic association with mouths and eyes and presents the raw and sacramentally unmediated image of Mary almost vampirically putting her mouth upon Christ's wounds. Though the eucharistic program of such a tableau is clear, the effect is much the same as in the circumcision ode: we are left with the distasteful proximity of the devout mouth and Christ's blood, a relation whose insistent corporeality flouts doctrine even as the drama it narrates—the adoration of Christ in his sacrificial function—is completely orthodox.

Crashaw's poetics represents the logical conclusion of the argument at play in the wider field of the seventeenth-century devotional lyric. Crashaw is only too aware of the ways in which the word presents as an artifact in and of itself, an object in which a kind of presence inheres. For Crashaw, such a substantiated sign does not hold out the promise of facilitating communion with the absent divine but rather proclaims itself so inescapably as to interrupt that communion. Like the Eucharist itself, the word—substantially present in its own right and shot through with sensory distractions—is inherently antiabsorptive. If the Eucharist, as the holiest of symbolaries, resists interpretive access, denies our absorption through transparent symbols to the heart of their sacred meanings, Crashaw's verse exposes the frustrations of eucharistic worship in a poetics precisely calibrated to the ritual's competing demands of spiritual signification and surface resistance. Crashaw's writing produces hermeneutic arrest, amplifying the corporeal, symbolically indeterminate registers of his language until it becomes referentially opaque.

To underscore the degree to which sacramental signification is subordinated, in Crashaw's work, to the symbolic opacity of the somatic, we need

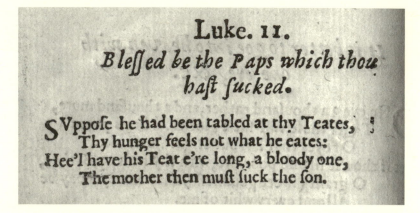

Figure 2: From Crashaw, *Steps to the Temple: Sacred poems, with other delights of the muses* (1648). Photo courtesy of the Newberry Library, Chicago; call number Case Y 185. C849, p. 24.

only glance at a contemporaneous edition of the epigram on Luke 11 (see Figure 2). Whatever transgressivities "suck" introduces into the physical relationship between Mary and Jesus by virtue of its extra-ritual terminology, this sense of indelicacy is intensified by a feature of early modern typography that appears in all seventeenth-century printings of Crashaw's epigram. The elongated initial "s" transforms "suck" into a verb whose frank corporeal valences preempt any possibility of reading Mary's act as a disembodied, spiritualized mingling with Christ. Beyond resisting assimilation into the sacramental (though it certainly does that too), the occasion of such transgressive corporeality in a poem whose sensuality is already troublingly extra-ritual completes the dislocation from the authorizing principle of sacramental abstractability. Moreover, the visual pun on "suck" occurs in the poem's inscription into its material expression. As the epigram is formed on the page, it becomes marked as finally, irrevocably unassimilable into the eucharistic symbolary. That is, the sacramentally inadmissable (and socially intolerable) suggestion of "fuck" in this context is only available when the poem takes physical form in the course of printing. Like the communicant's body itself in Crashaw's distressed translation of the "Adoro Te Devote," the poem as a material artifact devolves to the extra-ritual: it endures as a remainder, a troubling loose end in the dynamics of eucharistic worship, threatening to corrupt the attention into idolatry.[35] In each case, it is the obdurate medium that problematizes the experience of the divine, the recalcitrant materiality of both texts inserting itself irremediably into sacramental signification.[36]

In the Eucharist as Crashaw records it, the body persistently asserts itself where it doesn't belong, obstructing efforts to discern the holy beyond the diversions of sense-perception. It is just this difficulty into which Crashaw thrusts the reader of his poems on the Eucharist—poems concerning the very rite whose interplay of spiritual and physical so vexes him. Rendering spiritual principles in corporeal terms that repulse even as they invite interpretation, Crashaw's eucharistic poetics recapitulate for the reader the same hermeneutic challenge presented by the Sacrament of the Altar. His devotional arguments, defensibly orthodox though they may be, appear in symbols that emphasize such unyielding physicality that they preempt our efforts to read through them. Just as the accidents of bread and wine declare themselves to sense-perception, the corporeally substantial matter of Crashaw's symbols remains ineluctably apparent, activating the body's ports of perception in all their lavish and disturbing superfluity.

Crashaw's handling of the eucharistic symbolary enforces somatic awareness at the very moment we expect that materially apprehensible symbol should dissolve into spiritual substance. Crashaw's verse, like Crashaw the communicant, gets caught on the body, and in confronting the irreducible physicality of the sacrament's symbolic system discovers the alarming failure of the symbolic to function sacramentally—that is, to refer beyond the material to some kind of spiritual significance. In Christ's bloody penis and "Teat," in the blood-shot wounds of Christ's flesh, Crashaw offers a "taste" of the interpretive dilemma of eucharistic worship, forcing the reader to determine the significance of ritually unassimilable corporeality. The sacramentally indigestible details of his poems signal Crashaw's deliberate participation in the troubling hermeneutic method institutionalized in the Eucharist, and indicate a poetic strategy that exercises the rite's own interpretive challenges in order to replicate the difficulty of discerning Christ beneath the all-too-conspicuous veils of bread and wine.

When considered in the context of post-Reformation devotional poetry, the qualities of Crashaw's writing that have prompted readers to view him as an unrestrainedly baroque anomaly among his contemporaries, too quirkily ornate and luscious by half and altogether too indecorous and grotesque to reflect the poetic values of his age, do not seem so outlandish. In Crashaw's verse, we find many of the same principles of poetic resistance at work that we do in the purportedly more measured, and thereby more accessible, poetry of a writer like Herbert.[37] Indeed, in a fashion markedly similar to what we have observed in Herbert's poetry, Crashaw's poetics foregrounds the corporeal valences of his work to such a degree that the language he uses ceases to offer transparent access to spiritual principles, and consequently keeps hermeneutic focus on the unyielding surface of the text. The conspicuous and antiabsorptive substantiality of his descriptions asserts the poem as an object rather than a referential instrument. And while the manner in which he accomplishes this peculiar referential opacity may differ modally from Herbert's use of poetic form, or Taylor's aggregating structural scheme, or Donne's treatment of the metaphoric conceit, it nevertheless shares with these writers a sense of the urgency of conceiving the poem as an end in itself, as an object.

The phenomenon that recurs throughout the devotional lyric tradition of the early seventeenth century entails the persistent and often disorienting revaluing of the objective reality of the poetic text, an awareness of the word as a substantial thing that requires contemplation in and of itself rather than merely as an instrument for indicating a *something else*—in which that *something else* is the imperceptible site of meaning elsewhere to which the poetic text self-effacingly refers. The effect of the poetic strategies at work in Herbert's disruptive and self-aware formal innovations, in Taylor's argumentative reliance on the consistency of his lyric structure, in Donne's jarring antisymbolic metaphors, and in Crashaw's shockingly extra-ritual denotative embodiments is that interpretive absorption through the text to that ever-evasive *something else* is arrested, the attention refocused instead on the poem itself. Just as sunlight reflected off the surface of a lake prevents a view of the rocky bed beneath, so too do the outrageous surfaces of post-Reformation devotional poetry zealously refuse to yield in transparency to a ready representational ground, instead dazzling with poetic effects that interpose themselves into the operations of a more conventional semiology. In this formulation, sign does not politely bow to signified but instead never lets itself be overlooked, proclaiming its objective consequentiality for the poem's significative programs, its substantiality as an object in itself, its enduringly real presence.

It is not surprising that devotional poetry should become such an active site for considering these issues and for exploring the relationship between the representational capacities of the word and the perceptual processes of interpretation. Devotional poetry in particular reflects thematically the concerns and challenges that follow from an epistemological system whose primary stakes are in the objective reality of the perceptually absent—the sublime, the internal workings of the soul, and all those ever-intangible aspects of worship that make belief necessary, the material evasions to which faith responds scripturally as "the substance of things hoped for, the euidence of things not seen."[38] Beyond whatever confessional allegiances may lead a text to consider these questions, lyric poetry's inherent investment in rendering perceptible that which is perceptually unavailable, both as a function of its literariness and in its corporeal valences, makes of it an expressive form uniquely suited to navigating the problematics of Christianity's conflicted incarnationalism.[39] And because Christian incarnationalism, and by extension the value it assigns to the fleshly, is ultimately what is under negotiation in Reformation sacramental controversy, lyric poetry serves not just as a sensitive antenna to the pressures being brought to bear in the reform of sacramental worship but as a proving ground for the viability of the word to manifest presence.

What becomes striking when one considers the field of post-Reformation religious poetry for its poetic features rather than for whatever confessional territory seems to be under dispute from author to author, poem to poem, is that across all the varieties of style that one would expect to find distinguishing one writer from another, there persists a peculiar attentiveness to features that block interpretative absorption and disrupt referentiality. Though each of the poets under discussion here accomplishes it by different poetic means, these poems all display a remarkable resistance to their own interpretive dissolubility. These works push their poetics to the forefront of our attention, forcing us to confront the oddness of their conceits, the ostentation of their forms. And by interposing the technical elements of poetic utterance into the interpretive process, each of these poems asserts itself as a poem *qua* poem, a determinate object. Referentiality is preempted by the instance of poetics as an autonomous, self-substantiating entity—that is, by the poem as a made thing whose consequence lies in its own presence rather than in its service to a referential absence.

This poetics responds directly to the interpretive challenges of a ritual whose signification relies on the body's participation even as doctrine disavows—in any confessional tradition—the body's role in apprehending that act of signification. In a period when the efficacy of the material—in sacramental worship and beyond—is increasingly diminished, these sacramental poetics privilege the material as a site of presence. That these innovations persist across sectarian lines indicates that the fraught imperative to conceive of a perceptually inconceivable divine term—for which the Eucharist stands as a ritual distillation—is finally a representational rather than a theological problem. The poetics of post-Reformation devotional poetry grapples with meaningfulness and the significance of signs not in some other locality, some sphere beyond the ken of human apprehension, but in what is at hand. The determinedly materialist program seen in the poems of Crashaw, Donne, Taylor, and Herbert defies characterizations of seventeenth-century theology in England as committed to rejecting the material in faithful pursuit of an abstracted and disembodied piety. And while critics may have trawled around in the content of Renaissance devotional poetry to demonstrate an author's perceived fidelity to Calvinism or nostalgia for long-lost Catholicism, the dearth in recent decades of sustained critical attention to how poems communicate *as poems*, rather than as tracts, has obscured the complicated relationship between the flesh and the word that these poems bespeak. Indeed, taking the poetics of the post-Reformation lyric on its own terms, one becomes mystified by the kinds of assertions that accumulate around critical demarcations of "sacramental poetics," as when Regina Schwartz insists that the defining characteristic of sacramental poetry is that it "points to a meaning greater than and beyond itself," it "takes the hearer *beyond*" its own signs, ever pointing beyond itself, or when Judith H. Anderson suggests that sacramental metaphor "openly *transacts* the shift into another register [e.g., from literal to spiritual] and thereby initiates the sublation so fundamental to the reformers' understanding, and indeed to their performing, of the sacraments and specifically of Communion."[40] But as the work I have been examining makes clear, the post-Reformation lyric displays everywhere a mistrust of a view of poetry that would reduce the text to a set of signs that directs hermeneutic attention "beyond itself," and seeks rather to bring significance to presence, and presence to significance.

This concern with the meaningfulness and substantiality of text, and with the capacities of the word to manifest meaning in and of itself, would be notable in the work of a single author; its presence across the body of devotional poetry in the seventeenth century argues for a more pervasive aesthetic response to the problem of sacramental representation. The religious lyric makes explicit the connection between a poetics that prioritizes signs over signifieds and the immanence effects of eucharistic worship because it generates its innovations within a context of theological reconsideration. That is, religious poetry, by the very field of its survey, alerts us to the proximity between the work of poetic representation and the modes by which the divine might be made manifest in the world. But while the negotiation of this problem may be most readily apparent in the religious lyric because of its thematic investment in manifestations of the divine, poetic inquiry into the word's capacity to produce signifying presence is not limited to the poetic output of devout poets alone. The general neglect of poetics *as poetics* rather than as a misnomer for thematic content—what we might describe as a critical unwillingness to prioritize poetic signs over their signifieds—has excluded a productive perspective on the strangely resistant literature that pervades the period. The kind of sacramental poetics I have been exploring in the work of Crashaw and his devotional peers is a phenomenon that extends beyond poetry that aspires to holy themes, indicating the degree to which literary production generally in the post-Reformation period is engaged in a reconsideration of the status of the sign. The influence of the eucharistic debates and the attendant widespread cultural concern with the presencing efficacy of signs percolates into texts both spiritual and secular, and an acknowledgment of this commerce between theology and the aesthetic helps not only to explain the antiabsorptive poetics that arises in the wake of Reformation controversies but also reveals how inextricable the two categories are.

Chapter 5

Immanent Textualities in a
Postsacramental World

The explicit stake of post-Reformation devotional poetry in the capacities of the word to produce a kind of immanent presence also registers in the contemporary literary culture more broadly. It is hardly surprising that Reformation-era theological anxieties about the sign, which undergird the interrogations of the materializing potentialities of language we see in Donne and Herbert and their devotional fellows, should ramify into the field of nondevotional literature; religious writing may have a thematic affinity for the particular representational concerns of sacramental worship, but the semiotic interrogations of sixteenth-century religious discourse had implications for sign-making in general. The eucharistic debates of the sixteenth century are finally about the ways in which a sign's meaningfulness inheres not only in the way it redirects interpretation to an absent term but in its own status as an object—and not just a sacramental object, but an *object as such*. Accordingly, the early seventeenth century sees the widespread development of a poetics that announces its investment in the objective artifact of the poem, a poetics whose materializing elaborations suggest the creeping effects of the Reformation's sustained engagement with the expressive status of signs. Contemporaries of Donne and Herbert, Crashaw and Taylor, who treat secular rather than sacred subjects nevertheless reveal, in the peculiarities of their poetic innovation, a marked sympathy to the triangulation of matter, meaning, and textuality that comes under scrutiny in devotional contexts. The wider literary culture of seventeenth-century England cultivates a poetics that resists hermeneutic transparency and places a premium on poetic objecthood and antiabsorption.

A recognition of the complex and enduring relationship between sacramental theology and hermeneutics following the Reformation illuminates
the rather abrupt shift around the turn of the seventeenth century from a
cultural aesthetic that privileged decorum and pellucidity in poetry to one
that was increasingly characterized by hermeneutic interruption. The gen-
tlemen who authored handbooks of poetry and literary criticism in the
sixteenth century were careful to frame out the parameters of what was, in
George Gascoigne's terms, "lawfull" in verse; as George Puttenham puts it,
"our intent is to make this Art vulgar for all English mens vse, & therefore
are of necessitie to set downe the principal rules therein to be obserued."
In pursuit of such legitimate art, Gascoigne advises that the writer should
pursue a smooth and inviting poetic method, and avoid techniques that
might alienate or discompose the reader: "frame your stile to *perspicuity*
and to be sensible: for the haughty obscure verse doth not much delight."[1]
Thomas Wilson, whose *Arte of Rhetorique* preceded and influenced the
poetic theories of Gascoigne and Puttenham, stipulated that an author must
construct his text such "that the hearers maie well knowe what he meaneth,
and understande him wholly, the whiche he shall with ease do, if he utter
his mind in plain wordes, suche as are usually received, and tell it orderly,
without goyng about the busshe."[2] Such characterizations of poetic decorum articulate the Horatian dual mandate that poetry ought to be "dulce"
and "utile," sweet and profitable, a formulation that makes the instructive
utility of a work of art contingent upon its digestibility.[3] But as we have
seen, the model that emerges in the post-Reformation period displaces easy
consumption for indigestibility and perspicuity for obstruction, indeco-
rously asserting the unassimilable objecthood of texts in order to substantiate them, to make them present.

This poetic pivot toward the nontransparency of the discursive surface
provides some perspective on the work of Robert Herrick, whose virtuoso
formal performances are matched by a disorienting investment in surfaces,
in both thematics and style. Readers have long acknowledged Herrick's fascination with palpable objects and sensual textures.[4] Especially for many of
the poet's early-twentieth-century critics, Herrick's seductive poetic surfaces bespoke a lack of depth, a shallowness of thought that excluded him
from being categorized among the great "metaphysical" poets of his age.[5]
But Herrick's commitment to a poetics that promotes and celebrates the
exteriors of things indicates his susceptibility to the same aesthetic forces
that shape his contemporaries. Herrick's scintillations direct attention to

the lustrous superstratum, not only of the objects he examines with such minute concentration—his considerations moving "piece by piece," as he says by way of introduction in "The Argument of His Book"—but also of the poems themselves as objects.[6] By enacting the very distractions of superficial opulence and texture that his poems delight to describe, Herrick's work reifies the materiality and substantiality of his text.

Herrick hints at his investment in the materializing capacities of the poetic text in the prefatory poem to his volume *Hesperides*, in which he describes his book as a collection of *"Immortall Substances."*[7] The gesture toward poetic immortality is familiar enough, but Herrick's claim for the substantive nature of the poems anticipates the recurrent priority throughout his volume on the significative value of ornamentation. And Herrick's poems are nothing if not dazzlingly invested in ornament. His most frequently adored poetic mistress, Julia, is depicted bedizened by dews and by gemstones, wound in silks and in ribbons, decked with bracelets and belts. She wears a "Chaplet" in one poem, an "Azure Robe" that parts in swoon-inducing gaps over a secret *"Petticoat"* in another, and a "silken bodies," or bodice, in a third.[8] Such thoroughgoing attention to Julia's wardrobe may feel like the exercising of a fetish on the part of Herrick, but its effect is to direct interpretive focus not toward Julia herself but toward the sartorial flourishes that might otherwise work to suggest her metonymically. These poems devote effusive detail to the textiles and textures of adornment, but among the sensorily lush descriptions of her accoutrements, Julia herself remains remarkably unregarded, as when Herrick's lavish gaze lingers upon her jewelry rather than herself in "To Julia":

How rich and pleasing thou my *Julia* art
In each thy dainty, and peculiar part!
First, for thy *Queen-ship* on thy head is set
Of flowers a sweet commingled Coronet:
About thy neck a Carkanet is bound,
Made of the *Rubie, Pearle* and *Diamond*:
A golden ring, that shines upon thy thumb:
About thy wrist, the rich *Dardanium*.
Between thy Breasts (then Doune of Swans more white)
There playes the *Saphire* with the *Chrysolite*.
No part besides must of thy selfe be known,
But by the *Topaz, Opal, Calcedon*.

While the poem may promise to survey each of Julia's dainties, it spends its delight instead upon the "peculiar part" of her baubles, leaving very little of Julia on display. Indeed, the poem concludes by explicitly declaring Julia's perceptual inaccessibility within the context of this poem; she is known only by what she wears. But even as Julia recedes, the poem fairly glistens, recalling another poem, "*Upon* Julia's *haire fill'd with Dew*," in which water droplets sit vividly "spangled" (2) upon Julia's head, and

> glitter'd to my sight,
>> As when the Beames
> Have their reflected light,
>> Daunc't by the Streames. (5–8)

The light that plays across these lines does not illuminate Julia; rather, it reflects to the sight, bouncing off the surface of both stream and sign. The poem coruscates as an exercise in opacity, and the effect is the same as in the poem on Julia's jewelry. That is to say, surface is all the substance that we have in these verses—and perhaps all that we care to have, given the enthralled delectations of Herrick's catalogue. As the chrysolite and chalcedony remain the sumptuous objects of the gaze, Julia retreats into interpretive indifference, the surface supplanting what it might be expected to signify.

Just as Herrick's work thematizes an interest in material surfaces, so too does his language glitter ostentatiously, shards of it reflecting the attention away from, rather than providing a way into, the poem's ostensible object of praise. The ribbon around Julia's waist is "that *Zonulet* of love, / Wherein all pleasures of the world are wove."[9] The site of pleasures, naturally enough, but "*Zonulet*"? Herrick's conspicuous nonce interrupts the easy sensuality of the scene, focusing attention on the word itself, as with the jewelry poem's "*Chrysolite*" and "*Dardanium*"—the latter of whose hermeneutic strangeness Herrick's own text emphasizes by providing a marginal gloss for it: "*A Bracelet, from Dardanus so call'd*," he informs us, albeit spuriously. This turn to self-consciously strange, even unprecedented, language persists throughout the volume of *Hesperides*: in Julia's breath "all the Spices of the East / Are circumfused."[10] Julia's breasts exhibit a "circummortal purity."[11] Julia's head is decorated with an "*Inarculum*," which term Herrick must again gloss to clarify: "*A twig of Pomgranat, which the queen-priest did use to weare on her head at sacrificing.*"[12] Herrick's famous meditation "*Upon* Julia's *Clothes*" finds him reflecting not on Julia's body, nor even on her clothes per se, but on "That liquefaction of her clothes."[13] The term "liquefaction" cannot be literalized into the poem's descriptive program, in part because of its technical specificity and in part because its motions conflict with the "brave Vibration each way free" that describes the movement of Julia's clothes just two lines later. Neither "liquefaction" nor "Vibration" resolves texturally into the idea of fabric, nor do their competing actions resolve into one another, and so they remain indissolubly present to the interpretive awareness. And when Herrick meditates *"Upon* Julia's *unlacing her self,"* the accumulation of impediments between the poem's register of perception and Julia's body work virtually to re-lace her, re-covering what she uncovers with a veritable cabinet of nouns that overwrite any suggestion of unmediated access:

> Tell if thou canst, and truly, whence doth come
> This *Camphor, Storax, Spikenard, Galbanum:*
> These *Musks,* these *Ambers,* and those other smells,
> (Sweet as the *Vestrie of the Oracles.)*
> Ile tell thee; while my Julia did unlace
> Her silken bodies, but a breathing space:
> The passive air such odour then assum'd (1–7)

The names by which Julia's "scent" (10) is identified are simply too particularized, too specialized to yield easily to a harmoniously blended suite of olfactory stimuli; the praise reads more nearly like an apothecary's shopping list. Far from communicating a coherent praise of the divine odor that suffuses the senses when Julia uncases her body, this poem emphasizes the substance of the stuff that covers Julia's body—and covers her all the more from direct sensory apprehension the more uncovered she is.

Herrick's language self-consciously emphasizes the lapidary constructedness of each text as a text, such that the objective artifact of the poem is ever present to the interpretation. Again, this poetics keeps us on its surfaces, and resists strategies that would make it more transparent. It keeps our gaze upon the sign, an approach that Herrick articulates as an *ars poetica* in his short poem *"On* Julia's *Picture"*:

> How am I ravisht! When I do but see
> The Painters art in thy *Sciography?*
> If so, how much more shall I dote thereon,
> When once he gives it incarnation?

The marrow of Herrick's art is precisely in what he slyly names here as *Sciography*, a technical term lifted from the art of perspective that describes a method of shadowing, of playing the surface to create the illusion of depth. Herrick's depictions of Julia are all surface illusion, all sign and trapping and decoration, with very little attention spared for Julia incarnate. Indeed, the "incarnation" this poem anticipates is not Julia in the flesh but Julia's painted image upon the canvas. This oddly two-dimensional devotion venerates the sign in seeming indifference to the figure it would signify. And by describing this self-substantiated, meaningful sign as an "incarnation," Herrick reveals his propinquity to the sacramental discourse that pervades his period. Herrick is operating within a representational system that responds to the shift in objective efficacy from signified to sign by activating the incarnational valences of the sign. That is to say, the incarnation that the poem offers is not Julia's but its own, and its advertisement of its own surfaces constitutes a kind of sciography for its own sake. Here, as throughout his poetic corpus, Herrick keeps his attention firmly fixed upon the superficies of representation. Treating the silks and the spangles as ends in themselves, Herrick correspondingly suggests that the stuff of metonymy is likewise an end in itself and dotes upon the substantializing potentialities of his "Painters art," a poetics characterized by its ravishing—and unyielding—surfaces.

This investment in surface resistance and opacity finds a sympathetic aesthetic in the work of the man that Herrick calls "Father *Johnson*."[14] The poems whose publication Ben Jonson oversaw in the 1616 folio edition of his *Workes* flaunt their intractability to interpretation as a virtue. This is particularly true of the *Epigrammes*, those poems to which Jonson gives pride of place in the volume and that he describes in the book's dedication to the Earl of Pembroke as "the ripest of my studies."[15] The *Epigrammes* set their prickly interpretive difficulty as an overt challenge to the reader in the collection's short first poem, "To the Reader," in which Jonson couches his invitation as an anticipatory reproach: "Pray thee, take care, that tak'st my booke in hand / To reade it well; that is, to understand." The imperative to understand—that is, to read well—purports to sift the qualified reader from the uninitiated masses. But the poems themselves seem deliberately to impede the process of moving from reading well to understanding (if we define "understanding" as reading "through" the poem to grasp its referent), and not merely because they participate in the usual referential evasions of satire. Jonson's *Epigrammes* supplement the referential exclusivity of their milieu with a persistent focus on names, which prompts in the uninitiated reader a desire to scramble after the illumination of a footnote. No editorial intervention, however, will overcome the poems' accumulating argument that names constitute a kind of self-sufficient sign and substance in one, standing in Jonson's own formulation as both poem in miniature and object with inherent force: "I Doe but name thee Pembroke, and I find / It is an *Epigramme* on all man kind."[16] In Jonson's epigrams, the name becomes the expressive material of the poem, substantiating a significance that supersedes title or character.

The self-sufficiency of names as signs governs Jonson's treatment of the figures he turns his verse to praise. Implied in these brief lines is that the name of "Pembroke" manifests the nobility of Jonson's patron more fully than could an encyclopedia of the Earl of Pembroke's qualities, and glosses the category of nobility in order to delineate its application to humanity in general. That is to say, the sign of "Pembroke" signifies as such, independent of any reference to title or deed. This same principle is in evidence in Jonson's epigram "To Mary Lady Wroth," which celebrates the maiden name that connects Wroth to the distinguished house of her uncle Philip and aunt Mary. The name of Sidney serves as the representational ground of her being, and requires no ornaments of superfluous description to communicate its substance:

> And being nam'd, how little doth that name
> Need any *Muses* praise to give it fame?
> Which is, it selfe, the *imprese* of the great,
> And glory of them all, but to repeate! (5–8)

The name of Sidney works like an *impresa*, whose visible image was described by one of its contemporary philosophers as its "poétique," or poetics.[17] For Jonson, the name is the apprehensible medium that contains its own significative end. As he writes, "My praise is plaine" (13)—both unadorned and clarion—because it remains fixed upon the fullness of the name: "Forgive me, then, if mine but say you are / A Sidney" (9–10).

Thus, when Jonson's muse instructs him how to frame the creature he could "most desire / To honor serve and love" as his patron and literary inspiration, after he concludes his litany of excellencies ("Of greatest bloud, and yet more good than great," possessed of both a "softer bosome" and a "manly soule"), the muse directs him to a self-substantiated name: "My

Muse bad, *Bedford* write, and that was shee."[18] The Countess of Bedford's name not only contains Jonson's ideals, it also generates the poem's catalogue of praise, becoming itself the authorizing ground for the epigram's metaphoric invention. Lucy extends her beams from her "lucent seat" (8) throughout the poem, engendering both Jonson's reflection in this poem that "I meant the day-starre should not brighter rise" (7), and in another poem that the countess is the "brightness of our sphere" and "Life of the Muses' day, their morning star!"[19] The name of Lucy is itself the referential ground of the poems' elaborations, just as the name of his addressee is the referential end in Jonson's epigram "To Thomas Earl of Suffolk," in which Jonson constructs his flights of commendation upon the significative ground of the name of Howard ("high warden or guardian") when he exhorts:

> Stand high, then, HOWARD, high in eyes of men,
> High in thy bloud, thy place, but highest then,
> When, in men's wishes, so thy virtues wrought,
> As all thy honors were by them first sought:
> And thou design'd to be the same thou art. (5–9)[20]

In these poems, significance inheres in the sign of the name itself. As Linda Gregerson writes, in Jonson's poetic praise, the name becomes both "sign and substance, . . . [it] constitutes the poem from every angle."[21] The principle of the name as a self-substantiating sign extends beyond Jonson's explicitly identified patrons into the more circumspectly satiric epigrams in the collection: as Jonson names the objects of his scorn—variously, "Brainhardy," "Doctor Empiric," "Sir Annual Tilter," "Don Surly," "Captain Hungry," and "Sir Voluptuous Beast"—the names he assigns actively resist referring to an external sign. By design, they are referential ends, obstructing identification with some figure external to the poem— obstructing, that is, their transparency. Our sense of referential exclusion is not merely a consequence of our being left out of his social circle, nor does it follow from our being prevented from appreciating his etymological jokes because we have little Latin and less Greek; it is rather of a piece with his period's generalized investment in the significance of the sign. We need look no further than the massive architectural title page of Jonson's *Workes* (Figure 3) to appreciate his sense of the substantiality of the poetic text. There, in the center of a monument drawn as if it were carved from marble,

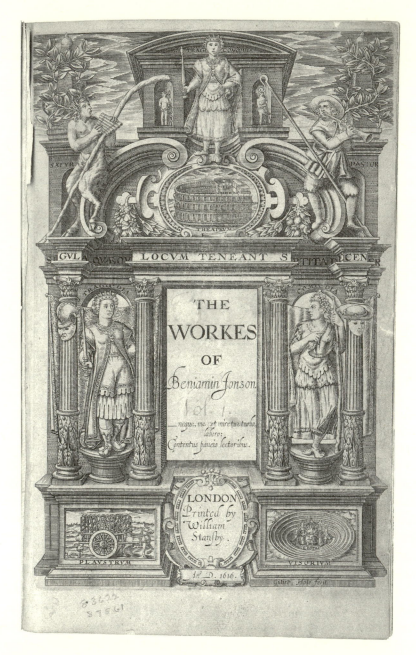

Figure 3: Title page of *The Workes of Beniamin Jonson* (1616). Photo courtesy of the Newberry Library, Chicago; call number Case Y 135. J735 v. 1.

displaying embodiments of tragedy, comedy, pastoral, and other literary arts, the words stand as if engraved: *The Workes of Beniamin Jonson*, the material heft of what's to come asserted by the image's marmoreal heraldry.[22] These poems are things, Jonson's title page declares, not to be seen through but to be seen, to be appreciated as artifacts with mass of their own, necessary to be confronted rather than treated as a mere instrument toward some elsewhere significance.

Even for those writers whose subjects reside away from the front lines of religious controversy, then, the representational implications of sacramental reform register as an insurgent priority on the sign as such and on the presence and significance of the text as an object. The effects of this aesthetic shift can be felt in a surprisingly broad range of texts, impossible to evaluate comprehensively within the scope of the present study but suggested by the works I have been examining here, tendrilling out from the lyric into a variety of contiguous literary modes.[23] Indeed, in William Shakespeare's most lyric-obsessed play, *Love's Labour's Lost*, the seductive substantiality of signs is the very matter that drives the comedy. In its liberal peppering with sonnets, *Love's Labour's Lost* renders as a feature of style a concern with poetic signs as self-substantiating objects that likewise threads through its plot. James L. Calderwood has observed that "nowhere else in Shakespeare do we find words so ascendant over matter," and he goes on to explain that in this comedy, "The referential role of words as pointers to ideas or things is consistently subordinated" to their status as signs, and consequently, "throughout the play, we are reminded that words, like poems, not only mean but are." Calderwood realizes that the consequence of such a significative scheme is to prevent transparency, to shift meaningfulness into words "as visual and as phonic objects." The play enforces our awareness that "The stuff of language, like that of mercers, has a surface texture."[24] Calderwood's survey of the play focuses explicitly upon its poetics, its devices of rhyme and rhythm, assonance and alliteration, and all the paronomasiac play that emphasizes the words as opaque "stuff" rather than referential vessels of meaning. The interpretively obscure affectations of Holofernes and the flourishes of the rhetorically obtuse Armado serve as dialogic exempla of the sign's capacity to be opaque, and the play thematizes the word's obstructions in the response of Costard, the failure of whose literalist hermeneutics to penetrate such linguistic extravagances demonstrates the incorrigibility of the sign. "I do confess much of the hearing it," as Costard admits, "but little of the marking of it."[25] Costard speaks for us all here: his commentary recognizes that the language of the play offers a sumptuous and flamboyant display of signs that do not yield readily to designative meaning. The interpretive resistance of signs culminates, of course, in the play's hyperbolic final scene, in which the French ladies' masquerade plot succeeds precisely because the visual markers of their individual identities become disjoined from what they are meant to signify. As the women exchange masks, their suitors (whose enchantment seems spurred by poetry itself rather than the women they decide to pursue) get caught on the significative surfaces and mistake their intended beloveds. Berowne makes clear the linguistic implications of this slapstick as he laments, "The ladies did change favours, and then we / Following the signs, wooed but the sign of she" (5.2.468–469).

Wooing the sign is, I would argue, the very response produced by the kind of antiabsorptive poetics that gains prominence in the post-Reformation period, for its focus on textual objecthood accomplishes a materialist program that supplants the instabilities of the absent and refractory signified with the stability of presence. The implications of this aesthetic phenomenon concatenate the lyric with a wide-ranging set of interests and practices of the period, from the age's fashion for hieroglyphs, to its developing theologies of the printed text, to its fascination with invented languages.[26] James Kearney's excellent study on the material artifact of the book prefaces its investigation of how concerns about idolatry affected printed culture by acknowledging that "Language cannot fail to have a material dimension; it cannot avoid being flesh or image."[27] Kearney is interested in the ways in which this notion resonates, sometimes comfortably but often uncomfortably, with the status of the written artifact as an object in itself, especially within the context of a larger Protestant iconoclasm, and he accordingly attends to what he sees as a general "ambivalence" about textual materiality as it is thematized in literary works of the period.[28] Yet at the root of the ambivalence Kearney identifies is a pervasive sense of the power of the text as a present object, its capacity to intrude into the more transcendent (read: disembodied) mode of devotional practice characteristic of Protestant theologies all the more consequential because of its bald objective perceptibility. A text is inevitably, as Kearney's title stipulates, incarnate, because its mode of transmission is corporeal, because one can hold a text physically in one's hand, activating all the senses to the condition of its presence. The poetics I have outlined in *Made Flesh* capitalizes on the textual materiality that Kearney treats so thoroughly, exercising as it does the corporeal valences of poetic expression with the effect of emphasizing the objecthood of poems. Indeed, even as Kearney argues that post-Reformation texts grapple with the imperative to distinguish between signs and signifieds—that is, to discern the transcendent meaning "behind" the palpable sign—his argument acknowledges the ineradicable substantiality of the textual: "there are," as he puts it, "no signs that are not carnal," and any effort to arrive at the spirit behind the letter must confront that "the letter is never transcended, never overcome."[29]

The post-Reformation lyric, then, exploits what cannot be overcome, making use of the nonreferential dimensions of poetic utterance to relocate immanence to the sign. In part, the difference between the thematic ambivalence that Kearney's study charts and the phenomenon of deliberately pronounced objecthood I have been examining may be attributable to generic difference. Kearney focuses primarily on texts (including *The Faerie Queene* and plays by Marlowe and Shakespeare) whose communicative priority is necessarily on their narrative development, while my focus has remained steadfastly upon the lyric, a genre whose always-already investment in manifesting presence—or "the presence of presence"—precedes any narrative it may dramatize.[30] As Mutlu Konuk Blasing explains, "The lyric works with the material experience of the somatic production and reproduction of words as sounds and sounds as words." The poetic features of the lyric, she elaborates, "serve to foreground its material reality and put up an organized resistance to meaning," an effect that guarantees "an experience of linguistic materials that are in excess of what can be categorically processed." The lyric's primary investment is in manifesting its own presence as utterance—that is, prior to referentiality and narrative content—and poetics is the mechanism by which the lyric accomplishes that end. Such resistant materiality, as Blasing states, "is the very substance of lyric language."[31]

Blasing's work is part of a theoretical trend toward articulating the ways in which lyric departs from a mimetic model that understands the poem as a kind of monologue, dramatizing a subjectivity or expressing an intensely personalized experience—a model in which the poem is, in John Stuart Mill's famous formulation, an utterance that is not so much "heard" as "*overheard*": "Poetry is feeling, confessing itself to itself in moments of solitude, and embodying itself in symbols, which are the nearest possible representations of the feeling in the exact shape in which it exists in the poet's mind."[32] And though the New Criticism would reject Mill's privileging of "the poet's mind" to describe the poem instead as the fictional utterance of a fictional speaker, its proponents nevertheless hewed to the implications of that mono-logic view in their conviction that each poetic artifact's nondenotative fea-tures resolve fully into its thematic and narrative concerns. But such a model subordinates what Donne might call "the poetry of the poem" to its thematic content, and, as Jonathan Culler has noted, "deprives rhythm and sound patterning of any constitutive role."[33] The corrective Blasing offers in her recognition that the resistance of poetics to referential transparency has self-substantiating effects for the poem is consonant with the argument of a num-ber of contemporary lyric theorists, who are attempting to account for the interpretive effects of those "impermeable textual elements" that Charles Bernstein identifies as he develops his sense of antiabsorptive poetics, and to appreciate the ways in which a poem's poetics is not subsidiary to but consti-tutive of its meaning.[34] In its demand for attention to the poem as an artifact whose myriad communicative devices are not necessarily unitary, and in its recognition that such variances often generate a poem's interpretive tensions, the approach modeled by Bernstein, Blasing, and others seeks to remedy the neglect of what Northrop Frye calls the *melos* and *opsis* of a poem, those verbal elaborations and the sonic play that are distinct from the denotative content of the text—terms he domesticates as *babble* and *doodle*. Frye's insis-tence upon the discursive surfaces of the lyric dovetails with his description of the poem as "an object of sense experience," which promotes an awareness of language as a thing in itself.[35]

Such critical refinements help flesh out the disruptive effects of poetic language and provide a vocabulary that can help sharpen attention on the communicative properties of the sign as such. Yet it is interesting to note that most of the dominant current thinking on the phenomenon of antiab-sorptive poetics either explicitly or implicitly identifies the starting point for such considerations in the innovations of Modernism. Blasing's excellent analysis of lyric resistance begins with T. S. Eliot and Ezra Pound. Veronica Forrest-Thomson's influential study *Poetic Artifice: A Theory of Twentieth-Century Poetry* likewise focuses its investigation of the poetic features that produce hermeneutic arrest on Pound and Eliot, though she does offer an introductory treatment of one of Shakespeare's sonnets to set up her case. And Charles Altieri provides a list of the qualities that signal the Modern poets' "substantial break from what they inherited," though he might well be describing Herbert or Taylor, Donne or Crashaw: "an insistence on the primacy of developing the material properties of its linguistic medium, an emphasis on the disruption of standard syntactic 'meaning,' a call for ideo-grammic method or other juxtapositional modes that replace conceptual connections with structures organized by the play of feeling and sensation, and, as a consequence of the work of these structures, a celebration of experience (rather than understanding) as the domain in which a presenta-tional art takes on significance."[36] Like Altieri and Bernstein, Marjorie Per-loff and Ron Silliman focus primarily on the avant-garde experimentalism of the American Postmodern, whose genealogies they each trace to the poetries and philosophies of the Modern era.[37] Each of these critics reveals a debt, often acknowledged, to aesthetic and historical divisions imagined by Roland Barthes, who distinguishes Modern poetry from its predecessors precisely by the substantiality of its signs: "Classical conceits involve rela-tions, not words: they belong to an art of expression"—by which Barthes means non-disruptive referentiality—and "they have lost their density," while modern poetry "destroys the spontaneously functional nature of lan-guage, and leaves standing only its lexical basis." The language of Modern poetry, Barthes declares, in terms that would be very much at home in Reformation exegesis, "lasts only to present the Word . . . it is a sign which stands."[38] Again, while his project is clearly to outline aesthetic discontinu-ities between the modern era and its historical predecessors, it is intriguing to recognize that Barthes's argument about the substantiating poetics of the Modern era adopts the fraught terminology of the sixteenth century to make that case.

Whether it is an accident or an inevitable consequence of disciplinary periodization, the rich and exciting turn to the discontinuities and disrup-tions of the discursive surface among Modernist and Postmodernist literary critics has largely resisted percolating into the discussion about poetic texts in the early modern period. Still, while the most consistent conversation about antiabsorptive poetics trains its gaze on twentieth-century writing with only occasional backward glances into longer literary history, some scholars of Renaissance literature consistently invite readers to reconsider the strategies by which poetic features "draw attention to the ontological status of the text."[39] This phrase is Heather Dubrow's, and her important book *The Challenges of Orpheus* devotes part of its far-reaching study of the lyric to the many disjunctive strategies and devices by which early modern poetry emphasizes the mediating materiality of its discursive surfaces—a topic that Dubrow also notes is thriving in discussions of contemporary American poetry.[40] Dubrow's ambitious work brings together the semiotic concerns of theology and humanism, the paratextual contributions of current print and manuscript studies, and perspectives from art history and musicology in her synthesis of the long historical theoretics on the lyric, and it is significant that much of the argument she constructs looks to lyric as a mode committed to an aesthetic principle of presence, toward which principle its emphasis on "mediation," which is her term for antiabsorptive poetics, explicitly strives.[41] Indeed, the most sensitive readers of poetry in early modern literary studies are alive to the ways in which the period's verses resist readerly absorption, arresting the reader on the discursive surface and thwarting hermeneutic transparency. I am thinking of Stephen Booth's body of work, including his splendidly subtle readings of the tensions and difficulties of Shakespeare's sonnets; Richard Strier's constant insistence on the ways in which texts resist or subvert unitary readings, as well as the painstaking blend of historicism and formalism he models; Debora Shuger's commitment to the particularities of historical texts; Heather Asals's enduring interest in "ontological language"; Brian Cummings's magisterial treatment of the cultural and theological significance of grammatical structures; Jeff Dolven's attentions to the perplexities of style; Ryan Netzley's argument that poetic texts demand a model of engagement that makes of reading an activity for its own sake, without the mercenary end of acquiring meaning; Rayna Kalas's interest in the aesthetic *matter* of metaphor; and Dubrow's own critical example of what she terms a "new formalism," an approach that understands "aesthetic issues as related, not inimical, to history."[42]

Still, the outstanding work being done by these scholars stands out in part because it tacks against the dominant critical drift in early modern studies. The past many decades have been witness to the development of critical perspectives that register impatience with the generally ahistorical, materially indifferent fixations of the New Criticism.[43] The lyric, privileged as that most well-wrought urn by the New Critics—aesthetically hermetic, unsusceptible to the pressures of culture, independent from the authorial mind—seemed to become for some time the proverbial baby that got tossed out with the bathwater of culturally unconcerned early-twentieth-century readings. But in the course of the important and necessary widening of critical methodologies, what Stephen Greenblatt famously called "cultural poetics" has supplanted a serious and sustained engagement with actual poetics.[44] It is surprising, however, that the focus on poetics that enriches studies of Modern and Postmodern literature has gone generally so neglected in the critical conversation about Renaissance literature, particularly given that recent and developing critical approaches have generated such a wealth of attention to the material artifacts of early modern culture. The substantiating program of post-Reformation poetics particularly gives the lie to the purported disaffinity between cultural and philological approaches to literary texts.[45] Moreover, by acknowledging the poem as a substantial artifact, the seventeenth-century lyric exposes as not inevitable the transition between the discursive and the semiotic, which has implications for cultural poetics' ballyhooed intersection of the formation of subjects in language and the fashioning of selves. A poetics that asserts presence is, in other words, not just about the location of meaning but about the fundamental and objective status of being.

When understood from this perspective, it is clear that the aesthetic and philosophical underpinnings of post-Reformation poetics align well after all with the ideas that animate the discontinuities and disjunctions of Modern and Postmodern poetics. The features of those later poetries that have provoked such a robust critical conversation about poetic objecthood do not spring unparented from the mind of Eliot and Pound, but trace their poetic genealogies back to the interpretively and epistemologically tumultuous effects of the Reformation era. Indeed, Eliot makes clear this legacy in his 1926 Clark Lectures at Cambridge, when he praises the post-Reformation lyric (which he calls by John Dryden's not entirely complimentary term "metaphysical") as a kind of utterance that foregrounds "sensible form," an effect that Eliot goes on to describe as "the *Word made Flesh*, so to speak."[46] In a later lecture, Eliot recognizes that the "sensible" (by which he means *sense-able*) poetics he so admires in the early seventeenth century is continuous with literary practice in his own day, describing their manifestation, "in Donne and in some of our contemporaries, in an affected, tortuous, and often over-elaborate and ingenious manner of speech."[47] My point, and Eliot's, is that there are clear aesthetic continuities between the indecorous, obstructive poetics of the post-Reformation period and the disjunctive innovations of the twentieth century, and that these continuities are only amplified as the seventeenth-century lyric ascends to critical prominence in the Modern period.[48]

As surely as antiabsorptive features pervade Eliot's own work, as Blasing and other critics have demonstrated, so too does the idea that the poem is a substantial object manifest itself in the work of his contemporaries. Pound packs his *Cantos* with Greek graphemes and Chinese characters, keeping the focus opaquely on the very shapes that constitute language, an effect that William Carlos Williams describes as redirecting interpretive focus "away from the word as symbol toward the word as reality."[49] And Gertrude Stein's 1914 tour de force *Tender Buttons* devises texts whose sentences block referentiality in order to emphasize the unyielding sign over some deferred signified. The first section of that volume, suggestively titled "Objects," leads off with a poem ("A CARAFE, THAT IS A BLIND GLASS") that foregrounds the tension between transparency and referentiality. "A kind in glass and a cousin, a spectacle and nothing strange a single hurt color and an arrangement in a system to pointing," Stein begins, balancing the substance of the carafe against its capacity to indicate meaning ("a system to pointing"). The effect is to obstruct that pointing, to offer up not glass but "BLIND GLASS," impeding the hermeneutic impulse and retraining readerly attention instead upon the impermeable object of the text itself.[50] The materializing program of post-Reformation poetics filters through the self-conscious and backward-gazing textuality of Modernism into the broad field of twentieth- and now twenty-first-century lyric production. Its heirs in our contemporary poetic context, displaced though they may be by time and culture from the religious controversies of sixteenth-century Europe, continue to register the competing claims of referentiality and objecthood, which arose as competing in the course of Reformation efforts to reimagine the Eucharist.[51]

Little wonder, then, that we hear echoes of Reformation-era exegesis in twentieth-century poet Archibald MacLeish's lyric "Ars Poetica," which ends by decreeing that "A poem should not mean / But be."[52] Or, as Wallace Stevens phrased it, "The poem is the cry of its occasion, / Part of the res itself and not about it."[53] These sentiments have become rallying cries for the poetries of our current literary-historical moment, and in their reiteration of the poetic ideals of a Donne or a Crashaw, they suggest that what we define, in our secular postmodernity, as the field of poetics is ultimately indebted to antiabsorptive strategies that developed out of the Reformation's probing of the relationship between the material and the sublime, between signification and referentiality. My project here has been in part to demonstrate that in the poetic tradition that follows upon the representational revolutions of sixteenth-century theology, the aesthetic artifact that is the poem imagines itself as not merely saying something but as *being* something, and offers an experience that subtends the synthesis of material and semantic into a singular hermeneutic experience. And in my claim that poetics offers one method by which that argument is accomplished, I hope to encourage a greater alertness to poetics in the wider conversation about literature, a fuller recognition that *how* a poem says communicates meaningfully beyond *what* a poem says. As the poet James Schuyler reminds us,

> How the thing said
> Is in the words, . . .
> The words are themselves
> The thing said.[54]

I hope also to suggest that current critical investments in the multivalent connections among subjects and objects, materiality and the distribution of meaning, representation and ontology, social determinants and literary production might be enriched by a renewed attentiveness to poetic structure, not as if it existed in a well-wrought vacuum but as an instrument for registering the spectrum of cultural pressures and habits of mind.

A focus on the ways in which the poetic features of a poem may obstruct its transparency might not always appear to be congenially allied to the work of literary criticism; after all, literary criticism often conceives of its explicative role as making literature more transparent to readers. But poetics is not the noise that one must penetrate in order to get at the "real meaning" of the text, and to overlook its communicative and constitutive contributions is to settle for a halfway understanding of any poem. Poetry itself has ever been bound up in its own durability, a "monumentum aere perennius" whose monumental capacity to outlast bronze is a function of its textuality, its fusion of material and meaning.[55] The poetic innovations of the post-Reformation period offer novel strategies in response to this age-old concern with poetry as an object that endures. My aim has been to show that these poems are *made flesh*, self-consciously constructed and substantially embodied artifacts, and they invite a hermeneutic encounter that honors the meaningfulness of presence. And what they argue, finally, is that poetry *matters*.

Notes

Introduction

1. Malcolm Ross, *Poetry and Dogma: The Transfiguration of Eucharistic Symbols in Seventeenth Century English Poetry*, 50–64. Ross's purpose is to trace the poetic consequences of what he calls "Cranmer's mutilation of the liturgy" (59) and to document the ways in which Anglican poetry "dissolves into bloodless abstraction" (228) following what is, in Ross's view, Calvinism's devaluation of religious symbol.

2. See also "The Poetics of the Eucharist: Poetry That Matters," the fourth chapter of Frances Cruickshank's *Verse and Poetics in George Herbert and John Donne*. Standing behind these and other studies is the work of Stephen Greenblatt, who in a set of influential pieces on the anxiety generated by the Eucharist has articulated the rite's relevance to literary texts. In his essay "The Mousetrap," Greenblatt distills the relationship between literature and sacrament into three linked propositions: "First, most of the significant and sustained thinking in the early modern period about the nature of linguistic signs centered on or was deeply influenced by eucharistic controversies; second, most of the literature that we care about from this period was written in the shadow of these controversies; and third, their significance for English literature in particular lies less in the problem of the sign than in what we will call 'the problem of the leftover,' that is, the status of the material remainder" (in Catherine Gallagher and Greenblatt, *Practicing New Historicism*, 141; see also Greenblatt's essay "Remnants of the Sacred in Early Modern England"). In a crucial refinement of Greenblatt's formulation, I will be arguing that in post-Reformation poetry, the sign becomes indistinguishable from the material remainder.

3. Molly Murray, *The Poetics of Conversion in Early Modern English Literature*, 24–25.

4. See Louis Martz, *The Poetry of Meditation: A Study in English Religious Literature of the Seventeenth Century*, and Barbara K. Lewalski, *Protestant Poetics and the Seventeenth-Century Religious Lyric*. Studies that follow Martz in identifying a catholically inflected, or Anglo-Catholic, view of early modern English poetry include Anthony Raspa's *The Emotive Image: Jesuit Poetics in the English Renaissance*, Anthony Low's *Love's Architecture: Devotional Modes in Seventeenth-Century English Poetry*, and R. V. Young's *Doctrine and Devotion in Seventeenth-Century Poetry*. Likewise, a number

of critical works argue for a thoroughgoing aesthetic Protestantism, including William Halewood, *The Poetry of Grace: Reformation Themes in English Seventeenth-Century Poetry*, and Andrew Weiner, *Sir Philip Sidney and the Poetics of Protestantism*. A catalogue of critical studies that seek specifically to establish the theology of Donne or Herbert everywhere along the spectrum from Catholic to Calvinist would overwhelm this already overlong note; many of these texts will be addressed over the course of the present book.

5. George Herbert, "Love Unknown," 41–45, from *The English Poems of George Herbert*, edited by Helen Wilcox. Subsequent references to this poem will be cited parenthetically.

6. Strier, *Love Known*, 163.

7. Ibid., 164.

8. "Apostasy," the first chapter of John Carey's biographical study *John Donne: Life, Mind, and Art* begins memorably: "The first thing to remember about Donne is that he was Catholic; the second, that he betrayed his faith" (1). For a more nuanced claim that Donne's Catholic affinities informed his religious identity throughout his confessional peregrinations, see Dennis Flynn, "Donne's Catholicism: I" and "Donne's Catholicism: II." For a Calvinist take on Donne, see Donald Doerksen, *Conforming to the Word: Herbert, Donne, and the English Church Before Laud*; Doerksen's phrase "Calvinist mainstream" appears on page 19 of that work. For his part, Raymond-Jean Frontain recognizes that critics of Donne may overlook his "liminalized" position and "polarize where he tried so desperately to unify" ("'Make all this All': The Religious Operations of John Donne's Imagination," 19).

9. For a brief history of these different names and their derivation from antiquity, see Eugene LaVerdiere, *The Eucharist in the New Testament and the Early Church*, 1–3.

10. Church of England, *Articles*, B3v–B4r.

11. Original and translation from the Blackfriars edition of Thomas Aquinas, *Summa Theologiae* (New York: Blackfriars/McGraw-Hill, 1975), 3a.73.1. All references are to this edition of the *Summa Theologiae* and will indicate part, question, and article numbers.

12. Unless otherwise indicated, all biblical passages in this study will be quoted from the 1611 *Holy Bible, conteyning the Old Testament, and the New, newly translated out of the originall tongues, and with the former translations diligently compared and reuised, by His Maiesties speciall comandement*—more commonly known as the King James Bible, the translation in standard use for the English church during most of the period examined by this study. All translations from the commentary tradition, if no translator is identified, are mine.

13. Luke 22.19.

14. Gary Macy notes that "the famous 'bread of life' passage in the Gospel of John (6:22–59)—itself the centre of much scholarly debate—may well have been written to clarify certain controversies over the understanding of how one might 'eat the flesh of

the Son of Man, and drink his blood'" (*The Theologies of the Eucharist in the Early Scholastic Period*, 18).

15. 1 Corinthians 11.24–25, 29.

16. Origen, *In Leviticum*, Homilia 7.5.

17. These passages are quoted from two of Ignatius of Antioch's epistles: Πρός Τράλλιανους, 8. and Πρός Φιλαδελφευσιν, 5.

18. Tertullian, *Liber de Resurrectione Carnis*, 37.

19. Clement of Alexandria, Παιδαγωγός, 1.6.45.

20. Ibid., 2.2.1.

21. For investigations into the varieties of sacramental theology through the fourteenth century, see Miri Rubin, *Corpus Christi: The Eucharist in Late Medieval Culture*, and Macy, *Theologies of the Eucharist in the Early Scholastic Period*. For commentary on the oldest negotiations about the manner of Christ's participation in the Eucharist, see LaVerdiere, *The Eucharist in the New Testament and the Early Church*. For a survey of the rite's development from the ante-Nicene period through the Reformation, see Edward J. Kilmartin's *The Eucharist in the West* and especially Darwell Stone's exhaustive, two-volume *History of the Doctrine of the Holy Eucharist*.

22. Ambrose of Milan, *De sacramentis*, 4.4.16.

23. Augustine, *Enarrationes in Psalmos*, 3.1.

24. Augustine, *De Doctrina Christiana*, 3.15.24.

25. Augustine, *In Iohannis evangelium*, tractatus 26.6.

26. Thomas Aquinas, *Summa Theologiae*, 3a.75.1, 3a.75.2, 3a.75.1, 3a.60.2, 3a.76.7, and 3a.75.1.32.

27. Huldreich Zwingli, *Ad Carolum Rom. Imperatorem, Fidei Huldrychi Zvingli ratio*, B3r [translated as *An Account of the Faith of Huldreich Zwingli Submitted to the German Emperor Charles VC, at the Diet of Augsburg*, July 3, 1530, in Clarence Nevin Heller, ed., *The Latin Works and the Correspondence of Huldreich Zwingli*, 2.48].

28. Ibid., B8r [and 2.55].

29. Zwingli, chapter 5 of *Christian Fidei a Huldrycho Zvinglio Praedicatae, brevis et clara expositio*, B8v [translated as *A Short and Clear Exposition of the Christian Faith Preached by Huldreich Zwingli, Written by Zwingli Himself Shortly Before His Death to a Christian King; Thus Far Not Printed by Anyone and Now for the First Time Published to the World. Matthew 11: "Come Unto Me," Etc.*, 1536, July 1531, in Heller, ed., *Latin Works and Correspondence of Huldreich Zwingli*, 2.257].

30. Ibid., C2r [and 2.259].

31. Stephen Gardiner, *An Explication and assertion of the true Catholique fayth, touchyng the most blessed Sacrament of the aulter*, B1r. Richard Hooker, likewise, coolly insists "that the Eucharist is not a bare signe or figure onely . . . as if the name of his body did import but the figure of his body" (*Of the lawes of ecclesiasticall politie*, 5.67 [page 177]; hereafter, this work will be cited by book and chapter number, with a parenthetical indication of page number keyed to the 1593 edition).

32. For an examination of the interlocking interests of linguistic history and Reformation theology and an account of the Zwingli's own forays into linguistic theory, see Judith H. Anderson, *Translating Investments*, especially chapter 3, "Language and History in the Reformation: Translating Matter to Metaphor in the Sacrament" (36–60).

33. John Calvin, *Institutio Christianae Religionis*, 4.17.5, 4.17.10, in *Joannis Calvini Opera Selecta*. All citations will be from this edition, indicated by book, chapter, and section numbers.

34. Calvin, *A Treatise on the Sacrament of the Body and Blood of Christ*, 441.

35. Calvin, *Institutio Christianae Religionis*, 4.14.6. Calvin refers to Augustine's *In Iohannis evangelium,* tractatus 80.3: "Accedit verbum ad elementum, et fit Sacramentum, etiam ipsum tamquam visibile verbum" [The word is added to the eucharistic element, and there results a Sacrament, itself even as a visible word].

36. Nicholas Ridley, *A Brief Declaration of the Lord's Supper*, 10; the final phrase, related in John Foxe's *Actes and Monuments of These Latter and Perillous Dayes*, is quoted in Anderson, *Translating Investments*, 54.

37. Edwin Sandys, *The Sermons of Edwin Sandys*, 88.

38. For a thorough examination of the influence of continental eucharistic reforms on the developing liturgy of the institutional Church of England, see Bryan D. Spinks, *From the Lord and "The Best Reformed Churches."*

39. Hooker, *Of the lawes of ecclesiasticall politie* 5.67 (176–179).

40. Lancelot Andrewes, "A Sermon Preached Before the King's Majesty, at Whitehall, on Thursday, the Twenty-Fifth of December, A.D. MDCXXIII. Being Christmas Day," in *Ninety-Six Sermons by the Right Honourable and Reverend Father in God, Lancelot Andrewes*, 1.282.

41. Ryan Netzley, *Reading, Desire, and the Eucharist in Early Modern Religious Poetry*, 15, 23.

42. Schwartz, *Sacramental Poetics*, 119, emphases in original.

43. The terms of my argument throughout this book will advertise my intellectual debt to the work of art historian Michael Fried, especially *Art and Objecthood* and *Absorption and Theatricality: Painting and Beholder in the Age of Diderot.*

44. Mutlu Konuk Blasing, *Lyric Poetry: The Pain and the Pleasure of Words*, 14; emphasis in original.

45. George Puttenham describes the action of figurative language as a process by which speech is "estranged" from meaning, "sometime by way of surplusage, some by defect, sometime by disorder, or mutation," in *The Arte of English Poesie*, 3.10. Though Puttenham does not intend the term "estranged" as a compliment, the project of this book is to demonstrate that post-Reformation poetics emphasizes such estrangements, flouting the decorum championed by Puttenham and other compositional manuals of his period.

46. Blasing, *Lyric Poetry*, 15.

47. Charles Bernstein, "Artifice of Absorption," in *A Poetics*, 64.

48. Ibid., 86.

49. Ibid., 86–87. Bernstein invokes, and inverts, Maurice Merleau-Ponty's argument in *The Visible and the Invisible*: "It is that the thickness of flesh between the seer and the thing is constitutive for the thing of its corporeity; it is not an obstacle between them, it is their means of communication" (135).

50. Susan Stewart, *Poetry and the Fate of the Senses*, 2.

51. Allen Grossman, Summa Lyrica, 6.2, republished in *The Sighted Singer: Two Works on Poetry for Readers and Writers*. The title of Grossman's work indicates his preoccupation with the overlap between theological and poetic questions of presence.

52. Again, Grossman acknowledges the proximity between poetic reading and sacramental worship when he describes the poetic encounter as an act of "'cooperation' with grace which is the precondition of the experience of grace" (*Summa Lyrica*, 18.5). His phrase "the presence of presence" appears in *Summa Lyrica*, 6.2.

53. For perhaps the most influential contemporary exposition on the aptness of divinity to the craft of poetry, see Phillip Sidney's *An Apologie for Poetrie*, especially B4r–C1v, where he notes that "among the Romans a Poet was called *Vates*, which is as much a Diuiner, Fore-seer, or Prophet . . . so heauenly a title did that excellent people bestow upon this heart-rauishing knowledge," and invokes "holy Dauids Psalmes" as the model of "a diuine Poem."

54. These poetic strategies represent a pointed departure from the immediately preceding generations of English poetry, which privileged decorum and transparency over bumptious antiabsorption. George Gascoigne's "Certayne notes of Instruction concerning the making of verse or ryme in English" advised that poets ought to use "just measure," or consistent meter, with "every worde . . . in his natural *Emphasis*"; that figurative language should be used judiciously, "aptly" and "modestly"; that "ryme" should be used with reason; that sentences should retain "their mother phrase and proper *Idióma*." In short, counsels Gascoigne, poetry should conduct itself in a manner that is "lawfull or commendable": "frame your stile to *perspicuity* and to be sensible: for the haughty obscure verse doth not much delight" (*The Posies of George Gascoigne Esquire*, 291r–295v). Gascoigne's priority on "naturall" language is reinforced by Puttenham, whose robust project, in *The Arte of English Poesie*, is to outline practices that will preserve decorum in poetic language, to ensure that poetic language may be "nothing the more vnseemely or misbecomming, but rather decenter and more agreable to any ciuill eare and vnderstanding" (3.1). Roughly contemporary with these works, Sidney's *Apologie for Poetrie* commits its final movement to demarcating what he terms the "rules" of decorum for sundry poetic modes and to censuring as indecorous such antiabsorptive features as assertive rhyme and a disregard for the unities of time and space (I3r–L3r).

55. Brian Cummings, *The Literary Culture of the Reformation: Grammar and Grace*, 281.

56. Joseph Addison famously criticized as instances of what he called "*false Wit*" frequent features of Herbert's style, including "Anagrams, Chronograms, Lipograms,

and Acrosticks: Sometimes of Syllables, as in Ecchos and Doggerel Rhymes: Sometimes of Words, as in Punns and Quibbles; and sometimes of whole Sentences or Poems, cast into the Figures of *Eggs, Axes,* or"—pointedly—"*Altars*" (*The Spectator*, no. 62, par. 3; reprinted at 1.103 of *The Works of Joseph Addison*). Edmund Gosse, likewise, writes of Herbert that "his greatest fault lay in an excessive pseudo-psychological ingenuity, which was a snare to all these lyrists, and in a tasteless delight in metrical innovations, often as ugly as they were unprecedented" (*A Short History of Modern English Literature*, 147).

Chapter 1. "The Bodie and the Letters Both"

1. The theological tensions of the Jacobean church have stimulated a number of fine historical studies, which, in their very disagreement, provide a glimpse into the confused ecclesiastical positioning of the period; see Patrick Collinson's *The Religion of Protestants: The Church in English Society, 1559–1625*; Peter Lake's *The Boxmaker's Revenge: "Orthodoxy," "Heterodoxy" and the Politics of the Parish in Early Stuart London*; Nicholas Tyacke's *Anti-Calvinists: The Rise of English Arminianism, c. 1590–1640*; and Peter White's *Predestination, Policy, and Polemic: Conflict and Consensus in the English Church from the Reformation to the Civil War*. The opposing views of these scholars find some synthesis in the essay collection edited by Kenneth Fincham, *The Early Stuart Church, 1603–42*; and in Charles Prior, *Defining the Jacobean Church: The Politics of Religious Controversy, 1603–1625*. In literary studies of the period, the most influential texts to read Herbert as writing out of a Reformed sensibility include Barbara K. Lewalski's *Protestant Poetics and the Seventeenth-Century Religious Lyric* and Richard Strier's *Love Known: Theology and Experience in George Herbert's Poetry*. For Herbert as Anglo-Catholic, see Louis Martz, *The Poetry of Meditation: A Study in English Religious Literature of the Seventeenth Century*, and R. V. Young, *Doctrine and Devotion in Seventeenth-Century Poetry*.

2. Richard Hooker, *Of the lawes of ecclesiasticall politie*, 5.67 (181).

3. C. A. Patrides, *The English Poems of George Herbert*, 17. Robert Whalen's *The Poetry of Immanence: Sacrament in Donne and Herbert* provides a comprehensive catalogue of eucharistic references in Herbert's language; see especially chapters 4 through 6 of that study.

4. George Herbert, "The H. Communion" (Williams MS version), lines 1–6. All quotations from Herbert's English verse are from *The English Poems of George Herbert*, edited by Helen Wilcox, and will be referenced textually by line number. For the relationship between the manuscript editions of Herbert's poetry and the volume that was published in 1633, see Greg Miller, "Scribal and Print Publication: The Case of George Herbert's English Poems," and Mario Di Cesare, "The Bodleian Manuscript and the Text of Herbert's Poems."

5. Michael C. Schoenfeldt, *Bodies and Selves in Early Modern England*, 98.

6. Ibid.

7. Thomas Cranmer, *An answer of the Most Reuerend Father in God Thomas Arch-ebyshop of Canterburye . . . vnto a crafty and sophisticall cauillation deuised by Stephen Gardiner*, 42. Hooker likewise describes the effects of the sacrament as inscribed by the body's need for "corporall nourishment" in *Of the lawes of ecclesiasticall politie*, 5.67 (173).

8. Whalen, *Poetry of Immanence*, 125.

9. Ibid., 124.

10. See Daniel W. Doerksen, *Conforming to the Word: Herbert, Donne, and the English Church Before Laud*; and Gene Veith, *Reformation Spirituality: The Religion of George Herbert*.

11. John Calvin, *Institutio Christianae Religionis*, 4.14.1, in *Joannis Calvini Opera Selecta*. Calvin references Augustine *De Civitate Dei*, 10.19: "haec ita signa esse illorum, sicut verba sonantia signa sunt rerum" [these (visible sacrifices) are signs of those (invisible things), as the words we utter are the signs of things].

12. Ibid., 4.14.6.

13. Theological discussions of the sacramental distinction between accidents and substance—the materially perceptual species of bread and wine and the ontologically irreducible spiritual essence on which they are contingent—are ultimately indebted to Aristotle's philosophies of matter. It is worth noting, given the argument of the present study, that Aristotle rejects the notion that the material itself can be considered οὐσία, or substance: rather, that which can be sensed is predicated upon an ultimate substratum, an essence that is "τῆς ὕλης πρότερον καὶ μᾶλλον" [prior to matter and of a higher degree of matter]; the material world is to this ultimate substratum a predicate—or, to use the term that will become familiar in discussions about sacramental signification, an "accident" (Aristotle's term is "συμβεβηκὸς"; see *Τὰ Μετὰ Τὰ Φυσικὰ* [*Metaphysics*] Z.1029a, 1031b).

14. Herbert, *A Priest to the Temple, or, The Countrey Parson His Character and Rule of Holy Life*, in F. E. Hutchinson's edition of *The Works of George Herbert*, 257–58.

15. Charles Bernstein, "Artifice of Absorption," in *A Poetics*, 86.

16. Indeed, in his essay "George Herbert and the Incarnation," Richard E. Hughes argues of Herbert that "the Incarnation is, without question, the central issue of his poetry" (23), which Hughes describes as expressed in Herbert's concern with "form overcoming inchoate matter, reason overcoming incomprehensibility" (28).

17. See Ephesians 2.20; see also 1 Corinthians 10.4, which offers a eucharistic interpretation of Exodus 17.6.

18. Throughout this chapter, biblical references are to the 1611 *Holy Bible, conteyning the Old Testament, and the* New, commonly referred to as the King James or Authorized Version, which was the translation in standard use for Herbert.

19. Bernstein, "Artifice of Absorption," in *A Poetics*, 86.

20. Nicholas Ferrar, *Materials for the Life of Nicholas Ferrar*, 76. For a fuller account of the textual experiments of Little Gidding, see Joyce Ransome, "Monotessaron: The Harmonies of Little Gidding." In his essay "'So rare a use': Scissors, Reading, and Devotion at Little Gidding," Paul Dyck discusses the construction of these

concordances as manifesting "the theological in the material" (67) and suggests that the spatial (re)arrangement of biblical narratives emphasizes the reading of signs as a devotional practice, and encourages the material participation with text as a spiritually edifying activity.

21. Joseph H. Summers, *George Herbert: His Religion and Art*, 148.

22. Though Strier opines that "The best critics of 'The Altar' have recognized that it does not in any way refer to the Eucharist" (*Love Known*, 191), such a dismissal almost willfully ignores the drama of sacramental preparation that the structure of *The Temple* enacts. Once we enter "The Church" proper (having moved across "The Church Porch" to be sprinkled by the "Perirrhanterium"), the calculated focus of the gaze is the sacramental altar, at which we arrive to "sit and eat" by the end of this central section of Herbert's book. "The Altar" may not mention sacramental worship explicitly, but its place in the book's architecture is itself one way the poem refers to the Eucharist.

23. Summers, *George Herbert*, 123.

24. Ibid., 143. In Summers's view, the poem's visual form operates counter to any sacramental program: "The shape of Herbert's poem was intended to hieroglyph the relevance of the old altar to the new Christian altar within the heart. It was fittingly, therefore, a modification of the traditional shape of a classic altar rather than of what Herbert knew as the Communion Table" (142).

25. For M. Thomas Hester, "the final shape of 'The Altar' is *both* an *altar* and an *I*—an image of the speaker's self and his Christ" ("Altering the Text of the Self," 112). Elizabeth McLaughlin and Gail Thomas argue that Herbert's poem transforms all references to external ritual into an internal offering: "The sacrificial altar or communion table is in the heart" ("Communion in *The Temple*," especially 116), while Doerksen rejects any echo of ritual worship, stating flatly that "The Altar" is "a poem clearly about the speaker's heart" (*Conforming to the Word*, 97). For Anthony Low, the shape of "The Altar," being "finished, perfect and symmetrical" represents the perfection for which the regenerate heart groans (*Love's Architecture: Devotional Modes in Seventeenth-Century English Poetry*, 93).

26. Stanley Fish, *Self-Consuming Artifacts: The Experience of Seventeenth Century Literature*, 207.

27. See Fish, *Self-Consuming Artifacts*, 206–15, whose reading of "The Altar" summarizes the poem's renunciations this way: "In losing the poem Herbert also loses, happily, the prideful claims it made silently in his name" (215). Strier similarly describes the poem as "turning away" from human art in *Love Known* (see especially 191–95).

28. In addition to the critical readings already mentioned, see Achsah Guibbory, who in *Ceremony and Community from Herbert to Milton* identifies similarities between Herbert's altar and the stone altars of the Israelites.

29. For a provocative discussion of "The Altar" in the context of Herbert's demonstrable commitment to the meaningfulness of the physical architecture of

churches, see Paul Dyck's essay "Locating the Word: The Textual Church and George Herbert's *Temple*"; the author argues that Herbert's reliance on concrete church structures in *The Temple* finds a material reflection in the poet's practice of inscribing actual churches (three of which he participated in rebuilding) with text. Though Dyck diverges from the present study in his contention that such concrete structures "were arranged to move the worshippers' attention past the material and to the spiritual" (237), his felicitous description of both church and textual architecture as "edifying structures" (238) aligns with my own claims.

30. It is a poem's *sense-ability*—its ability to be perceived by the senses—that T. S. Eliot intends when he describes the "sensible form" of a poetic text. See Eliot, *The Varieties of Metaphysical Poetry*, 54.

31. Martin Elsky, "George Herbert's Pattern Poems and the Materiality of Language," 252. See also "'The bodie and the letters both': 'blending' the rules of early modern religion," by Patricia Canning, who makes use of linguistics to expand Elsky's argument about the speaker's construction of meaning out of sound units and to claim that Herbert's "blended network" (198) of form and meaning generates "a kind of linguistic transubstantiation" (197).

32. I take the phrase "hieroglyphic riddle" from Fish, *The Living Temple: George Herbert and Catechizing*, 28.

33. Whalen, *Poetry of Immanence*, 124. For the argument that Herbert's book instructs a reader catechetically toward spiritual truth, see Fish, *Living Temple*.

34. Fish, *Living Temple*, 29. See also Richard Todd, *The Opacity of Signs: Acts of Interpretation in George Herbert's* The Temple, which follows and expands Fish's argument that in "Love-joy" the sign "*JESUS CHRIST*" serves as a figure for "*Joy*" and "*Charitie*," and vice versa.

35. *Oxford English Dictionary*, 2nd ed., s.v. "Tent."

36. Louis H. Leiter, "George Herbert's Anagram," 544.

37. Robert Reiter reminds us that "the Greek verb *eskenosen* [ἐσκήνωσεν] . . . literally means 'pitched a tent.'" The familiar biblical explanation of the Incarnation in John 1.14 "thus can be rendered 'and the word became flesh and *pitched his tent* among us'" ("George Herbert's 'Anagram': A Reply to Professor Leiter," 60).

38. Heather A. R. Asals, *Equivocal Predication: George Herbert's Way to God*, 9, 36; emphases in original.

39. Ibid., 11; emphases in original.

40. John Chrysostom, Ὑπόμνημα εἰς τόν Ἅγιον Ματθαῖον τόν Εὐαγγελιστήν, homily 82.5.

41. For other examples of this well-trod pun, see the opening lines of Shakespeare's *Richard III*, and—with more specific reference to Christ—Donne's "Hymn to god the father": "at my death thy sonne / Shall shine as he shines now, and heretofore" (15–16; this spelling of the pun follows the 1633 manuscript, printed in Herbert Grierson's edition side by side with the variant text from Izaak Walton's *The Lives of Doctor John Donne, Sir Henry Wotton, Mr. Richard Hooker, Mr. George Herbert, and Doctor*

Robert Sanderson, in which the pun tips toward its other signification: "thy Sunn / Shall shine as it shines nowe"). And despite the praise Herbert devotes to the punning capacity of English in "The Sonne," it is also worth noting that Herbert's gloss of "sun" as "light" gestures toward the Greek pun in the prologue to the Gospel of John: "καὶ τὸ φῶς ἐν τῇ σκοτίᾳ φαίνει, καὶ ἡ σκοτία αὐτὸ κατέλαβεν" [And the light shineth in darkness; and the darkness comprehended it not, as the King James Version translates it (1.5)], where the word "φῶς" signifies both "light" and "mortal." This verse is located, not insignificantly, in the long passage that establishes the identity of Christ as Logos.

42. Elsky, "George Herbert's Pattern Poems and the Materiality of Language," 254; emphasis and brackets in original.

43. Matthias Bauer, "'A Title Strange, Yet True': Toward an Explanation of Herbert's Titles," 108.

44. See especially Luke 22.24, which notes that Jesus's sweat "was as it were great drops of blood falling down to the ground." For a consideration of the relationship between the Ignatian meditative practice of *compositio loci* and the practice of devotional poetry, see Martz, *Poetry of Meditation*, 25–39.

45. In *A Reading of George Herbert*, on pp. 117–33, Rosemond Tuve documents the sacrificial iconography of "The Agonie" and other works, tracing the poetry's figures to the biblical narrative of the Passion. Tuve's reading strategy, however, insists upon the referential function of Herbert's language; she says Herbert's "physical or sensuous" devices "would seem fanciful, quaint, and more ingenious than moving, if not seen instantly *as* what they signify" (131).

46. Ibid., 128.

47. Helen Vendler, *The Poetry of George Herbert*, 73. Critics have noted that the poem also communicates the theme of the tortured body in its form, which pictures the shape of a winepress; see Edmund Miller, *Drudgerie Divine: The Rhetoric of God and Man in George Herbert*, 92; and J. Max Patrick, "Critical Problems in Editing George Herbert's *The Temple*," 17–28. Again, such arguments acknowledge that Herbert emphasizes the opacity of the material artifact on the page.

48. Strier, *Love Known*, 43–44.

49. Young, *Doctrine and Devotion*, 118.

50. Strier, *Love Known*, 47. Coleridge's commentary can be found in *Coleridge on the Seventeenth Century*, 536. For his part, Young declares that Herbert's figure leaves him "open to Catholic interpretation" (*Doctrine and Devotion*, 116).

51. Ryan Netzley, "'Take and Taste': Sacramental Physiology, Eucharistic Experience, and George Herbert's *The Temple*," 190, 183. See also Christopher A. Hill, "George Herbert's Sweet Devotion," which identifies physical delight as an animating principle of Herbert's aesthetic.

52. See Schoenfeldt, "'That Ancient Heat': Sexuality and Spirituality in *The Temple*," the sixth chapter of *Prayer and Power* (230–70). For another perspective on the

erotics of "Love (III)," see Chana Bloch's discussion of the poem in *Spelling the Word: George Herbert and the Bible*, 108–12.

53. Asals, *Equivocal Predication*, 90; Whalen, *Poetry of Immanence*, 159.

54. Netzley, "'Take and Taste,'" 204.

55. Herbert's collection of Latin poems, *Musae Responsoriae* is reprinted in the Hutchinson edition of *The Works of George Herbert*.

56. Jonathan Goldberg, *Voice Terminal Echo: Postmodernism and English Renaissance Texts*, 115.

57. Fish, *Self-Consuming Artifacts*, 194–96.

Chapter 2. Edward Taylor's "Menstruous Cloth"

1. Louis Martz discusses the similarities between Edward Taylor and George Herbert in his foreword to *The Poems of Edward Taylor*, edited by Donald E. Stanford, xiii–xiv.

2. Donald Stanford, *Edward Taylor*, 22.

3. Taylor, *Preparatory Meditations* 2.81.13–20. All citations from Taylor's poetry are from Stanford's 1960 edition of *The Poems of Edward Taylor* and will be referenced textually by series, meditation, and line numbers.

4. Among the sparse property of Taylor's library was a 1634 edition of the King James Bible, which was printed, like the 1611 edition, in London by Robert Barker. Taylor apparently brought this volume with him when he emigrated from England to America, and it seems to have been the text he used throughout his ministry. See Francis Murphy, "A Letter on Edward Taylor's Bible."

5. Caroline Walker Bynum explains the binary logic that situates the soul as feminine: "God was (as he has been to most of the pious throughout the long Christian tradition) metaphorically male—father or judge, Bridegroom or friend—and the soul (partly because of the linguistic gender of *anima*) was frequently symbolized or described as female" (*Holy Feast and Holy Fast: The Religious Significance of Food to Medieval Women*, 282). We can extend Bynum's passing observation that the "linguistic gender of *anima*" is feminine to include the Tanakh's Hebrew נפש, and the New Testament's Greek ψῡχή: each of these terms is linguistically feminine, each denotes the seat of spiritual life, in opposition to the body, and each is rendered in most biblical translations as "soul."

6. Karen Rowe, *Saint and Singer: Edward Taylor's Typology and the Poetics of Meditation*, 207.

7. This chapter will discuss the drama of self-feminization within the context of the Puritan regeneracy paradigm particularly, but in their gendered description of the relationship between God and humankind, the Puritans are hardly original. Indeed, Bynum reports that so prevalent was the eroticization of devotion in medieval writing that worshippers coined a term to describe the use of nuptial and erotic imagery to represent the soul's ecstatic union with God: *Brautmystik*, or bride-mysticism (see Bynum, *Jesus as Mother: Studies in the Spirituality of the High Middle Ages*, 141). In

addition to the valuable scholarship of Bynum on the widespread use of female symbols within medieval Catholic culture to register human dependence on and submission to God (for which see also *Holy Feast and Holy Fast*, 282–94), Debora Shuger examines the Renaissance fascination with Mary Magdalene as a devotional model and traces the overlap between the voice of the Bride of Canticles and of the Magdalene in early modern literature and exegesis (see especially chapter 5, "Saints and Lovers," in *The Renaissance Bible: Scholarship, Sacrifice, and Subjectivity*). What distinguishes the Puritan treatment of this commonplace is the extension of the erotic narrative into reproduction in the discourse surrounding regeneracy. And though Nathan Hitchcock argues in his essay "Saving Edward Taylor's Purse: Masculine Devotion in the *Preparatory Meditations*" that Taylor engages in a performance of self-feminization in order to receive by imputation Christ's uncompromisingly masculine authority, as we shall see, Taylor's structural strategies serve precisely as a provision against the failure of self-feminization—and, by extension, against exclusion from the explicitly reproductive regeneracy that follows from becoming the Bride.

8. For a full examination of the Half-Way Covenant and its historical urgency, see Robert G. Pope, *The Half-Way Covenant: Church Membership in Puritan New England*, and E. Brooks Holifield, *The Covenant Sealed: The Development of Puritan Sacramental Theology in Old and New England, 1570–1720*, chapters 5, 6, and especially 7. For a thorough account of Stoddard's efforts to reform New England sacramental policy and Taylor's opposition to any such reform, see *Edward Taylor vs. Solomon Stoddard: The Nature of the Lord's Supper*, a series of relevant primary documents edited by Thomas and Virginia Davis. Stoddard articulates his position most publicly, and at greatest length, in his 1687 treatise *The Safety of Appearing at the Day of Judgement, in the righteousness of Christ, opened and applied*.

9. See Matthew 22.2–12.

10. Taylor, *Treatise Concerning the Lord's Supper*, 14. All references to this text will be to Norman Grabo's edition of the *Treatise*.

11. Ibid., 36.

12. Ibid., 17, emendations in original.

13. For a helpful survey of ancient and patristic sources for and instances of this convention, see Claude Chavasse, *The Bride of Christ: An Enquiry into the Nuptial Element in Early Christianity*.

14. Cornelius Hoen's text comes from the first section of his 1525 *Epistola christiana*; the translation is mine.

15. Taylor, *Treatise Concerning the Lord's Supper*, 179. Throughout the *Treatise*, Taylor's own biblical citations appear parenthetically.

16. Ibid., 29.

17. Ibid., 58.

18. Ibid., 19. Here the *Treatise* quotes 2 Corinthians 11.2; Taylor, whose Greek was good, would have recognized that the Greek word usually translated as "virgin" in this passage, παρθένος, denotes specifically a marriageable maiden.

19. Ibid., 48. Taylor's association of the amorous relationship (or relationships) dramatized in the Song of Songs with the Bride and Bridegroom of Christian allegorical parable (see Matthew 25.1–13; Mark 2.19; Ephesians 5.23) has long precedent. Augustine's writings are riddled with often self-excoriating ejaculations containing versions of the Bride/lover metaphor. "Cogitans de pulchro et apto," he writes dreamily at one point, "et stare cupiens et audiere te et gaudio gaudere propter vocem sponsi" [As I pondered over beauty and proportion, I wanted to stand still and listen to you and rejoice at hearing the voice of my Bridegroom] (*Confessionum* 4.15). Bernard of Clairvaux remains, of course, the standard-bearer for sacred eroticism; his massive commentary on Canticles vividly explicates the love-relationship between the Bride and divine Bridegroom, representing Christ as both husband and lover: "et cum ipsos cogitatis amantes," Bernard instructs us, "non virum et feminam, sed Verbum et animam sentiatis oportet" ["and when you consider the lovers themselves, think not of a man and a woman but of the Word and the Soul] (*Sermones in Cantica Canticorum*, 61.2)—the Word here being the Logos, Christ himself.

20. Isaiah 62.5.

21. Taylor, *Treatise Concerning the Lord's Supper*, 172.

22. Ibid., 38.

23. Ephesians 5.22.

24. This drama of bridal self-feminization would, of course, constitute more of a "conversion" of the self in male worshippers than in female worshippers. Ivy Schweitzer investigates the gendered discourse of Puritan conversion and its privileging of the male experience in her book *The Work of Self-Representation: Lyric Poetry in Colonial New England*, asking wryly, "Can women dream of becoming what they already are?" (18).

25. Margaret W. Masson, "The Typology of the Female as a Model for the Regenerate: Puritan Preaching, 1690–1730," 309–10. Masson quotes from Cotton Mather's *A Glorious Espousal: A Brief Essay to Illustrate and Prosecute the Marriage, Wherein Our Great Saviours Offers to Espouse unto Himself the Children of Men*.

26. Peter Bulkeley, *The Gospel-Covenant*, 50. In *The Language of Puritan Feeling: An Exploration in Literature, Psychology, and Social History*, David Leverenz examines from a psycholanalytical perspective the pervasive use of gendered language in Puritan conversion and salvation rhetoric, finding evidence of a Freudian family romance in the culture that produced such language. "Puritans," he argues," tried to resolve ambivalences about parental and social authority in a fantasy of dependence" (105).

27. Bulkeley, *Gospel-Covenant*, 50.

28. John Winthrop's private correspondence is collected in *Life and Letters of John Winthrop: Governor of the Massachusetts-Bay Company at their Emigration to New England*, edited by Robert C. Winthrop, 1.105.

29. Schweitzer devotes the opening chapter of *Work of Self-Representation* to describing this process of submission and concludes that self-effacement constitutes the Puritan ideal of what she calls "redeemed subjectivity"; see pages 1–39 of that

study. For additional perspectives on the Puritan premium on self-feminization as a sign of submission, see Albert Gelpi, *The Tenth Muse: The Psyche of the American Poet*, especially pages 36–37, and Jeffrey Hammond, *Edward Taylor: Fifty Years of Scholarship and Criticism*, especially page 137.

30. Thomas Foxcroft, *A Funeral Sermon Occasioned by Several Mournful Deaths*, 27. Richard Godbeer examines the celebration of what minister Samuel Willard delicately termed "conjugal union" as a model for the soul's espousal in his essay " 'Love Raptures': Marital, Romantic, and Erotic Images of Jesus Christ in Puritan New England, 1670–1730."

31. Mather, *Elizabeth in her Holy Retirement: An Essay to Prepare a Pious Woman for her Lying-in*, 31.

32. Leverenz, *Language of Puritan Feeling*, 130.

33. Mather, *Elizabeth in her Holy Retirement*, 19. Mather's exclamation is not exotic to the Puritan rhetoric of regeneracy. In her essay "Mothers in Israel: The Puritan Rhetoric of Child-Bearing," Margaret Thickstun examines tropes of pregnancy and childbirth in Puritan pastoral texts to demonstrate how women are encouraged to find spiritual instruction in their own reproductive events.

34. Taylor, *Treatise Concerning the Lord's Supper*, 44.

35. Ibid., 83, 58, 46, 44, 150.

36. Ibid., 45–46., 44, 46 (emphasis added), 153, 157.

37. Taylor, "Theological Notes," 27r.

38. Taylor, *Treatise Concerning the Lord's Supper*, 156, 158, emphasis added. Taylor's thinking conforms to the provisions of the 1662 Synod regarding conversion and admission to the Lord's Supper, but opinions regarding assurance, which term itself is applied differently throughout the Puritan tradition, varied widely in seventeenth-century New England. For clarification about the range of spiritual states signified by the word "assurance," see Michael Joseph Schuldiner, *Gifts and Works: The Post-Conversion Paradigm and Spiritual Controversy in Seventeenth-Century Massachusetts*, 18 n. 3. Schuldiner's study explains the doctrine's roots in Calvin (17–22), and traces the forms of its interpretation in early America, including in Taylor's work.

39. Taylor, *Treatise Concerning the Lord's Supper*, 150.

40. See "Church Records" in *Edward Taylor's "Church Records" and Related Sermons*, edited by Thomas M. and Virginia L. Davis, 97–104.

41. Taylor, *Treatise Concerning the Lord's Supper*, 187.

42. Ibid., 157.

43. Ibid., 173–75.

44. In appropriating the Bride figure from the Song of Songs, Taylor participates in a sort of poetic fad of the post-Reformation period, which climaxed in England in the early seventeenth century. Stanley Stewart's *The Enclosed Garden: The Tradition and the Image in Seventeenth-Century Poetry* and Noam Flinker's *The Song of Songs in English Renaissance Literature*, both useful examinations of the literary and interpretive traditions surrounding the book of Canticles, provide a sense of the wealth of poetic

borrowings from the biblical text with special focus on the seventeenth-century religious lyric; Stewart's study pays particular attention to Taylor's enthusiastic engagement with the Song of Songs.

45. Barbara K. Lewalski, *Protestant Poetics and the Seventeenth-Century Religious Lyric*, 417.

46. A number of critics have explored the early modern reliance on ocular proof of the father in the countenance of the child; see especially Katharine Eisaman Maus, "Horns of Dilemma: Jealousy, Gender, and Spectatorship in English Renaissance Drama," and Lawrence Danson, "Shakespeare and the Misrecognition of Fathers and Sons."

47. Karl Keller, *The Example of Edward Taylor*, 95.

48. William Scheick, *The Will and the Word: The Poetry of Edward Taylor*, 166.

49. Grabo, *Edward Taylor*, 83.

50. The term "primitive" is Keller's, a description he promotes in *The Example of Edward Taylor* (239–45). That Keller intends the term to be not altogether complimentary is evident when he bases his judgment on what he considers to be Taylor's poetic oddity and regards the successes of his verse as "unintended" (247). Of course, Keller also announces on his first page that the subject of his study "is a second-string poet, perhaps even a poor poet" (3), so one should not perhaps be surprised to find in his work a lack of appreciation for Taylor's poetic strategies.

51. Taylor, *Treatise Concerning the Lord's Supper*, 152.

52. See Leviticus 15.19–28, which proscribes against contact with menstruating women (and their furniture) and imposes strict ritual purification procedures both for women following the period of menstruation and for those who touch women during the period of their uncleanness.

53. Walter Bruele, *Praxis medicinae, or, the physicians practice*, 363.

54. Nicholas Fontanus, *The Womans Doctour*, 1–2.

55. William Salmon, *Aristotles Complete and Experience'd Midwife*, 96.

56. Thomas Shepard, *The Sound Believer: A Treatise of Evangelical Conversion*, 130.

57. Thomas Goodwin, *Aggravation of Sinne: and Sinning Against Knowledge/Mercie*, 22; and *The tryall of a Christians growth in mortification, or, purging out corruption, vivification, or bringing forth more fruit*, 13.

58. Quotations from the Hebrew Bible refer to the Jewish Publication Society's 1917 edition of the *Tanakh*, based on the Masoretic Text.

59. See Leviticus 15.25, where "issue of blood" (as the King James Bible translates this phrase) refers specifically to menstrual discharge and requires cleansing: "And if a woman haue an issue of her blood many dayes out of the time of her separation, or if it runne beyond the time of her separation, all the dayes of the issue of her vncleannesse, shall be as the dayes of her separation: she shalbe vncleane."

60. Taylor, *Treatise Concerning the Lord's Supper*, 152.

61. John Donne likewise invests himself in the positive effect of anxiety as a devotional practice. My next chapter examines the ways in which Donne, like Taylor, puts his trust in the medium of a materially invested textuality in order to secure the vagaries of spiritual practice that imagines meaning as inhering primarily beyond the phenomenal world, replacing uncertain referentiality with ostentatiously durable signs.

62. In a chapter on John Milton, Ryan Netzley discusses the challenge of attending to and celebrating in signs that which has already occurred, arguing that in that event both sacrament and poetry become "unnecessary, purposeless activity" (*Reading, Desire, and the Eucharist in Early Modern Religious Poetry*, 157). For Taylor, I would argue, the burden of discerning whether regeneracy has already occurred keeps his poetic activity both necessary and purposeful.

Chapter 3. Embracing the Medium

1. Allen Grossman, *Summa Lyrica*, 6.2, republished in *The Sighted Singer: Two Works on Poetry for Readers and Writers*.

2. Henry Peacham, *The Garden of Eloquence . . .* , C2r. For an examination of metaphor as a practice of imaginative and semantic organization within the context of Renaissance theology and biblical typology, see the second chapter of Frances Cruickshank's book *Verse and Poetics in George Herbert and John Donne*.

3. John Donne, *The Sermons of John Donne*, edited by George Potter and Evelyn Simpson, 6.55. All quotations from Donne's sermons will be to this edition, hereafter referenced by volume and page number.

4. Donne, *Sermons of John Donne*, 3.144.

5. Ibid., 3.105.

6. Ibid., 10.233, 235.

7. Ibid., 10.231.

8. Ibid.

9. Ramie Targoff, *John Donne, Body and Soul*, 167.

10. Donne, *Sermons of John Donne*, 3.109.

11. Targoff, *John Donne, Body and Soul*, 173.

12. Donne, *Sermons of John Donne*, 10.236. Donne's authority for this doctrine is Acts 2.31.

13. Ibid., 10.238.

14. Ibid.

15. All quotations from biblical text will refer to the 1611 King James Bible.

16. Donne, *Sermons of John Donne*, 10.239–240.

17. Ibid., 10.245, 246, 247, 248.

18. Donne, Holy Sonnet 9, line 3. This chapter follows Helen Gardner's edition of Donne's *The Divine Poems*.

19. William Empson wondered with revulsion nearly half a century ago, "Is a man in the last stages of torture so beautiful, even if blood hides his frowns?" (*Seven*

Types of Ambiguity, 146). John Carey simply calls the poem "gruesome" (*John Donne: Life, Mind, and Art*, 47). R. V. Young attempts to soften the image's difficulty by demonstrating its continuity with an aesthetic tradition that glorifies the crucified Christ in art; nevertheless, he admits, "To find such a tearful, bloody visage 'beauteous' is not an obviously natural or spontaneous response. To appreciate it in a detached fashion as a work of art requires a trained, or at least an acquired, aesthetic sensibility" (*Doctrine and Devotion in Seventeenth-Century Poetry*, 25). Donald M. Friedman's reading, elegantly cognizant of the paradoxes inherent in Christian theology, suggests that Donne's argument transvalues beauty. The picture of Christ crucified is a "beauteous form" because in that image the compassion of divine mercy replaces the strictures of justice, and the "horrid shape" of human sin is displaced by the mark of Christ's image ("Christ's Image and Likeness in Donne").

20. William Kerrigan, "The Fearful Accommodations of John Donne," 351.

21. Ibid., 348; Kerrigan quotes Donne's phrase "reverentiall feare" from a 1627 sermon on Psalm 65.5 (*Sermons of John Donne*, 7.316).

22. See John 6.51–52 for the earliest recorded resistance to the eucharistic symbolary, where Jesus declares, "I am the liuing bread, which came downe from heauen. If any man eate of this bread, he shall liue for euer: and the bread that I will giue, is my flesh, which I will giue for the life of the world. The Iewes therefore stroue amongst themselues, saying, How can this man giue vs his flesh to eate?" Thomas Aquinas, in the *Summa Theologiae*'s meticulous and definitive articulation of transubstantiation, acknowledges the problematics of Christ's essential bodily presence under the species of bread and wine; for the implications of that recognition, see the discussion of the Angelic Doctor's "Adoro Te Devote" (and Crashaw's response to it) in the next chapter of the present study. For a critical perspective on the theme of cannibalism as it relates to eucharistic worship, see Maggie Kilgour's far-reaching work *From Communion to Cannibalism: An Anatomy of Metaphors of Incorporation*, as well as Merrall Llewelyn Price, *Consuming Passions: The Uses of Cannibalism in Late Medieval and Early Modern Europe*, which addresses the many theological and social crises that follow from the doctrine of divine body-eating.

The tradition of recognizing the intimate bodily encounter of the Eucharist as erotic finds articulation within a number of spiritual traditions, of which, as we have seen, Edward Taylor's own work stands as one example. Huldreich Zwingli's landmark treatise *Ejn klare Underrichtung vom Nachtmal Christi* (1526) describes the rite as a sort of marriage ring, a pledge of love in token of fidelity—God's to us, and ours to God: "das sy dik Brot und wyn den lychnam und Blůt Christi genennet habend / wie wol sy die nun für ein Bedütung und vermanung des lychnâs und Blůts Christi verstanden habend / Glych als das fromm wyb, den ring den ir der hingezogen oder gestorben gmahel zů gedechtnus sin gelassen hatt / offtiren man nennet / Das ist min man saelig / der doch nun ein manůg des mans ist" ["they have called the bread and wine the body and blood of Christ, but what we should understand is that they are a representation and memorial of Christ's body and blood, even as a devoted wife, whose dead husband has left her a ring as a remembrance, often refers to the ring as her husband, saying, This is my departed husband, although what she means is that it is her husband's reminder" (Article 3, I4v)]. For a survey of instances in which erotic language is used to describe sacramental communion with God, see Claude Chavasse, *The Bride of Christ: An Enquiry into the Nuptial Element in Early Christianity*.

23. Donne, *Sermons of John Donne*, 10.245.

24. For an examination of the iconographic tradition that depicts Christ in his eucharistic function as a nursing mother, see Caroline Walker Bynum, *Jesus as Mother* and *Holy Feast and Holy Fast*, especially chapter 9.

25. After spending a chapter ("O Taste & See") documenting the doctrinally inconsistent and blurred formulation of the Eucharist that emerges from Donne's sermons, Jeffrey Johnson determines that "Donne's theology is marked by an eclecticism that defies assigning him too precise a sectarian designation" (*The Theology of John Donne*, 146). Jeanne Shami considers that such theological "eclecticism" allows Donne to arrive at "a more inclusive understanding of religious identity" that helps to temper confessional distinctions; see her essay "Troping Religious Identity: Circumcision and Transubstantiation in Donne's Sermons," especially pages 115–17.

26. Barbara K. Lewalski's assertion, in *Protestant Poetics and the Seventeenth-Century Religious Lyric*, of Donne's manifest "Calvinism" is expanded by a number of other critics. See, among many others, Paul R. Sellin, *John Donne and "Calvinist" Views of Grace*; John Stachniewski, "John Donne: The Despair of the 'Holy Sonnets'"; and Paul Cefalu, "Godly Fear, Sanctification, and Calvinist Theology in the Sermons and 'Holy Sonnets' of John Donne." On the other hand, the influence on Donne of the Roman church is central to John Carey's argument in *John Donne: Life, Mind, and Art* and to Dennis Flynn's brace of articles on "Donne's Catholicism," as well as his book *John Donne and the Ancient Catholic Nobility*.

27. Robert Whalen, *Poetry of Immanence*, 85.

28. Ibid., 108–109.

29. Donne, *Sermons of John Donne*, 7.293.

30. Whalen, *Poetry of Immanence*, 107–109.

31. From Samuel Johnson's chapter on "Cowley," in *Lives of the English Poets*, 6.

32. Donne, *Sermons of John Donne*, 2.282.

33. Ibid., 7.295.

34. For a representative sampling of critics who seek to synthesize a systematic sacramental theology from Donne's sermons, with particular focus on the Christmas 1626 sermon, see Young, *Doctrine and Devotion*, 94–99; Eleanor McNees, "John Donne and the Anglican Doctrine of the Eucharist," especially pages 100–101; Theresa DiPasquale, *Literature & Sacrament: The Sacred and the Secular in John Donne*, 70–73; chapter 5 of Jeffrey Johnson, *Theology of John Donne*; and chapter 3 of Whalen, *Poetry of Immanence*.

35. Donne, *Sermons of John Donne*, 3.259–260.

36. Ibid., 4.87, 5.144.

37. Ibid., 7.294.

38. Ibid., 8.220. It is worth remarking, if only in passing, that the relationship between rhetoric and substance is a topic to which Donne notably returns in sermons occasioned by the church's festival observances of Christ's Incarnation: Christmas and Easter.

39. Ibid., 8.229.

40. Ibid., 8.231.

41. Ibid., 6.62. Precisely to my point is the observation of Brian Cummings, in *The Literary Culture of the Reformation*, that literalness is finally a function of language, and "depends upon a process inevitably interpretative, properly speaking 'literary'"; thus, what is literal insists upon its own reified textuality. As Cummings succinctly distills his argument, "What is literal is made up of letters, of words" (5).

42. Donne, *Sermons of John Donne*, 6.63.

43. For Ryan Netzley, this disorientation and disordering of perception provokes readerly anxiety. Netzley argues that cultivating a disposition of godly fear—fear as a devotional state, and as an end in itself—is Donne's proposition. Netzley goes on to suggest that one strategy by which Donne produces interpretive anxiety is through the indeterminacy of his grammar and syntax, which directs readerly attention not to what Netzley calls the "communicated payload" of the poem but rather to the "relations" between words (*Reading, Desire, and the Eucharist in Early Modern Religious Poetry*, 143). While Netzley's primary concern is with reading strategies and mine is with poetic strategies, we share an interest in the displacement of semantic content by discursive surfaces.

44. Claude J. Summers, "The Bride of the Apocalypse and the Quest for True Religion: Donne, Herbert, and Spenser," 77. The Book of Revelation's most familiar depictions of the Bride can be found at 19.7–8 and 21.9–11.

45. Much of the critical discussion about this sonnet echoes the sentiment of Frank Kermode: "Perhaps we dislike this metaphor because the image of the Church as the Bride is no longer absolutely commonplace; but having accepted the image we are still unwilling to accept its development, even though we see that the main point is the *glorious* difference of this from a merely human marriage" (*John Donne*, 39). Kerrigan's article teases out Kermode's opinion, and cites the poem as an example of what he calls "dangerous anthropomorphism" ("Fearful Accommodations of John Donne," 351). Summers asserts that the sonnet's conclusion is ludicrous precisely so that "attempts to identify the competing Churches with Christ's spouse are similarly revealed as ludicrous." Summers continues, "The daring and moving conclusion to the sonnet beautifully expresses Donne's sincere desire for communion with Christ's spouse the Church, but the extended sexual conceit simultaneously exposes the poet's recognition of the preposterous irony involved in any quest for true religion that identifies Christ's spouse with a temporal institution" ("Bride of the Apocalypse and the Quest for True Religion," 79, 81).

46. Isaiah 62.5, 54.5; 2 Corinthians 11.2. For other biblical passages that employ marital imagery to adumbrate the relationship between the divine and the human, see Isaiah 61.10, Jeremiah 31.32, James 4.4, and the first three chapters of Hosea.

47. Kerrigan, "Fearful Accommodations of John Donne," 359.

48. Donne, "Satire 3," line 43, from *The Poems of John Donne*, edited by Herbert Grierson.

49. For Young, that unifying principle is the desire for grace; see *Doctrine and Devotion*, 17. Targoff argues that metaphor subsides to metaphor to enact "personal regeneration," thus countering Donne's fear of dissolution (*John Donne, Body and Soul*, 123). For a generous survey of the abundant commentary on this poem's metaphors, see the *Variorum Edition of the Poetry of John Donne*, volume 7.1, 221–261.

50. Richard Strier considers how this difference between "weake" or "untrue" reason redounds to the confessional sympathies of this poem in "John Donne Awry and Squint: The 'Holy Sonnets,' 1608–1610," 376.

51. Richard Rambuss describes this poem as pleading for "a trinitarian gang-bang" (*Closet Devotions*, 50), and Stanley Fish is only too happy to inform us that Donne's supplicant "spreads his legs (or cheeks)" in a show of holy sadomasochism ("Masculine Persuasive Force: Donne and Verbal Power," 242).

52. Kerrigan, "Fearful Accommodations of John Donne," 353, 354.

53. Targoff, *John Donne, Body and Soul*, 123.

54. Donne, *Sermons of John Donne*, 7.295.

55. Ibid., 7.320.

56. James Baumlin defines an "incarnational rhetoric" as a "linguistic theology" in which the word makes *the thing it represents* truly present (*John Donne and the Rhetorics of Renaissance Discourse*, 17).

57. DiPasquale, *Literature & Sacrament*, 39–40.

58. Ibid., 40.

59. Ibid., 44–46. In her attempt to answer this problem, DiPasquale turns from her excellent demonstration of the way the poem facilitates textual encounters with the cross to an argument that seemingly undercuts her own insights when she suggests that Donne's poem renders indifferent its artifactual status by emphasizing its "sermon-like qualities," appealing not to its own materiality as a site of meaningfulness but to its moral (46).

60. Donne, *Sermons of John Donne*, 8.220, emphasis in original.

61. Though he resists the notion that Reformed sacramental theologies were invested in communicating presence, Young's *Doctrine and Devotion* offers perhaps the most sustained critique of the applicability of Derridean notions of *différance* to a sacramentally inflected poetics.

62. Donne, *Sermons of John Donne*, 8.75.

63. Ibid., 5.320, 5.326–327.

64. Ibid., 327.

65. Donne, "A Valediction: forbidding Mourning," lines 25–26. I rely on Helen Gardner's edition of *The Elegies and the Songs and Sonnets*.

66. M. Thomas Hester quotes contemporary Protestant disputants to claim that the poem's language bears "the hallmark of Popery," and argues that the poem's lover "pleads that his 'divine' lady rely on the Catholic Mass instead of the 'mere signs' of the Protestant Supper as a model for their love, to reject analogically the 'glass and lines' of Protestantism's symbolic reading of the Feast in favor of the transubstantiation of Real Presence which the Catholic reading affirms" (" 'this cannot be said': A Preface to the Reader of Donne's Lyrics," 375). For her part, DiPasquale considers the poem "a parody of the Catholic Mass," calculated to debunk the Roman doctrine of Real Presence as idolatry *(Literature & Sacrament*, 202).

67. Baumlin, *John Donne and the Rhetorics of Renaissance Discourse*, 183–84.

68. Elaine Scarry considers how this attentiveness to the window's surface makes union possible in the glassy reflection, noting the intersection of bodily images and nouns. See her essay "Donne: But yet the body is his booke," in *Literature and the Body: Essays on Populations and Persons*, 80–84.

69. For Hester's excellent discussion of "The Flea," see " 'this cannot be said': A Preface to the Reader of Donne's Lyrics," 377–82.

70. DiPasquale devotes a chapter of *Literature & Sacrament* to her argument that in "The Flea" Donne makes use of sacramentally charged language in order to accomplish his erotic ends, which conclusion seems to ignore the larger theological and representational import of the poem's eucharistic program, ultimately making the poem, for all DiPasquale's sensitivity to the sacramental echoes of its language, merely a clever courtly seduction poem. See chapter 6 of that book, " 'The Flea' as Profane Eucharist," 173–86.

71. Hester, " 'this cannot be said,' " 379.

72. Donne's grammatical ambiguities, argues Netzley, "drive readers to a focus not on what the poem means, but the syntactical, structural, grammatical, even possessive relations that obtain within it" (*Reading, Desire, and the Eucharist in Early Modern Religious Poetry*, 143), cultivating in Netzley's view a nonteleological mode of reading—that is, reading not for the aim of content but for the sake of reading, which transforms reading into an act of devotion, of love.

73. Baumlin articulates this position when he writes that "the lady's moral dilemma becomes an interpretive problematic for the reader as well, who, like the lady, must ask whether he or she will *allow* such a word as 'honor' to be so disabled or dislocated from its conventional meaning (*John Donne and the Rhetorics of Renaissance Discourse*, 254).

74. The poem's investment in the indissoluble substantiality of signs is reinforced by its orthographic puns on the elongated Elizabethan *s* of line 3's "suck": "It suck'd me first, and now sucks thee." As Hester observes, this material substitution "inscribes the English sign for sexual intercourse in the body of the text" (" 'this cannot be said,' " 379). What Hester doesn't say is that Donne's pun transfers semantics to the

material sign, as "fuck" specifies the action that Donne's flea metaphor veils. The poem's sexual agenda, like its representational agenda, is worn on its poetic surface. For a related discussion of similar orthographic puns in the work of Richard Crashaw, see my next chapter.

75. Donne, Expostulation 19, from *Devotions upon Emergent Occasions*, 99.

76. For Thomas Aquinas's influential discussion of the relationship between the *verba* of the sacramental sign and the *res* of its substance, a discussion to which sacramental theologians on all sides were compelled to respond, see *Summa Theologiae* 3a.60.6–7.

77. Donne, Expostulation 19, from *Devotions upon Emergent Occasions*, 100.

78. Donne, *Sermons of John Donne*, 7.296.

Chapter 4. Richard Crashaw's Indigestible Poetics

Note to epigraph: All quotations from Richard Crashaw's poetry refer to *The Complete Poetry of Richard Crashaw*, edited by George Walton Williams.

1. Williams's comments appear in his edition of *The Complete Poetry of Richard Crashaw*, 14.

2. Williams refers to Robert Adams, "Taste and Bad Taste in Metaphysical Poetry: Richard Crashaw and Dylan Thomas," 69, and William Empson, *Seven Types of Ambiguity*, 221. Williams's objections to this latter text seem not to recognize the compliment Empson pays Crashaw by identifying his epigram as an example of the seventh, and most verbally and psychologically complex, type of ambiguity—an ambiguity activated in this case in order "to show the unearthly relation to earth of the Christ, and with a sort of horror to excite adoration." Earlier in the paragraph from which Williams takes the offending quotation, Empson muses that the ambiguity of Crashaw's verse arises in part because "the ideas involved are so unfamiliar" and "are used in his judgments with such complexity" (221).

3. In Crashaw, *Complete Poetry of Richard Crashaw*, 14. Some critics have followed Williams's lead in attempting to spiritualize Crashaw's imagery, chastening us away from scurrilous readings by asserting the theological orthodoxy of Crashaw's epigram. See Eugene R. Cunnar, "Opening the Religious Lyric: Crashaw's Ritual, Liminal, and Visual Wounds": "Read against the theology of the wounds and the profound gender reversal that most likely came about from the liminal experience, this poem simply merges oretic and normative ritual imagery in order to emphasize the salvific effect of the Eucharist. Moreover, the mother in Luke 11 becomes a positive and parallel image of the nourishing Christ" (260). Maureen Sabine's *Feminine Engendered Faith* likewise affirms the safe and unshocking religiosity of Crashaw's eucharistic program, identifying in the epigram's final couplet "allusions to the communion in which Christ as proto-Mother continually nurses his children" (186).

4. R. V. Young, *Doctrine and Devotion in Seventeenth-Century Poetry*, 156.

5. The principle of physical intimacy with the divine gives rise to a number of exegetical reflections on the Eucharist that express sacramental contact in explicitly

erotic terms. In *The Doctrine of the Real Presence, as Contained in the Fathers, Vindicated, In Notes on a Sermon, "The Presence of Christ in the Holy Eucharist,"* Edward Bouverie Pusey accumulates a massive compendium of erotic descriptions of the Eucharist from the patristic period. See pages 315–715 of that volume.

6. For familiarity's sake, I will use the translations by Phyllis S. Bowman from Williams's edition of *The Complete Poetry of Richard Crashaw*, which, while occasionally awkward, communicate the literal meaning of the Latin.

7. Though these words are elided into "&c" in many sixteenth-and seventeenth-century printings of the *Missale Romanum*, they are spoken during the section of the Mass set down in "De Canone Missae usque ad Consecrationem," from the "Ritus Servandus in Celebratione Missae."

8. Caroline Walker Bynum's influential work surveys the feminine imagery associated with Jesus in *Jesus as Mother*, and pays particular attention to Christ's pierced breast as a source of nourishment (see pp. 115–125), a topic she returns to with a more intensive focus in the third chapter of her *Fragmentation and Redemption*.

9. Thomas Healy, *Richard Crashaw*, 64.

10. Crashaw, of course, is well aware of the distinction between language that reifies the body's corporeality and language that renders the body symbolic; his poetry contains more than forty instances of the word *breast* and its forms, of which almost none refer specifically to the organs of lactation. Instead, almost invariably, he uses *breast* to denote the abstract principle of passion, or the heart as a seat of affection, as in the "Hymne to Sainte Teresa": "Her weake brest heaves with strong desire" (40). By contrast, Crashaw uses "Teat" (and "Teates") only in "Blessed be the paps."

11. Healy, *Richard Crashaw*, 64.

12. Ibid., 139–40. Healy quotes from John Cosin's treatise *The history of Popish transubstantiation . . .* (pp. 110–11). Laudian though he may be, Cosin's description of eucharistic participation as feeding with the heart clearly echoes Cranmer: "as we see with our eyes and eat with our mouths very bread, and see also and drink very wine, so we lift up our hearts unto heaven, and with our faith we see Christ crucified with our spiritual eyes, and eat his flesh thrust through with a spear, and drink his blood springing out of his side with our spiritual mouths of our faith"; and again, "Faithful Christian people, such as be Christ's true disciples, continually from time to time record in their minds the beneficial death of our Saviour Christ, chawing it by faith in the cud of their spirit, and digesting it in their hearts, feeding and comforting themselves with that heavenly meat" (Cranmer, *The answer of Thomas Archbishop of Canterbury &c. against the false calumniations of Dr. Richard Smyth*, in *The Remains of Thomas Cranmer*, 2.318, 3.130).

13. Healy, *Richard Crashaw*, 140.

14. Gary Kuchar, *Divine Subjection: The Rhetoric of Sacramental Devotion in Early Modern England*, 105.

15. As Richard Rambuss has observed, the conjunction of images and actions in the epigram's last line is both discomfiting and disorienting, presenting a body that is

determinedly physical even as its physicality becomes transgressively indeterminate: Jesus "bears a wound—one somehow concave and convex at once—that also functions as a protrusion; he is endowed with a 'Teat' that is both mammary and phallic" (*Closet Devotions*, 38). Rambuss's sense of the physical confusion of the image is ultimately indebted to the remark of Empson's that provoked Williams to defend Crashaw: "a wide variety of sexual perversions can be included in the notion of sucking a long bloody teat which is also a deep wound" (*Seven Types of Ambiguity*, 221).

16. Here as elsewhere throughout this book, I rely on the Latin text and English translation in the Blackfriars edition of *Summa Theologiae*, 3a.75.5. All references will indicate part, question, and article numbers.

17. For biblical figures that link the crucifixion with the winepress and Jesus's blood with wine, see Isaiah 63.3: "I haue troden the winepresse alone," and John 15.1–7, which includes and elaborates on the famous "I am the true vine" parable.

18. Rambuss, *Closet Devotions*, 34.

19. Ibid., 7. Rambuss continues his exploration of Crashaw's habit of "converting operations of the soul into spectacles of the body" as a response to the mysteries of the Incarnation in "Sacred Subjects and the Aversive Metaphysical Conceit: Crashaw, Serrano, Ofili," especially pages 501–507. In many ways, Rambuss's examinations of "aversive" conceits in contemporary visual art are indebted to Leo Steinberg's seminal study *The Sexuality of Christ in Renaissance Art and in Modern Oblivion*.

20. Historically speaking, this dogma was slow to be institutionally canonized. In addition to writing an excellent monograph on developing formulations of eucharistic worship through the medieval period, *The Theologies of the Eucharist in the Early Scholastic Period*, Gary Macy has more recently coedited a useful collection of essays that outline the overlapping and competing forces that helped shape what would become institutional eucharistic theology. See *A Companion to the Eucharist in the Middle Ages*, edited by Ian Christopher Levy, Macy, and Kristen Van Ausdall.

21. Miri Rubin suggests that Thomas Aquinas did not write the hymn that has been for so long attributed to him. See *Corpus Christi* (156 n. 437), where Rubin points to arguments found in André Wilmart's *Auteurs spirituels et textes dévots du moyen-âge latin: études d'histoire littéraire* and in music historian Joseph Szöffervy's *Die Annalen der lateinischen Hymnendichtung* to support this historical revision. Despite these perspectives, the present study will refer to the hymn's authorship as Crashaw believed it to be.

22. Critical assertions of Crashaw's baroque sensibility trace their genealogy to Mario Praz's *The Flaming Heart*. Paul Parrish wishes to disentangle such baroque ecstasies from Crashaw's conversion to Catholicism but determines nevertheless that "The God celebrated in [Crashaw's] hymns is a Baroque God who is approached through the fullest realization of the senses" (*Richard Crashaw*, 119–20).

23. I refer to the text of the Latin hymn as printed in the Williams edition of Crashaw's poems. Throughout this chapter, the passages translated directly from the "Adoro Te Devote" that are not identified as Crashaw's work are my own.

24. In his essay "Oral Devotion: Eucharistic Theology and Richard Crashaw's Religious Lyrics," Ryan Netzley explores what he sees as Crashaw's habit of diffusing the physical mouth into nonlocalizable and abstract sites of contact with the divine, arguing that the poet employs this strategy in an attempt to redeem the mouth from its taint of sacramental cannibalism. He concludes that the phrase "vitall gust" in Crashaw's translation shifts "the locus of eucharistic eating away from the corporeal mouth and the teeth" and "defangs Protestant polemic built around the grotesquerie and crudeness of the bodily mouth and teeth" (254). But as we have seen, and especially as it departs from its Latin source, Crashaw's use of "gust" posits a particularly oral form of tasting, and stands in contrast to the truly diffused orality of Aquinas's original. Netzley refines this argument in his book *Reading, Desire, and the Eucharist*, positing that "Crashaw returns to 'gust' after the condemnation of 'gustus' in the Latin hymn so as to erase the distinction between spiritual and sensual domains on which the *sapere-gustare* separation is founded" (234 n. 41), which corresponds more nearly to my own contention that Crashaw locates meaningfulness in the material.

25. For an overview of this poem's progression through sensory emphases as a movement from longing to consummation, see Parrish, *Richard Crashaw*, 134–36. For a detailed outline of the ways in which this sensory division maps onto the distinct phases of Ignatian meditation, see Louis Martz, *The Poetry of Meditation*, 331–52.

26. Remembering Crashaw's own poetic treatment of the circumcision, in which the flesh remains transgressively, stubbornly extra-ritual, it is intriguing to note that this hymn was likely composed for the Feast of the Holy Name, which commemorates the circumcision and naming of the infant Jesus (see Parrish, *Richard Crashaw*, 133).

27. Crashaw's friend Thomas Car, who saw the 1652 volume into posthumous print, mentions "the pictures in the following Poemes which the Authour first made with his owne hand," a grammatically ambiguous declaration that leaves open the possibility that Crashaw was himself the artist of all twelve emblems in his book (Car's comments are reported in L. C. Martin's edition of *The Poems English, Latin and Greek of Richard Crashaw*, xlvii). This seems not to have been the case; there are stylistic variances across the engravings, and some of the etchings appear to be marked with their respective artist's initials. Still, a couple of the book's images may well have been drawn by Crashaw himself, and the ciborium emblem is among those that bear no artist's marks or initials.

28. From the section "De Canone Missae usque ad Consecrationem" of "Ritus Servandus in Celebratione Missae," in the *Missale Romanum, ex Decreto Sacrosancti Concilii Tridentini*.

29. Rambuss, *Closet Devotions*, 2.

30. Steinberg describes the Incarnation as God's "condescension to kinship" (*Sexuality of Christ*, 47), and Bynum identifies the "intensely physical" devotions of the mystics she studies as a corporeal attempt at *imitatio Christi*: "And because the pain of God's bodiliness is the instrument of salvation, imitation of that God is through

the wounds, laughter, tears, suffocation, and hunger" experienced by the body (*Holy Feast and Holy Fast*, 165).

31. Rambuss, *Closet Devotions*, 34.

32. For a sampling of critics who find in Crashaw's work what Rambuss calls "a seriously sensationalist body of poetry" ("Sacred Subjects," 507), see Joan Bennett, who notes that "Crashaw loves to elaborate sensations" (*Five Metaphysical Poets: Donne, Herbert, Vaughan, Crashaw, Marvell*, 94); James M. Bromley, who declares that "Crashaw's devotional subject welcomes the corporeal" ("Intimacy and the Body in Seventeenth-Century Religious Devotion," par. 1); and Ernest Gilman, who says that Crashaw "is not only content but often deliriously happy to dissolve himself" in his elaborate corporeal figures (*Iconoclasm and Poetry in the English Reformation: Down Went Dagon*, 148). Kuchar follows Healy in arguing that Crashaw's work reflects a Laudian program of "spiritualizing the physical," yet remarks that Crashaw's verse "openly revels" in carnality (*Divine Subjection*, 107). Each of these assessments resorts to an almost romantic idiom to describe Crashaw's praxis, as if the luxuriance of physical details in his poetry could only signal the poet's undiluted affection for the body.

33. It has become something of a ritual in Crashavian criticism to nod to Adams's complaint about Crashaw's "bad taste" ("Taste and Bad Taste," 66), as well as to Ruth Wallerstein's no less florid admission that the poet's work "comprehends passages of the worst taste, not merely in rhetoric but in spirit, perhaps to be found in the whole range of English poetry" (*Richard Crashaw: A Study in Style and Poetic Development*, 112). Often, this practice allows the critic either to smirk about such callow and undiscerning dismissals of Crashaw's misunderstood greatness or to displace onto the seeming remove of a bold earlier reader one's own qualms about Crashaw's style. But it is worth acknowledging here that Adams's argument is that Crashaw's difficult imagery functions to represent the incongruity between the limited perceptual capacities of the mortal flesh and the absurdly unfamiliar and inhuman logic of divinity: "One laughs at the images, but one squirms under them too; and this effect can, if Crashaw's art is art and not accident, be taken as meaningful" (69). Adams's conclusion is finally not too far afield from my own argument about Crashaw's deliberately disruptive deployment of the liturgical symbolary.

34. Adams, "Taste and Bad Taste," 68.

35. Stephen Greenblatt is sensitive to the problem of "the remainder" in eucharistic theology, though his use of the term refers more to the digestive implications of the transubstantial rite (see "The Mousetrap," the fifth chapter of *Practicing New Historicism*, edited by Catherine Gallagher and Greenblatt, 141–51). My own use of the term aligns more with the concerns of James Kearney, whose book *The Incarnate Text: Imagining the Book in Reformation England* extends Reformation-era admonitions about the propensity of material representations to inspire dangerous veneration

and idolatry of literary texts themselves, the printed book made suspect as an alluring object whose power must be abjured; see especially Kearney's fourth chapter, on the uneasy fetishizing of Prospero's books.

36. As I indicated in my discussion of Donne, M. Thomas Hester treats the effects of this same orthographic feature in "The Flea." His purpose is to note that the elongated Elizabethan *s* presents the reader with a hermeneutic choice about how to read the poem's signs, and to suggest that this decision corresponds to the hermeneutic conundrum of distinguishing between competing doctrinal designations of the Eucharist as a metonymy or a literal event ("'this cannot be said,'" 379). My point here is to seize upon a remark Hester makes in passing, which is that this visual pun "inscribes" the significance of its signs "on the body of the text"—or, in the terms of the present study, it refocuses interpretation onto the discursive surface, the medium overtaking the content, the sign made opaquely substantial.

37. For his part, Crashaw seems to have considered himself aligned with Herbert's poetic project in *The Temple*; the later poet announced his sense of his close aesthetic affiliation with Herbert's work in the title of his collection of devotional poetry, *Steps to the Temple*.

38. Hebrews 11.1.

39. Brian Cummings acknowledges that literariness emphasizes the word as a self-perpetuating and self-actualizing artifact, and explicitly connects the increasingly consequential textuality of the literary in the early modern period to its material dissemination in books. See his discussion of Luther as "a bibliolater, a textual fetishist" in *The Literary Culture of the Reformation: Grammar and Grace*, 28–47. For an extended examination of poetry's corporeal valences, see Susan Stewart, *Poetry and the Fate of the Senses*; see also "Music," the fifth chapter of Robert Von Hallberg's *Lyric Powers*.

40. Regina Schwartz, *Sacramental Poetics at the Dawn of Secularism: When God Left the World*, 6–7, and Judith H. Anderson, *Translating Investments: Metaphor and the Dynamic of Cultural Change in Tudor-Stuart England*, 75; it is difficult to understand how the semiotics Schwartz describes as "sacramental" differs from standard-issue, nonsacramental Derridian semiotics. See also James Baumlin, who links sacramental theology with a "Poetics of Absence" (see especially chapter 5 of *John Donne and the Rhetorics of Renaissance Discourse*, 159).

Chapter 5. Immanent Textualities in a Postsacramental World

1. George Puttenham, *The Arte of English Poesie*, 1.10; George Gascoigne, *The Posies of George Gascoigne Esquire*, 291r–295v. Though George Chapman defends interpretive complexity, denying "that Poesy should be as peruiall as Oratorie" and stating that poets "must lymn" their expression to make it artful, he yet reaffirms the importance of decorum as he inveighs against "Obscuritie in affection of words, & indigested concets" as "pedanticall and childish," not "utterd with fitnes" to its content (from the dedicatory epistle "To the Truly Learned, and my worthy Friende, Ma.

Mathew Royden," in *Ovids Banquet of Sence: A Coronet for his Mistresse Philosophie, and his amorous Zodiacke*, A2r). For the argument that such regulation of style was understood as necessary to distinguish English verse from the extravagances of foreign influence, and was thus a nationalist project, see Wayne A. Rebhorn, "Outlandish Fears: Defining Decorum in Renaissance Rhetoric."

2. Thomas Wilson, *The Arte of Rhetorique*, 14.

3. Horace offers his now proverbial perspective in the *Ars Poetica*, lines 343–44: "omne tulit punctum qui miscuit utile dulci / lectorem delectando pariterque monendo" [He has won every point who mingles profit and pleasure, / delighting and instructing the reader all at once].

4. Norman K. Farmer, Jr., draws parallels between what he describes as Herrick's painterly interest in detail and the ancient principle of *ut pictura poesis* as expressed in the era's fashion for emblems, hieroglyphics, icons, and *imprese*, and notes in suggestive passing the effect of Herrick's descriptive minutiae is that "something seemingly so insubstantial in our actual experience takes on the permanence of substance" ("Herrick's Herperidean Garden: *ut pictura poesis* Applied," 45). L. E. Semler compares Herrick to a painterly "limner" ("Robert Herrick, the Human Figure, and the English Mannerist Aesthetic," 108); Alastair Fowler characterizes Herrick's enchantment with particularities as "microphilia" ("Robert Herrick," 245); and Ann Baynes Coiro draws attention to Herrick's enduring interest in the quirks of the body's surfaces as she explores his treatment of physical deformity: "Herrick is fascinated almost exclusively with physical grotesqueries" (*Robert Herrick's "Hesperides" and the Epigram Book Tradition*, 156).

5. The era of the New Critics was particularly and influentially unsympathetic to Herrick's ornamental style. F. R. Leavis disparages "the very triviality of Herrick's talent" (*Revaluation*, 36). Cleanth Brooks and Robert Penn Warren explain in a pedagogical anthology that Herrick's work is "rather simple," especially compared to the profundity of Donne's poetry (*Understanding Poetry: An Anthology for College Students*, 250). Douglas Bush's 1945 survey of seventeenth-century literature goes some way toward explaining how these dismissals relate to the opulence of Herrick's discursive surfaces, suggesting that Herrick's poetry might have been "underestimated because its smooth surface is deceptive; we suspect lack of stress and depth" (*English Literature in the Early Seventeenth Century, 1600–1660*, 118). One index of how widespread has been the opinion that Herrick's poems are all surface with little depth is that the introductory essay of a 1978 volume on Herrick (still the only scholarly collection devoted to Herrick alone) opens by protesting against such a view: "many of these poems exhibit patterns of intellectual significance and emotional depth beneath their polished and seemingly simple surfaces" (Roger B. Rollin, "Sweet Numbers and Sour Readers: Trends and Perspectives in Herrick Criticism," 3).

6. Robert Herrick, "The Argument of His Book," line 7. Quotations from Herrick's poetry reference L. C. Martin's edition of his *Poetical Works*.

7. Herrick, "To the most illvstriovs, and Most Hopefull Prince, CHARLES, Prince of *Wales*," 10.

8. Herrick, "*To* Julia, *the* Flaminica Dialis, *or* Queen-Priest," 3; "Julia's *Petticoat*," 1; "*Upon* Julia's *unlacing her self*," 6.

9. Herrick, "*Upon* Julia's *Riband*," 3–4.

10. Herrick, "*On* Julia's *breath*," 3–4.

11. Herrick, "*Upon* Julia's *breasts*," 2.

12. Herrick includes his marginal note for line 3 of "*To* Julia, *the* Flaminica Dialis, *or* Queen-Priest" in the text of *Hesperides*.

13. Herrick, "*Upon* Julia's *Clothes*," 3. In his essay "'Upon Julia's Clothes': Herrick, Ovid, and the Celebration of Innocence," John Roe recognizes that Herrick's depiction of Julia's clothes in these terms "appears to aim at something other than translucency" (351). Roe's larger point is that Herrick's poem avoids scurrilous voyeurism and maintains its innocence by abstracting Julia's form into a disembodied phenomenon, whereas I argue that Julia's form ceases to matter, in either sense of that term, as Herrick's opaque surfaces become themselves objects of attention and desire.

14. Herrick, "*The Apparition of his Mistresse calling him to* Elizium," 57.

15. Ben Jonson, *The Workes of Beniamin Jonson*, 767; all citations of Jonson's epigrams will refer to the 1616 edition.

16. Jonson, "To William Earle of Pembroke," 1–2.

17. The term is defined in Claude-François Menestrier's 1682 treatise *La Philosophie des Images*, quoted in Judi Loach, "Body and Soul: A Transfer of Theological Terminology into the Aesthetic Realm," 36. Loach's study situates early modern philosophies of the aesthetic within the context of the Counter-Reformation, and notes that emblem theory derives its provocatively theological lexicon from Thomas Aquinas, in which "essence" is distinct from "accident," the material image is a "body," and the immaterial signified is a "soul"—though these distinctions blur as the emblematic "body" increasingly comes to encompass both parts of the text, and as the material demands interpretive attention as such.

18. Jonson, "On Lucy, Countesse of Bedford," lines 3–4, 6, 12–13, 17–18.

19. Jonson, "To Lucy Countess of Bedford, with Master Donne's Satires," 1–2.

20. For the view that Jonson's naming reflects a general fixation on the uncertain relationship between the *res* and its *verbum* that is ultimately indebted (as the terminology indicates) to Augustine's own sacramentally inflected grapplings with signification, see the third chapter of Martin Elsky, *Authorizing Words: Speech, Writing, and Print in the English Renaissance*.

21. Linda Gregerson, "Ben Jonson and the Loathèd Word," 88–89; Gregerson's essay begins by describing Jonson's lyric project as staging the word itself as, among other things, "a hedge against transience" and "the ground of self-sufficiency" (86).

22. Sara van den Berg notes that "Missing from the allegorical sculptures on the frontispiece is poetry," and suggests that, rather than in the iconography of the monument, poetry is represented here as inhering in "the fourth theater, the printed page,"

which transforms the ephemera of the stage into a durable material artifact ("Ben Jonson and the Ideology of Authorship," 115–16).

23. On the relationship between the lyric and the emblem tradition, see Barbara K. Lewalski, "Emblems and the Religious Lyric: George Herbert and Protestant Emblematics," and Kristen L. Olson, "Picture-Pattern-Poiesis: Visuality, the Emblem, and Seventeenth-Century English Religious Lyric." For the argument that emblems and hieroglyphs fulfill a presencing function that counters their allegorical content, see Bradley J. Nelson, *The Persistence of Presence: Emblem and Ritual in Baroque Spain*: "In the emblem's transduction of the world of bodies into the world of souls, images into meaning, we recognize that signs themselves exhibit an analogous otherness with respect to meaning due to a material presence and incorrigibility that simultaneously exceeds and contributes to the mystification of knowledge whose reality comes about through a ritual process of selection, assemblage, and framing" (236). Seizing, as Nelson does, upon the symbolic similarities between emblems and masques, Stephen Orgel has rightly identified Jonson's investment in the pre-semantic communicative properties of Jonson's court dramas as a "poetics of spectacle," in which meaning inheres in the sign, and though Orgel argues in the essay of that title that the hieroglyphic features of both emblems and masques served to "conceptualize abstractions"—that is, that spectacle "is properly the *expression* of the meaning, the body of the work as the poetry is the soul" ("The Poetics of Spectacle," 371–72)—the implications of his work suggest that in the poetics of spectacle, figures intended to represent abstractions increasingly assert themselves as surfaces that demand to be looked at themselves, a point that Nathaniel Strout develops in "Jonson's Jacobean Masques and the Moral Imagination" (see especially 235).

24. James L. Calderwood, "*Love's Labour's Lost*: A Wantoning with Words," 317–18. Calderwood continues, "In perhaps no other play does language so nearly becomes an autonomous symbolic system whose value, somewhat like that of pure mathematics, lies less in its relevance to reality than in its intrinsic fascination"—that is, in the seductions of the sign as such. Gillian Woods glancingly connects the significative slippage and fracture in *Love's Labour's Lost* to the triangulation of "aesthetic, semantic, and theological value" in the Reformation era ("Catholicism and Conversion in *Love's Labour's Lost*," 112), a connection addressed rather more forcefully by Keir Elam, in *Shakespeare's Universe of Discourse: Language-Games in the Comedies*. Elam reflects that such semiotic ingenuities distributed, as he demonstrates, across Shakespeare's theatrical work are perhaps inevitable given "the degree to which the mystical reification of the sign had become familiar, or even codified" in post-Reformation discourse (129). Keir's analysis of signs in Shakespeare is shot through with terminology familiar from sacramental exegesis, leading tellingly to his theologically freighted declaration that "there is no doubt that one of the principal verbal activities of *LLL* is that of the hypostasization (whether knowing or guileless) of the word" (120).

25. William Shakespeare, *Love's Labour's Lost* 1.1.285–286. I refer to the text as printed in *The Riverside Shakespeare*.

26. In his essay "George Herbert's Pattern Poems and the Materiality of Language: A New Approach to Renaissance Hieroglyphics," Elsky explores the continuities between the twinned Renaissance fascinations with hieroglyphs and orthographics, and begins to consider how the attribution of significance to the material text corresponds to the search for stable material means of expressing spiritual mysteries. Joshua Calhoun explores the relationship between the inexpensive medium of the printed paper Bible and early modern anxieties about the transmission of doctrine. Calhoun investigates controversies about how material media might express—or, more concerningly, corrupt in the process of expressing—divine principles, noting that one complication to the idea that materiality stabilized presence arises from its very matter: "Texts tend toward corruption, and that corruption is due not only to human error but also to material conditions. Paper is easily ripped, burned, and soaked. Bookworms are no respecters of crucial words, and knots of organic matter in the mage can interrupt typography" ("The Word Made Flax: Cheap Bibles, Textual Corruption, and the Poetics of Paper," 331). And it is Francis Bacon's unease with the material opacity of words that provokes him (and the Royal Society) into experiments with invented language, a form of communication that might express content transparently without the "intervention of words"; see Margreta de Grazia, "Words as Things," in which she quotes this passage from the *Works of Francis Bacon* on pages 231–32.

27. James Kearney, *The Incarnate Text: Imagining the Book in Reformation England*, 22.

28. Ibid., 53. While both de Grazia and Calhoun more directly address the cultural and theological anxieties produced by the materiality of texts, Kearney focuses rather on how these anxieties redound to the literary portrayal of texts as having materially consequential force arising from their substantial presence.

29. Kearney, *Incarnate Text*, 171, 135.

30. Allen Grossman, *Summa Lyrica*, 6.2, republished in *The Sighted Singer: Two Works on Poetry for Readers and Writers*.

31. Mutlu Konuk Blasing, *Lyric Poetry*, 27, 119.

32. John Stuart Mill, "Thoughts on Poetry and Its Varieties," 95. Revisiting Mill in order to posit an alternative to the mimetic model of lyric expression, Virginia Jackson describes "Thoughts on Poetry and Its Varieties" as "the most influentially misread essay in the history of Anglo-American poetics" (9), and notes that Mill muddies his own formulation of poem as soliloquy when he attempts to account for the devices that mediate between poem and audience (*Dickinson's Misery: A Theory of Lyric Reading*, 129–33).

33. Jonathan Culler, "Why Lyric?" 202. Culler's essay appears as part of a special topics discussion on the lyric in the January 2008 issue of *PMLA*, which developed out of Marjorie Perloff and Craig Dworkin's 2006 MLA Presidential Forum on "The Sound of Poetry/The Poetry of Sound," calling for renewed scholarly attention to "Poetic language" as "language made strange, made somehow extraordinary by the use of verbal and sound repetition, visual configuration, and syntactic deformation"

(753; the text of Perloff and Dworkin's introductory remarks appears in the May 2008 issue of *PMLA*). In another essay in which he reflects on the New Criticism's retooling of the mimetic model, Culler notes that even "To think of lyrics as fictional representations of possible historical utterances makes it harder to explore them as ingenious artifacts" ("Changes in the Study of the Lyric," 41). For a discussion about the productive obstructions of what Donne calls "the poetry of the Sermon," as distinct from "the Sermon of the Sermon" (*The Sermons of John Donne*, 7.293), see Chapter 3.

34. Charles Bernstein, "Artifice of Absorption," in *A Poetics*, 29. For the assertion that the nonreferential features of a poem are in fact inseparable from its semantics, see Perloff and Dworkin, "The Sound of Poetry/The Poetry of Sound," 754. Critics whose work is helping to turn focus onto the self-substantiating and phenomenally constitutive qualia of poetics include Culler and Jackson, as well as Jennifer Ashton (*From Modernism to Postmodernism: American Poetry and Theory in the Twentieth Century*), Sharon Cameron (*Lyric Time*), and Christopher Nealon (*The Matter of Capital: Poetry and Crisis in the American Century*). In *How to Read a Poem*, Terry Eagleton argues against readings that "treat the poem as *language* but not as *discourse*"; the distinction that Eagleton intends here has to do precisely with the materializing valences of a poem's poetic features, for he says that awareness of a poem as discourse "means attending to language in all its material density, whereas most approaches to poetic language tend to disembody it" (2).

35. Northrop Frye, *Anatomy of Criticism*, 275, 280. Though Frye echoes Mill in describing lyric as "preeminently the utterance that is overheard" (275), his emphasis on *melos* and *opsis* reflects his resistance to any formulation that would imagine poetics as a mere extension of thematics: "Recurrently in the history of rhetoric some theory of a 'natural' relationship between sound and sense turns up. It is unlikely that there is any such natural relation" (262).

36. Charles Altieri, "What Theory Can Learn from New Directions in Contemporary American Poetry," 67. Altieri's argument is that the discursive surface offers a potential site for integrating aesthetic concerns and the construction of cultural identities, a position to which I am obviously sympathetic.

37. Perloff's major contributions on the subject of antiabsorptive poetics in the Modern and Postmodern age include *The Poetics of Indeterminacy: Rimbaud to Cage*, which argues that poetry after Modernism privileges surfaces over depth, and *Radical Artifice: Writing Poetry in the Age of Media*, which roots the development of a Postmodern poetics "Against Transparency" (as her third chapter is titled) in the interpretively obstructive innovations of Ezra Pound. The features that Perloff enumerates as central to the contemporary poetries she describes bear striking resemblance to the strategies I have been examining throughout *Made Flesh*: "To emphasize the Word as Such is, inevitably, to pay special attention to sound patterning, to phonemic play, punning, rhythmic recurrence, rhyme," Perloff writes, and while the subject of her sentence here is the late-twentieth-century school of L=A=N=G=U=A=G=E poetry, she could easily be describing the post-Reformation lyric (*The Dance of the*

Intellect: Studies in the Poetry of the Pound Tradition, 228). In *The New Sentence*, Ron Silliman seeks to account for the structural and poetic strategies of Postmodern unlineated verse; he argues that in these texts, sentences become structural components which, by refusing syllogistic integration, become objects in themselves, more akin to rhythmic devices than referential instruments. Significantly, he locates the germ of such structural foregrounding in the work of Gertrude Stein and, by extension, in the *fin de siècle* French poets that inspired her (see especially Silliman's essay "The New Sentence" in the volume of the same title).

38. Roland Barthes, *Writing Degree Zero*, 45–47. Barthes's language announces in striking echo its continuities with the discourse surrounding sacramental representation, an association he emphasizes when he describes the transparency of "classical language" as reducing signs to "accidents of form and disposition" (45) and complains that this symbolic redundancy prevents the "inner reality" of a sign from being "consubstantial to its outer configuration" (44).

39. Heather Dubrow, *The Challenges of Orpheus: Lyric Poetry and Early Modern England*, 128.

40. "Early modern antecedents to characteristics frequently and sometimes exclusively associated with the experimental writing of our own age, such as an emphasis on the visual appearance of the poem, could help us better understand the poetry of both periods" (Dubrow, *Challenges of Orpheus*, 237).

41. Dubrow's most sustained engagement with the mediating effects of poetics occurs in the third chapter of *The Challenges of Orpheus*, "The Craft of Pygmalion: Immediacy and Distancing" (106–55).

42. See Stephen Booth, *Shakespeare's Sonnets* and "Poetic Richness: A Preliminary Audit," among others; Richard Strier, *Resistant Structures: Particularity, Radicalism, and Renaissance Texts*, among others; Debora Shuger's *Sacred Rhetoric: The Christian Grand Style in the English Renaissance* and *Habits of Thought in the English Renaissance: Religion, Politics, and the Dominant Culture*, among others; Heather Asals, *Equivocal Predication* and "Crashaw's Participles and the 'Chiaroscuro' of Ontological Language," among others; Brian Cummings, *Literary Culture of the Reformation*; Jeff Dolven, "Reading Wyatt for the Style"; Ryan Netzley, *Reading, Desire, and the Eucharist*; Rayna Kalas, *Frame, Glass, Verse: The Technology of Poetic Invention in the English Renaissance*; and Dubrow, *A Happier Eden: The Politics of Marriage in the Stuart Epithalamium*, where she introduces the designation "new formalism" on page 269.

43. However, as Strier and Dubrow each note, William Empson, long regarded as one of the preeminent figures of the New Criticism (whose methods he derides as a "campaign to make poetry as dull as possible" [*Essays on Renaissance Literature: Volume 1, Donne and the New Philosophy*, 122]), provides an early model for a critical approach that synthesizes text and culture. Strier demonstrates Empson's method in the first essay of *Resistant Structures*, "Tradition"; see also Dubrow, *Challenges of Orpheus*, 239.

44. Stephen Greenblatt, *Renaissance Self-Fashioning: From More to Shakespeare*, 4–5. For a sprightly lamentation about the general infacility with poetics in contemporary criticism, see Simon Jarvis, "For a Poetics of Verse."

45. Again, as I indicated in my introductory chapter, Greenblatt himself recognizes the interinvolvement of early modern religio-political culture and concerns with the word's significative status; see Catherine Gallagher and Greenblatt, *Practicing New Historicism*, 141.

46. T. S. Eliot, *The Varieties of Metaphysical Poetry*, 54, 55. Dryden's comment that Donne "affects the metaphysics" appears in "A Discourse on the Original and Progress of Satire," 7.

47. Eliot, *Varieties of Metaphysical Poetry*, 120.

48. I recognize that I am skipping over two centuries' worth of poetry in connecting the antiabsorptive qualities of post-Reformation writing with Modernism's disruptions. I mean not to suggest that those intervening centuries offer no poetry relevant to these concerns, but rather to recognize that the Modern poets whose work critics most readily identify as innovating antiabsorptive tendencies themselves acknowledge a sympathetic aesthetic culture in the early modern period.

49. William Carlos Williams, "Excerpts from a Critical Sketch," in *Selected Essays*, 107. Williams's remarks concern the poems in Ezra Pound, *The Cantos of Ezra Pound*.

50. Gertrude Stein, *Tender Buttons*, 3. Stein herself reflects on the writing of *Tender Buttons* in *The Autobiography of Alice B. Toklas*, which she describes as a turn from an interest in "the insides of people" to "the visible world," from the representational function of language to its status as a reified medium: "It was a long, tormenting process, she looked, listened and described. She always was, she always is, tormented by the problem of the external and the internal. . . . The english language was her medium and with the english language the task was to be achieved, the problem solved. The use of fabricated words offended her, it was an escape into imitative emotionalism" (*The Selected Writings of Gertrude Stein*, 111–12).

51. Again, it is beyond the scope of the present study to trace the renegotiations of and responses to the indecorous poetics of the seventeenth century through all the years that follow. My point here is not to slight the eighteenth and nineteenth centuries, nor to suggest that such concerns are absent from the poetic tradition during that time, but to acknowledge that the main body of criticism on antiabsorptive poetic strategies focuses on Modernism and after. Interested readers who wish to pursue this topic into the centuries that intervene between the early modern and Modern periods should begin by consulting the work of Marshall Brown (*Preromanticism*), Margaret Anne Doody (*The Daring Muse: Augustan Poetry Reconsidered*), William Keach ("Rethinking Romantic Poetry and History: Lyric Resistance, Lyric Seduction"), Blanford Parker (*The Triumph of Augustan Poetics: English Literary Culture from Butler to Johnson*), Yopie Prins ("Historical Poetics, Dysprosody, and *The Science of English Verse*" and other works), and Susan Stewart (*Poetry and the Fate of the Senses*).

52. Archibald MacLeish, "Ars Poetica," 1–2, 23–24. MacLeish's poem appears in the collection *Streets in the Moon*.

53. Wallace Stevens, "An Ordinary Evening in New Haven," 73–74. Stevens's poem appears in *The Auroras of Autumn*.

54. James Schuyler, from "The Morning of the Poem," in *Collected Poems*, 268.

55. Horace, Ode 3.30, line 1, from *Odes and Epodes*.

Bibliography

Adams, Robert Martin. "Taste and Bad Taste in Metaphysical Poetry: Richard Crashaw and Dylan Thomas." *Hudson Review* 8 (1955): 61–77.

Addison, Joseph. *The Works of Joseph Addison*. 3 vols. New York: Harper, 1845.

Altieri, Charles. "What Theory Can Learn from New Directions in Contemporary American Poetry." *New Literary History* 43.1 (2012): 65–87.

Ambrose of Milan. *De sacramentis*. Vol. 16, *Patrologia cursus completus, Series Latina*. Paris: J.-P. Migne, 1841–1903.

Anderson, Judith H. *Translating Investments: Metaphor and the Dynamic of Cultural Change in Tudor-Stuart England*. New York: Fordham University Press, 2005.

Andrewes, Lancelot. *Ninety-Six Sermons by the Right Honourable and Reverend Father in God, Lancelot Andrewes, Sometime Lord Bishop of Winchester*. Edited by J. P. Wilson. 11 vols. Oxford: John Henry Parker, 1841.

Aristotle. *Τὰ Μετὰ Τὰ Φυσικά*. Edited by W. Jaeger. Scriptorum Classicorum Bibliotheca Oxoniensis. Oxford: Clarendon, 1957.

Asals, Heather A. R. "Crashaw's Participles and the 'Chiaroscuro' of Ontological Language." In *Essays on Richard Crashaw*, edited by Robert M. Cooper, 35–49. Salzburg, Austria: Institut für Anglistik and Amerikanistik, Universität Salzburg, 1979.

———. *Equivocal Predication: George Herbert's Way to God*. Toronto: University of Toronto Press, 1981.

Ashton, Jennifer. *From Modernism to Postmodernism: American Poetry and Theory in the Twentieth Century*. Cambridge: Cambridge University Press, 2006.

Augustine of Hippo. *Confessionum*. Vol. 32, *Patrologia cursus completus, Series Latina*. Paris: J.-P. Migne, 1841–1903.

———. *De Civitate Dei*. Vol. 41, *Patrologia cursus completus, Series Latina*. Paris: J.-P. Migne, 1841–1903.

———. *De Doctrina Christiana*. Vol. 34, *Patrologia cursus completus, Series Latina*. Paris: J.-P. Migne, 1841–1903.

———. *Enarrationes in Psalmos*. Vol. 36, *Patrologia cursus completus, Series Latina*. Paris: J.-P. Migne, 1841–1903.

———. *In Iohannis evangelium tractatus CXXIV*. Edited by R. Willems. Vol. 36, *Corpus christianorum, series Latina*. Turnhout, Belgium: Typographi Brepols, 1954.

Bacon, Francis. *The Works of Francis Bacon.* Edited by James Spedding, Robert Leslie Ellis, and Douglas Denon Heath. London: Longmans, 1857.

Barthes, Roland. *Writing Degree Zero.* Translated by Annette Lavers and Colin Smith. New York: Hill and Wang, 1977.

Bauer, Matthias. "'A Title Strange, Yet True': Toward an Explanation of Herbert's Titles." In *George Herbert: Sacred and Profane,* edited by Helen Wilcox and Richard Todd, 103–17. Amsterdam: VU University Press, 1995.

Baumlin, James. *John Donne and the Rhetorics of Renaissance Discourse.* Columbia: University of Missouri Press, 1991.

Bennett, Joan. *Five Metaphysical Poets: Donne, Herbert, Vaughan, Crashaw, Marvell.* Cambridge: Cambridge University Press, 1966.

Bernard of Clairvaux. *Sermones in Cantica Canticorum.* Edited by H. Hurter. Innsbruck: Academica Wagneriana, 1888.

Bernstein, Charles. *A Poetics.* Cambridge, Mass.: Harvard University Press, 1992.

Blasing, Mutlu Konuk. *Lyric Poetry: The Pain and the Pleasure of Words.* Princeton, N.J.: Princeton University Press, 2007.

Bloch, Chana. *Spelling the Word: George Herbert and the Bible.* Berkeley: University of California Press, 1985.

Booth, Stephen. "Poetic Richness: A Preliminary Audit." *Pacific Coast Philology* 19.1–2 (1984): 68–78.

———. *Shakespeare's Sonnets.* New Haven, Conn.: Yale University Press, 1977.

Bromley, James M. "Intimacy and the Body in Seventeenth-Century Religious Devotion." *Early Modern Literary* Studies 11.1 (2005), 5.1–41. http://purl.oclc.org/emls/11–1/brominti.htm.

Brooks, Cleanth, and Robert Penn Warren. *Understanding Poetry: An Anthology for College Students.* 1938, revised edition. New York: Henry Holt, 1955.

Brown, Marshall. *Preromanticism.* Stanford, Calif.: Stanford University Press, 1993.

Bruele, Walter. *Praxis medicinae, or, the physicians practice vvherein are contained inward diseases from the head to the foote: explayning the nature of each disease, with the part affected; and also the signes, causes, and prognostiques, and likewise what temperature of the ayre is most requisite for the patients abode, with direction for the diet he ought to obserue, together with experimentall cures for euery disease. . . . Written by that famous and worthy physician, Walter Bruel.* London: John Norton, for William Sheares, 1632.

Bulkeley, Peter. *The Gospel-Covenant, or, The covenant of grace opened wherein are explained, 1. The differences betwixt the covenant of grace and covenant of works, 2. The different administration of the covenant before and since Christ, 3. The benefits and blessings of it, 4. The condition, 5. The properties of it / preached in Concord in New-England by Peter Bulkeley.* London: Sold by Tho. Parkhurst, 1674.

Bush, Douglas. *English Literature in the Early Seventeenth Century, 1600–1660.* Oxford History of English Literature. 2nd edition. Oxford: Oxford University Press, 1962.

Bynum, Caroline Walker. *Fragmentation and Redemption.* New York: Zone, 1991.

————. *Holy Feast and Holy Fast: The Religious Significance of Food to Medieval Women*. Berkeley: University of California Press, 1987.

————. *Jesus as Mother: Studies in the Spirituality of the High Middle Ages*. Berkeley: University of California Press, 1982.

Calderwood, James L. "*Love's Labour's Lost*: A Wantoning with Words." *Studies in English Literature, 1500–1900* 5.2 (1965): 317–32.

Calhoun, Joshua. "The Word Made Flax: Cheap Bibles, Textual Corruption, and the Poetics of Paper." *PMLA* 126.2 (2011): 327–44.

Calvin, John. *Joannis Calvini Opera Selecta*. Edited by Peter Barth, Wilhelm Niesel, and Dora Scheuner. 5 vols. Munich: Chr. Kaiser, 1926–52.

————. *A Treatise on the Sacrament of the Body and Blood of Christ*. Translated by Miles Coverdale. In *Writings and Translations of Miles Coverdale, Bishop of Exeter*. Edited by Rev. George Pearson for the Parker Society. Cambridge: Cambridge University Press, 1844.

Cameron, Sharon. *Lyric Time: Dickinson and the Limits of Genre*. Baltimore: Johns Hopkins University Press, 1981.

Canning, Patricia. "'The bodie and the letters both': 'blending' the rules of early modern religion." *Language and Literature* 17.3 (2008): 187–203.

Carey, John. *John Donne: Life, Mind, and Art*. Oxford: Oxford University Press, 1980.

Cefalu, Paul. "Godly Fear, Sanctification, and Calvinist Theology in the Sermons and 'Holy Sonnets' of John Donne." *Studies in Philology* 100.1 (2003): 71–86.

Chapman, George. *Ovids Banquet of Sence: A Coronet for his Mistresse Philosophie, and his amorous Zodiacke*. London: Printed by I. R. for Richard Smith, 1595.

Chavasse, Claude. *The Bride of Christ: An Enquiry into the Nuptial Element in Early Christianity*. London: Religious Book Club, 1940.

Chrysostom, John. Ὑπόμνημα εἰς τόν Ἅγιον Ματθαῖον τόν Εὐαγγελιστήν. Vol. 58, *Patrologia cursus completus, Series Graeca*. Paris: J.-P. Migne, 1857–66.

Church of England. *Articles. wherevpon it was agreed by the archbysshops and bisshops of both the prouinces, and the whole clergye . . . thauoydyng of the diuersities of opinions, and for the stablyshyng of consent touchyng true religion*. London: Richarde Jugge and John Cawood, 1563.

Clement of Alexandria. Παιδαγωγός. Vol. 8, *Patrologia cursus completus, Series Graeca*. Paris: J.-P. Migne, 1857–66.

Coiro, Ann Baynes. *Robert Herrick's* Hesperides *and the Epigram Book Tradition*. Baltimore: Johns Hopkins University Press, 1988.

Coleridge, Samuel Taylor. *Coleridge on the Seventeenth Century*. Edited by Roberta Florence Brinkley. Durham, N.C.: Duke University Press, 1955. Reprint, New York: Greenwood Press, 1968.

Collinson, Patrick. *The Religion of Protestants: The Church in English Society, 1559–1625*. Oxford: Oxford University Press, 1984.

Cosin, John. *The history of Popish transubstantiation, to which is premised and opposed, the Catholick doctrin of Holy Scripture, the ancient fathers and the Reformed churches, about the sacred elements, and presence of Christ in the blessed sacrament of the eucharist / written nineteen years ago in Latine, by the Right Reverend Father in God, John, late Lord Bishop of Durham, and allowed by him to be published a little before his death, at the earnest request of his friends.* Ttranslated by Luke de Beaulieu. London: Printed by Andrew Clark for Henry Brome, 1676.

Cranmer, Thomas. *An answer of the Most Reuerend Father in God Thomas Archebyshop of Canterburye, primate of all Englande and metropolitane vnto a crafty and sophisticall cauillation deuised by Stephen Gardiner doctour of law, late byshop of Winchester, agaynst the trewe and godly doctrine of the moste holy sacrament of the body and bloud of our sauiour Iesu Christe . . .* London: Reynold Wolfe, 1551.

———. *The answer of Thomas Archbishop of Canterbury &c. against the false calumniations of Dr. Richard Smyth.* In *The Remains of Thomas Cranmer,* edited by Henry Jenkyns, 4 vols. Oxford: Oxford University Press, 1833.

Crashaw, Richard. *Carmen Deo Nostro, te decet hymnus, sacred poems.* Paris: Peter Targa, 1652.

———. *The Complete Poetry of Richard Crashaw.* Edited by George Walton Williams. New York: New York University Press, 1972.

———. *The Poems English, Latin and Greek of Richard Crashaw.* 2nd edition. Edited by L. C. Martin. Oxford: Clarendon, 1966.

———. *Steps to the Temple: Sacred poems, with other delights of the muses.* London: Printed by T. W. for Humphrey Moseley, 1648.

Cruickshank, Frances. *Verse and Poetics in George Herbert and John Donne.* Farnham, Surrey, U.K.: Ashgate, 2010.

Culler, Jonathan. "Changes in the Study of the Lyric." In *Lyric Poetry: Beyond New Criticism,* edited by Chaviva Hošek and Patricia Parker, 38–54. Ithaca, N.Y.: Cornell University Press, 1985.

———. "Why Lyric?" *PMLA* 123.1 (2008): 201–6.

Cummings, Brian. *The Literary Culture of the Reformation: Grammar and Grace.* Oxford: Oxford University Press, 2002.

Cunnar, Eugene R. "Opening the Religious Lyric: Crashaw's Ritual, Liminal, and Visual Wounds." In *New Perspectives on the Seventeenth Century English Religious Lyric,* edited by John R. Roberts, 237–67. Columbia: University of Missouri Press, 1994.

Danson, Lawrence. "Shakespeare and the Misrecognition of Fathers and Sons." In *Paternity and Fatherhood: Myths and Realities,* edited by Lieve Spaas, 236–45. New York: St. Martin's, 1998.

Davis, Thomas and Virginia, eds. *Edward Taylor vs. Solomon Stoddard: The Nature of the Lord's Supper.* Vol. 2 of *The Unpublished Writings of Edward Taylor.* Twayne's American Literary Manuscripts Series. Boston: Twayne, 1981.

de Grazia, Margreta. "Words as Things." *Shakespeare Studies* 28 (2000): 231–35.

Di Cesare, Mario. "The Bodleian Manuscript and the Text of Herbert's Poems." *George Herbert Journal* 6.2 (1983): 15–35.

DiPasquale, Theresa M. *Literature & Sacrament: The Sacred and the Secular in John Donne*. Pittsburgh: Duquesne University Press, 1999.

Doerksen, Daniel W. *Conforming to the Word: Herbert, Donne, and the English Church Before Laud*. Lewisburg, Pa.: Bucknell University Press, 1997.

Dolven, Jeff. "Reading Wyatt for the Style." *Modern Philology* 105.1 (2007): 65–86.

Donne, John. *Devotions upon Emergent Occasions*. Edited by Anthony Raspa. New York: Oxford University Press, 1987.

———. *The Divine Poems*. Edited by Helen Gardner. Oxford: Clarendon, 1952.

———. *The Elegies and the Songs and Sonnets*. Edited by Helen Gardner. Oxford: Clarendon, 1965.

———. *The Poems of John Donne*. Edited by Herbert J. C. Grierson. 2 vols. Oxford: Clarendon, 1912.

———. *The Sermons of John Donne*. Edited by George Potter and Evelyn Simpson. Berkeley: University of California Press, 1953–62.

———. *The Variorum Edition of the Poetry of John Donne, Volume 7, Part 1: The Holy Sonnets*. Edited by Gary A. Stringer. Bloomington: Indiana University Press, 2005.

Doody, Margaret Anne. *The Daring Muse: Augustan Poetry Reconsidered*. Cambridge: Cambridge University Press, 1985.

Dryden, John. "A Discourse on the Original and Progress of Satire." In *Discourses on Satire and Epic Poetry*, 2–40. London: Cassell, 1888.

Dubrow, Heather. *The Challenges of Orpheus: Lyric Poetry and Early Modern England*. Baltimore: Johns Hopkins University Press, 2008.

———. *A Happier Eden: The Politics of Marriage in the Stuart Epithalamium*. Ithaca, N.Y.: Cornell University Press, 1990.

Dyck, Paul. "Locating the Word: The Textual Church and George Herbert's *Temple*." In *Centered on the Word: Literature, Scripture, and the Tudor-Stuart Middle Way*, edited by Daniel W. Doerksen and Christopher Hodgkins, 224–44. Newark: University of Delaware Press, 2004.

———. " 'So rare a use': Scissors, Reading, and Devotion at Little Gidding." *George Herbert Journal* 27.1–2 (Fall 2003–Spring 2004): 67–81.

Eagleton, Terry. *How to Read a Poem*. Oxford: Blackwell, 2007.

Elam, Keir. *Shakespeare's Universe of Discourse: Language-Games in the Comedies*. Cambridge: Cambridge University Press, 1984.

Eliot, T. S. *The Varieties of Metaphysical Poetry: The Clark Lectures at Trinity College, Cambridge, 1926, and the Turnbull Lectures at the Johns Hopkins University, 1933*. New York: Mariner Books, 1996.

Elsky, Martin. *Authorizing Words: Speech, Writing, and Print in the English Renaissance*. Ithaca, N.Y.: Cornell University Press, 1989.

———. "George Herbert's Pattern Poems and the Materiality of Language: A New Approach to Renaissance Hieroglyphics." *ELH* 50.2 (1983): 245–60.

Empson, William. *Essays on Renaissance Literature: Volume 1, Donne and the New Philosophy*. Edited by John Haffenden. Cambridge: Press Syndicate of the University of Cambridge, 1993.

————. *Seven Types of Ambiguity*. New York: New Directions, 1947.

Farmer, Norman K., Jr. "Herrick's Hesperidean Garden: *ut pictura poesis* Applied." In *"Trust to Good Verses": Herrick Tercentenary Essays*, edited by Roger B. Rollin and J. Max Patrick, 15–51. Pittsburgh: University of Pittsburgh Press, 1978.

Ferrar, John. *Materials for the Life of Nicholas Ferrar*. Edited by Lynette R. Muir and John A. White. Leeds, U.K.: Leeds Philosophical and Literary Society, 1996.

Fincham, Kenneth, ed. *The Early Stuart Church, 1603–42*. Stanford, Calif.: Stanford University Press, 1993.

Fish, Stanley. *The Living Temple: George Herbert and Catechizing*. Berkeley: University of California Press, 1978.

————. "Masculine Persuasive Force: Donne and Verbal Power." In *Soliciting Interpretation: Literary Theory and Seventeenth-Century English Poetry*, edited by Elizabeth D. Harvey and Katharine Eisaman Maus, 223–52. Chicago: University of Chicago Press, 1990.

————. *Self-Consuming Artifacts: The Experience of Seventeenth Century Literature*. Berkeley: University of California Press, 1972.

Flinker, Noam. *The Song of Songs in English Renaissance Literature*. Cambridge: D. S. Brewer, 2000.

Flynn, Dennis. "Donne's Catholicism: I." *Recusant History* 13 (1975): 1–17.

————. "Donne's Catholicism: II." *Recusant History* 13 (1975): 178–95.

————. *John Donne and the Ancient Catholic Nobility*. Bloomington: Indiana University Press, 1995.

Fontanus, Nicholas. *The womans doctour, or, An exact and distinct explanation of all such diseases as are peculiar to that sex with choise and experimentall remedies against the same: being safe in the composition, pleasant in the use, effectuall in the operation, cheap in the price / faithfully translated out of the works of that learned philosopher and eminent physitian Nicholas Fontanus*. London: John Blague and Samuel Howes, 1652.

Forrest-Thomson, Veronica. *Poetic Artifice: A Theory of Twentieth-Century Poetry*. Manchester, U.K.: Manchester University Press, 1978.

Fowler, Alastair. "Robert Herrick." *Proceedings of the British Academy* 66 (1980): 243–64.

Foxcroft, Thomas. *A Funeral Sermon Occasioned by Several Mournful Deaths*. Boston, 1722.

Foxe, John, ed. *Actes and monuments of these latter and perillous dayes, touching matters of the Church . . .* London: Day, 1563.

Fried, Michael. *Absorption and Theatricality: Painting and Beholder in the Age of Diderot*. Chicago: University of Chicago Press, 1980.

————. *Art and Objecthood*. Chicago: University of Chicago Press, 1998.

Friedman, Donald M. "Christ's Image and Likeness in Donne." *John Donne Journal* 15 (1996): 75–94.

Frontain, Raymond-Jean. "'Make all this All': The Religious Operations of John Donne's Imagination." In *John Donne's Religious Imagination: Essays in Honor of John T. Shawcross*, edited by Raymond-Jean Frontain and Frances M. Malpezzi, 1–27. Conway: University of Central Arkansas Press, 1995.

Frye, Northrop. *Anatomy of Criticism*. Princeton, N.J.: Princeton University Press, 1957.

Gallagher, Catherine and Stephen Greenblatt. *Practicing New Historicism*. Chicago: University of Chicago Press, 2000.

Gardiner, Stephen. *An Explication and assertion of the true Catholique fayth, touchyng the most blessed Sacrament of the aulter*. Rouen, France: Robert Caly, 1551.

Gascoigne, George. *The Posies of George Gascoigne Esquire. Corrected, perfected, and augmented by the Authour*. London: Richard Smith, 1575.

Gelpi, Albert. *The Tenth Muse: The Psyche of the American Poet*. Cambridge, Mass.: Harvard University Press, 1975.

The Geneva Bible: A Fascimile of the 1560 Edition. Madison: University of Wisconsin Press, 1969.

Gilman, Ernest B. *Iconoclasm and Poetry in the English Reformation: Down Went Dagon*. Chicago: University of Chicago Press, 1986.

Godbeer, Richard. "'Love Raptures': Marital, Romantic, and Erotic Images of Jesus Christ in Puritan New England, 1670–1730." In *A Shared Experience: Men, Women and the History of Gender*, edited by Laura McCall and Donald Yacovone, 51–77. New York: New York University Press, 1998.

Goldberg, Jonathan. *Voice Terminal Echo: Postmodernism and English Renaissance Texts*. New York: Methuen, 1986.

Goodwin, Thomas. *Aggravation of Sinne: and Sinning Against Knowledge/Mercie. Delivered in severall Sermons, and on divers occasions*. London: M. Flesher and John Rothwell, 1637.

———. *The tryall of a Christians growth in mortification, or purging out corruption, vivification, or bringing forth more fruit: a treatise affording some helps rightly to judge of growth in grace by resolving some tentations, clearing some mistakes, answering some questions about growth: together with other observations upon the parable of the vine, Iohn 15: 1, 2 verses*. London: Printed by M. Flesher for R. Dawlman and L. Fawne, 1641.

Gosse, Edmund. *A Short History of Modern English Literature*. New York: D. Appleton, 1898.

Grabo, Norman. *Edward Taylor*. New York: Twayne, 1961.

Greenblatt, Stephen. "Remnants of the Sacred in Early Modern England." In *Subject and Object in Renaissance Culture*, edited by Margreta de Grazia, Maureen Quilligan, and Peter Stallybrass, 337–48. Cambridge: Cambridge University Press, 1996.

———. *Renaissance Self-Fashioning: From More to Shakespeare*. Chicago: University of Chicago Press, 1980.

Gregerson, Linda. "Ben Jonson and the Loathèd Word." In *Green Thoughts, Green Shades: Essays by Contemporary Poets on the Early Modern Lyric*, edited by Jonathan F. S. Post, 86–108. Berkeley: University of California Press, 2002.

Grossman, Allen. *The Sighted Singer: Two Works on Poetry for Readers and Writers*. Baltimore: Johns Hopkins University Press, 1992.

Guibbory, Achsah. *Ceremony and Community from Herbert to Milton*. Cambridge: Cambridge University Press, 1998.

Halewood, William. *The Poetry of Grace: Reformation Themes in English Seventeenth-Century Poetry*. New Haven, Conn.: Yale University Press, 1970.

Hammond, Jeffrey. *Edward Taylor: Fifty Years of Scholarship and Criticism*. Columbia S.C.: Camden House, 1993.

Healy, Thomas F. *Richard Crashaw*. Leiden: E. J. Brill, 1986.

Hebrew-English Tanakh. Philadelphia: Jewish Publication Society, 1999.

Herbert, George. *The English Poems of George Herbert*. Edited by Helen Wilcox. Cambridge: Cambridge University Press, 2007.

———. *The Works of George Herbert*. Edited by F. E. Hutchinson. Oxford: Clarendon, 1941.

Herrick, Robert. *The Poetical Works of Robert Herrick*. Edited by L. C. Martin. London: Oxford University Press, 1965.

Hester, M. Thomas. "Altering the Text of the Self: The Shapes of 'The Altar.'" In *A Fine Tuning: Studies of the Religious Poetry of Herbert and Milton*, edited by Mary A. Maleski, 95–116. Binghamton, N.Y.: Medieval and Renaissance Texts and Studies 64, 1989.

———. "'this cannot be said': A Preface to the Reader of Donne's Lyrics." *Christianity and Literature* 39 (1990): 365–85.

Hill, Christopher A. "George Herbert's Sweet Devotion." *Studies in Philology* 107.2 (2010): 236–58.

Hitchcock, Nathan. "Saving Edward Taylor's Purse: Masculine Devotion in the *Preparatory Meditations*." *Literature and Theology* 22.3 (2008): 339–53.

Hoen, Cornelius. *Epistola christiana admodum ab annis quatuor ad quendam, apud quem omne iudicium sacrae scripturae fuit, ex Bathavis missa, sed spreta, longe aliter tractans coenam dominicam quam hactenus tractata est, ad calcem quibusdam adiectis Christiano homini pernecessariis, praesertim his periculosis temporibus. 1. Corinth. 11. Non potestis coenam dominicam manducare, quod unusquisque propriam coenam occupat in edendo*. Strassburg: Johann Knobloch, 1525.

Holifield, E. Brooks. *The Covenant Sealed: The Development of Puritan Sacramental Theology in Old and New England, 1570–1720*. New Haven, Conn.: Yale University Press, 1974.

The Holy Bible, conteyning the Old Testament, and the New, newly translated out of the originall tongues, and with the former translations diligently compared and reuised, by His Maiesties speciall comandement ; appointed to be read in churches. London: Robert Barker, 1611.

Hooker, Richard. *Of the lawes of ecclesiasticall politie, Eyght books.* London: Iohn Windet, 1593.

Horace. *Odes and Epodes.* Translated by Niall Rudd. Loeb Classical Library. Cambridge, Mass.: Harvard University Press, 2004.

———. *Satires, Epistles, and Ars Poetica.* Translated by H. Rushton Fairclough. Loeb Classical Library. Cambridge, Mass.: Harvard University Press, 1942.

Hughes, Richard E. "George Herbert and the Incarnation." *Cithera* 4.1 (1964): 22–32.

Ignatius of Antioch. Epistles. Vol. 5, *Patrologia cursus completus, Series Graeca.* Paris: J.-P. Migne, 1857–66.

Jackson, Virginia. *Dickinson's Misery: A Theory of Lyric Reading.* Princeton, N.J.: Princeton University Press, 2005.

Jarvis, Simon. "For a Poetics of Verse." *PMLA* 125.4 (2010): 931–35.

Johnson, Jeffrey. *The Theology of John Donne.* Studies in Renaissance Literature, vol. 1. Cambridge, U.K.: D. S. Brewer, 1999.

Johnson, Samuel. *Lives of the English Poets.* London: Jones, 1825.

Jonson, Benjamin. *The Workes of Beniamin Jonson.* London: Will Stansby, 1616.

Kalas, Rayna. *Frame, Glass, Verse: The Technology of Poetic Invention in the English Renaissance.* Ithaca, N.Y.: Cornell University Press, 2007.

Keach, William. "Rethinking Romantic Poetry and History: Lyric Resistance, Lyric Seduction." In *The Cambridge Companion to British Romantic Poetry,* edited by James Chandler and Maureen N. McLane, 217–38. Cambridge: Cambridge University Press, 2008.

Kearney, James. *The Incarnate Text: Imagining the Book in Reformation England.* Philadelphia: University of Pennsylvania Press, 2009.

Keller, Karl. *The Example of Edward Taylor.* Amherst: University of Massachusetts Press, 1975.

Kermode, Frank. *John Donne.* London: Longman, 1961.

Kerrigan, William. "The Fearful Accommodations of John Donne." *English Literary Renaissance* 4 (1974): 337–63.

Kilgour, Maggie. *From Communion to Cannibalism: An Anatomy of Metaphors of Incorporation.* Princeton, N.J.: Princeton University Press, 1990.

Kilmartin, Edward J. *The Eucharist in the West.* Englewood Cliffs, N.J.: Prentice-Hall, 1965.

Kuchar, Gary. *Divine Subjection: The Rhetoric of Sacramental Devotion in Early Modern England.* Pittsburgh: Duquesne University Press, 2005.

Lake, Peter. *The Boxmaker's Revenge: "Orthodoxy," "Heterodoxy" and the Politics of the Parish in Early Stuart London.* Stanford, Calif.: Stanford University Press, 2002.

LaVerdiere, Eugene. *The Eucharist in the New Testament and the Early Church.* Collegeville, Minn.: Liturgical, 1996.

Leavis, F. R. *Revaluation.* New York: W. W. Norton, 1963.

Leiter, Louis H. "George Herbert's Anagram." *College English* 26.7 (1965): 543–44.

Leverenz, David. *The Language of Puritan Feeling: An Exploration in Literature, Psychology, and Social History.* New Brunswick, N.J.: Rutgers University Press, 1980.

Levy, Ian Christopher; Gary Macy; and Kristen Van Ausdall, eds. *A Companion to the Eucharist in the Middle Ages.* Leiden, Netherlands: Brill, 2001.

Lewalski, Barbara K. "Emblems and the Religious Lyric: George Herbert and Protestant Emblematics." *Hebrew University Studies in Literature* 6 (1978): 32–56.

———. *Protestant Poetics and the Seventeenth-Century Religious Lyric.* Princeton, N.J.: Princeton University Press, 1979.

Loach, Judi. "Body and Soul: A Transfer of Theological Terminology into the Aesthetic Realm." *Emblematica: An Interdisciplinary Journal of Emblem Studies* 12 (2002): 31–60.

Low, Anthony. *Love's Architecture: Devotional Modes in Seventeenth-Century English Poetry.* New York: New York University Press, 1978.

MacLeish, Archibald. *Streets in the Moon.* Boston: Houghton Mifflin, 1926.

Macy, Gary. *The Theologies of the Eucharist in the Early Scholastic Period: A Study of the Salvific Function of the Sacrament according to the Theologians c. 1080-c. 1220.* Oxford: Clarendon, 1984.

Martz, Louis. Foreword. In *The Poems of Edward Taylor,* edited by Donald E. Stanford, xiii-xxxvii. New Haven, Conn.: Yale University Press, 1960.

———. *The Poetry of Meditation: A Study in English Religious Literature of the Seventeenth Century.* New Haven, Conn.: Yale University Press, 1954.

Masson, Margaret W. "The Typology of the Female as a Model for the Regenerate: Puritan Preaching, 1690–1730." *Signs: Journal of Women on Culture and Society* 2.2 (1976): 69–86.

Mather, Cotton. *Elizabeth in Her Holy Retirement: An Essay to Prepare a Pious Woman for her Lying-in.* Boston: 1710. Reprint in *The Colonial American Family: Collected Essays,* edited by David J. Rothman and Sheila M. Rothman. New York: Arno Press and the *New York Times,* 1972.

———. *A Glorious Espousal: A Brief Essay to Illustrate and Prosecute the Marriage, Wherein Our Great Saviours Offers to Espouse unto Himself the Children of Men. And thereupon to recommend from that grand pattern a good carriage in the married life among them. An essay proper and useful in the hands of those who travel on the noble design of espousing the souls of men unto their Saviour.* Boston: S. Kneeland, 1719.

Maus, Katharine Eisaman. "Horns of Dilemma: Jealousy, Gender, and Spectatorship in English Renaissance Drama." *ELH* 54.3 (1987): 561–83.

McLaughlin, Elizabeth, and Gail Thomas. "Communion in *The Temple.*" *Studies in English Literature* 15.1 (1975): 111–24.

McNees, Eleanor J. *Eucharistic Poetry: The Search for Presence in the Writings of John Donne, Gerard Manley Hopkins, Dylan Thomas, and Geoffrey Hill.* Lewisburg, Pa.: Bucknell University Press, 1992.

————. "John Donne and the Anglican Doctrine of the Eucharist." *Texas Studies in Literature and Language* 29.1 (1987): 94–114.

Menestrier, Claude-François. *La philosophie des images*. Paris, 1682.

Merleau-Ponty, Maurice. *The Visible and the Invisible, followed by working notes*. Edited by Claude Lefort, translated by Alphonso Lingis. Evanston, Ill.: Northwestern University Press, 1968.

Mill, John Stuart. "Thoughts on Poetry and Its Varieties." *Crayon* 7.4 (1860): 93–97.

Miller, Edmund. *Drudgerie Divine: The Rhetoric of God and Man in George Herbert*. Salzburg, Austria: Institut für Anglistik und Americanistik, 1979.

Miller, Greg. "Scribal and Print Publication: The Case of George Herbert's English Poems." *George Herbert Journal* 23 (1999–2000): 14–34.

Missale Romanum, ex Decreto Sacrosanci Concilii Tridentini. Ratisbonae, Italy: Pustet, 1906.

Murphy, Francis. "A Letter on Edward Taylor's Bible." *Early American Literature* 6.1 (1971): 91.

Murray, Molly. *The Poetics of Conversion in Early Modern English Literature: Verse and Change from Donne to Dryden*. Cambridge: Cambridge University Press, 2009.

Nealon, Christopher. *The Matter of Capital: Poetry and Crisis in the American Century*. Cambridge, Mass.: Harvard University Press, 2011.

Nelson, Bradley J. *The Persistence of Presence: Emblem and Ritual in Baroque Spain*. Toronto: University of Toronto Press, 2010.

Netzley, Ryan. "Oral Devotion: Eucharistic Theology and Richard Crashaw's Religious Lyrics." *Texas Studies in Literature and Language* 44.3 (2002): 247–72.

————. *Reading, Desire, and the Eucharist in Early Modern Religious Poetry*. Toronto: University of Toronto Press, 2011.

————. "'Take and Taste': Sacramental Physiology, Eucharistic Experience, and George Herbert's *The Temple*." In *Varieties of Devotion in the Middle Ages and Renaissance*, edited by Susan C. Karant-Nunn, 179–206. Arizona Studies in the Middle Ages and the Renaissance, vol. 7. Turnhout, Belgium: Brepols, 2003.

The New Testament in the Original Greek. New York: Macmillan, 1925.

The New Testament of Iesus Christ, Translated Faithfully into English, our of the authentical Latin, according to the best corrected copies of the same . . . in the English College of Rhemes. Rhemes: Iohn Fogny, 1582.

Olson, Kristen L. "Picture-Pattern-Poiesis: Visuality, the Emblem, and Seventeenth-Century English Religious Lyric." *Emblematica: An Interdisciplinary Journal of Emblem Studies* 17 (2009): 271–98.

Orgel, Stephen. "The Poetics of Spectacle." *New Literary History: A Journal of Theory and Interpretation* 2.3 (1971): 367–89.

Origen. *In Leviticum*. Vol. 12, *Patrologia cursus completus, Series Graeca*. Paris: J.-P. Migne, 1857–66.

Parker, Blanford. *The Triumph of Augustan Poetics: English Literary Culture from Butler to Johnson*. Cambridge: Cambridge University Press, 1998.

Parrish, Paul. *Richard Crashaw*. Boston: Twayne, 1980.

Patrick, J. Max. "Critical Problems in Editing George Herbert's *The Temple*." In *The Editor as Critic and the Critic as Editor: Papers Read at a Clark Library Seminar, November 13, 1971*, edited by John Max Patrick and Alan Roper, 3–24. Los Angeles: William Andrews Clark Memorial Library, University of California, 1973.

Patrides, C. A. Introduction. In *The English Poems of George Herbert*, 6–25. London: J. M. Dent/ Everyman's Library, 1974.

Peacham, Henry. *The Garden of Eloquence, Conteining the most excellent Ornaments, Exornations, Lightes, flowers, and formes of speech commonly called the Figures of Rhetorike*. London: R[ichard] F[ield] for H. Iackson dwelling in Fleetstrete, 1593.

Perloff, Marjorie. *The Dance of the Intellect: Studies in the Poetry of the Pound Tradition*. Cambridge: Cambridge University Press, 1985.

———. *The Poetics of Indeterminacy: Rimbaud to Cage*. Evanston, Ill.: Northwestern Univeristy Press, 1999.

———. *Radical Artifice: Writing Poetry in the Age of Media*. Chicago: University of Chicago Press, 1991.

Perloff, Marjorie, and Craig Dworkin. "The Sound of Poetry/The Poetry of Sound: The 2006 MLA Presidential Forum." *PMLA* 123.3 (May 2008): 749–61.

Pope, Robert G. *The Half-Way Covenant: Church Membership in Puritan New England*. Princeton, N.J.: Princeton University Press, 1969.

Pound, Ezra. *The Cantos of Ezra Pound*. New York: New Directions, 1996.

Praz, Mario. *The Flaming Heart: Essays on Crashaw, Machiavelli, and Other Studies in the Relations Between Italian and English Literature from Chaucer to T. S. Eliot*. Garden City, N.Y.: Doubleday, 1958.

Price, Merrall Llewelyn. *Consuming Passions: The Uses of Cannibalism in Late Medieval and Early Modern Europe*. New York: Routledge, 2003.

Prins, Yopie. "Historical Poetics, Dysprosody, and *The Science of English Verse*." *PMLA* 123.1 (2008): 229–34.

Prior, Charles. *Defining the Jacobean Church: The Politics of Religious Controversy, 1603–1625*. Cambridge: Cambridge University Press, 2005.

Pusey, Edward Bouverie. *The Doctrine of the Real Presence, as Contained in the Fathers, Vindicated, in Notes on a Sermon, "The Presence of Christ in the Holy Eucharist."* Oxford: John Henry Parker, 1855.

Puttenham, George. *The Arte of English Poesie*. London: Richard Field, 1589.

Rambuss, Richard. *Closet Devotions*. Durham, N.C.: Duke University Press, 1998.

———. "Sacred Subjects and the Aversive Metaphysical Conceit: Crashaw, Serrano, Ofili." *ELH* 71 (2004): 497–530.

Ransome, Joyce. "Monotessaron: The Harmonies of Little Gidding." *Seventeenth Century* 20.1 (2005): 22–52.

Raspa, Anthony. *The Emotive Image: Jesuit Poetics in the English Renaissance*. Fort Worth: Texas Christian University Press, 1983.

Rebhorn, Wayne A. "Outlandish Fears: Defining Decorum in Renaissance Rhetoric." *Intertexts* 4.1 (2000): 3–24.

Reiter, Robert. "George Herbert's 'Anagram': A Reply to Professor Leiter." *College English* 28.1 (1966): 56–60.

Ridley, Nicholas. *A Brief Declaration of The Lord's Supper, or a Treatise against the Error of Transubstantiation, written by Nicolas Ridley, Bishop of London, During his Imprisonment, A.D. 1555.* In *The Works of Nicholas Ridley*, edited by Henry Christmas, 5–45. Cambridge: University Press, 1841.

Roe, John. "'Upon Julia's Clothes': Herrick, Ovid, and the Celebration of Innocence." *The Review of English Studies*, New Series, 50.199 (1999): 350–58.

Rollin, Roger B. "Sweet Numbers and Sour Readers: Trends and Perspectives in Herrick Criticism." In *"Trust to Good Verses": Herrick Tercentenary Essays*, edited by Roger B. Rollin and J. Max Patrick, 3–14. Pittsburgh: University of Pittsburgh Press, 1978.

Ross, Malcolm. *Poetry and Dogma: The Transfiguration of Eucharistic Symbols in Seventeenth Century English Poetry.* New Brunswick, N.J.: Rutgers University Press, 1954. Reprint, New York: Octagon, 1969.

Rowe, Karen. *Saint and Singer: Edward Taylor's Typology and the Poetics of Meditation.* Cambridge: Cambridge University Press, 1986.

Rubin, Miri. *Corpus Christi: The Eucharist in Late Medieval Culture.* Cambridge: Cambridge University Press, 1991.

Sabine, Maureen. *Feminine Engendered Faith.* London: Macmillan, 1992.

Salmon, William. *Aristotle's complete and experienced midwife. In two parts: I. A Guide for Child-Bearing Women, in the Time of their Conception, Bearing, and Suckling their Children; with the best Means of Helping them, both in Natural and Unnatural Labours: Together with suitable Remedies for the various Indispositions of New-Born Infants. II. Proper and safe Remedies for the Curing all those Distempers that are incident to the Female Sex; and more especially those that are any Obstruction to their bearing of Children. A Work far more perfect than any yet Extant; And highly Necessary for all Surgeons, Midwives, Nurses, and Child-Bearing Women. Made English by W- S-, M.D.* London, 1782.

Sandys, Edwin. *The Sermons of Edwin Sandys, D.D., Successively Bishop of Worcester and London, and Archbishop of York, to which are added Some Miscellaneous Pieces by the Same Author.* Edited by John Ayre. Cambridge: University Press, 1842.

Scarry, Elaine. "Donne: But yet the body is his booke." In *Literature and the Body: Essays on Populations and Persons*, edited by Elaine Scarry, 70–106. Baltimore: Johns Hopkins University Press, 1986.

Scheick, William. *The Will and the Word: The Poetry of Edward Taylor.* Athens: University of Georgia Press, 1974.

Schoenfeldt, Michael. *Bodies and Selves in Early Modern England.* Cambridge: Cambridge University Press, 1999.

———. *Prayer and Power: George Herbert and Renaissance Courtship.* Chicago: University of Chicago Press, 1991.

Schuldiner, Michael Joseph. *Gifts and Works: The Post-Conversion Paradigm and Spiritual Controversy in Seventeenth-Century Massachusetts.* Macon, Ga.: Mercer University Press, 1991.

Schuyler, James. *Collected Poems.* New York: Farrar, Straus and Giroux, 1995.

Schwartz, Regina. *Sacramental Poetics at the Dawn of Secularism: When God Left the World.* Stanford, Calif.: Stanford University Press, 2008.

Schweitzer, Ivy. *The Work of Self-Representation: Lyric Poetry in Colonial New England.* Chapel Hill: University of North Carolina Press, 1991.

Sellin, Paul R. *John Donne and "Calvinist" Views of Grace.* Amsterdam: VU Boekhandel, 1983.

Semler, L. E. "Robert Herrick, the Human Figure, and the English Mannerist Aesthetic." *Studies in English Literature, 1500–1900,* 35.1 (1995): 105–21.

Shakespeare, William. *Love's Labour's Lost.* In *The Riverside Shakespeare,* 2nd edition. Edited by G. Blakemore Evans et al. Boston: Houghton Mifflin, 1997.

Shami, Jeanne. "Troping Religious Identity: Circumcision and Transubstantiation in Donne's Sermons." In *Renaissance Tropologies: The Cultural Imagination of Early Modern England,* edited by Jeanne Shami, 89–117. Pittsburgh: Duquesne University Press, 2008.

Shepard, Thomas. *The Sound Believer: A Treatise of Evangelical Conversion. Discovering the Work of Christs Spirit in reconciling of a sinner to God.* London: Andrew Crooke, 1659.

Shuger, Debora Kuller. *Habits of Thought in the English Renaissance: Religion, Politics, and the Dominant Culture.* Berkeley: University of California Press, 1990.

———. *The Renaissance Bible: Scholarship, Sacrifice, and Subjectivity.* Berkeley: University of California Press, 1994.

———. *Sacred Rhetoric: The Christian Grand Style in the English Renaissance.* Princeton, N.J.: Princeton University Press, 1988.

Sidney, Phillip. *An Apologie for Poetrie, Written by the right noble, virtuous, and learned, Sir Phillip Sidney, Knight.* London: Henry Olney, 1595.

Silliman, Ron. *The New Sentence.* New York: Roof, 1995.

Spinks, Bryan D. *From the Lord and "The Best Reformed Churches": A Study of the Eucharistic Liturgy in the English Puritan and Separatist Traditions, 1550–1633,* vol. 1. Rome: Edizioni Liturgiche, 1984.

Stachniewski, John. "John Donne: The Despair of the 'Holy Sonnets.'" *ELH* 48 (1981): 677–705.

Stanford, Donald. *Edward Taylor.* University of Minnesota Pamphlets on American Writers, no. 52. St. Paul: University of Minnesota Press, 1965.

Stein, Gertrude. *The Selected Writings of Gertrude Stein.* Edited by Carl Van Vechten. New York: Vintage, 1962.

———. *Tender Buttons*. New York: Claire Marie, 1914. Reprint, Mineola, N.Y.: Dover, 1997.

Steinberg, Leo. *The Sexuality of Christ in Renaissance Art and in Modern Oblivion*, 2nd edition, revised and expanded. Chicago: University of Chicago Press, 1996.

Stevens, Wallace. *The Auroras of Autumn*. New York: Alfred A. Knopf, 1950.

Stewart, Stanley. *The Enclosed Garden: The Tradition and the Image in Seventeenth-Century Poetry*. Madison: University of Wisconsin Press, 1966.

Stewart, Susan. *Poetry and the Fate of the Senses*. Chicago: Chicago University Press, 2002.

Stoddard, Solomon. *The Safety of Appearing at the Day of Judgement, in the righteousness of Christ, opened and applied*. Boston: Samuel Green, 1687.

Stone, Darwell. *History of the Doctrine of the Holy Eucharist*. 2 vols. London: Longmans, Green, 1909.

Strier, Richard. "John Donne Awry and Squint: The 'Holy Sonnets,' 1608–1610." *Modern Philology* 86.4 (May 1989): 357–84.

———. *Love Known: Theology and Experience in George Herbert's Poetry*. Chicago: University of Chicago Press, 1983.

———. *Resistant Structures: Particularity, Radicalism, and Renaissance Texts*. Berkeley: University of California Press, 1995.

Strout, Nathaniel. "Jonson's Jacobean Masques and the Moral Imagination." *Studies in English Literature, 1500–1900*, 27.2 (1987): 233–47.

Summers, Claude J. "The Bride of the Apocalypse and the Quest for True Religion: Donne, Herbert, and Spenser." In *"Bright Shootes of Everlastingnesse": The Seventeenth-Century Religious Lyric*, edited by Claude J. Summers and Ted-Larry Pebworth, 72–95. Columbia: University of Missouri Press, 1987.

Summers, Joseph H. *George Herbert: His Religion and Art*. Cambridge, Mass.: Harvard University Press, 1954.

Szöffervy, Joseph. *Die Annalen der lateinischen Hymnendichtung*. 2 vols. Berlin: E. Schmidt, 1964.

Targoff, Ramie. *John Donne, Body and Soul*. Chicago: University of Chicago Press, 2008.

Taylor, Edward. *Edward Taylor's "Church Records" and Related Sermons*. Vol. 1 of *The Unpublished Writings of Edward Taylor*. Edited by Thomas M. and Virginia L. Davis. Twayne's American Literary Manuscripts Series. Boston: Twayne, 1981.

———. *Edward Taylor vs. Solomon Stoddard: The Nature of the Lord's Supper*. Vol. 2 of *The Unpublished Writings of Edward Taylor*. Edited by Thomas M. and Virginia L. Davis. Twayne's American Literary Manuscripts Series. Boston: Twayne, 1981.

———. *The Poems of Edward Taylor*. Edited by Donald E. Stanford. New Haven, Conn.: Yale University Press, 1960.

———. "Theological Notes." In "Diary, Theological Notes, and Poems." Newport, R.I.: Redwood Library and Athenaeum MS.

————. *Treatise Concerning the Lord's Supper.* Edited by Norman S. Grabo. East Lansing: Michigan State University Press, 1966.

Tertullian. *Liber de Resurrectione Carnis.* Vol. 2, *Patrologia cursus completus, Series Latina.* Paris: J.-P. Migne, 1841–1903.

Thickstun, Margaret. "Mothers in Israel: The Puritan Rhetoric of Child-Bearing." In *Praise Disjoined: Changing Patterns of Salvation in Seventeenth-Century English Literature,* edited by William P. Shaw, 71–87. New York: Peter Lang, 1991.

Thomas Aquinas. *Summa Theologi;ae: Latin text and English translation, introductions, notes, appendices, and glossaries.* Edited by the Dominican Order of the Roman Catholic Church. 61 vols. Cambridge: Blackfriars, 1964.

Todd, Richard. *The Opacity of Signs: Acts of Interpretation in George Herbert's* The Temple. Columbia: University of Missouri Press, 1986.

Tuve, Rosemond. *A Reading of George Herbert.* Chicago: University of Chicago Press, 1952.

Tyacke, Nicholas. *Anti-Calvinists: The Rise of English Arminianism, c. 1590–1640.* Oxford: Clarendon, 1984.

Tyndale, William. *The New Testament: A Facsimile of the 1526 Edition.* London/Peabody, Mass.: British Library and Hendrickson Publishers, 2008.

van den Berg, Sara. "Ben Jonson and the Ideology of Authorship." In *Ben Jonson's 1616 Folio,* edited by Jennifer Brady and W. H. Herendeen, 111–37. Newark: University of Delaware Press, 1991.

Veith, Gene. *Reformation Spirituality: The Religion of George Herbert.* Lewisburg, Pa.: Bucknell University Press, 1985.

Vendler, Helen. *The Poetry of George Herbert.* Cambridge, Mass.: Harvard University Press, 1975.

Von Hallberg, Robert. *Lyric Powers.* Chicago: University of Chicago Press, 2009.

Wallerstein, Ruth C. *Richard Crashaw: A Study in Style and Poetic Development.* Madison: University of Wisconsin Press, 1959.

Walton, Izaak. *The Lives of Doctor John Donne, Sir Henry Wotton, Mr. Richard Hooker, Mr. George Herbert, and Doctor Robert Sanderson.* Chicago: Stone and Kimball, 1895.

Weiner, Andrew. *Sir Philip Sidney and the Poetics of Protestantism.* Minneapolis: University of Minnesota Press, 1978.

Whalen, Robert. *The Poetry of Immanence: Sacrament in Donne and Herbert.* Toronto: University of Toronto Press, 2002.

White, Peter. *Predestination, Policy, and Polemic: Conflict and Consensus in the English Church from the Reformation to the Civil War.* Cambridge: Cambridge University Press, 1992.

Williams, William Carlos. *Selected Essays.* New York: Random House, 1954.

Wilmart, André. *Auteurs spirituels et textes dévots du moyen-âge latin: études d'histoire littéraire.* Paris: Bloud et Gay, 1932.

Wilson, Thomas. *The Arte of Rhetorique.* London: George Robinson, 1585.

Winthrop, John. *Life and Letters of John Winthrop: Governor of the Massachusetts-Bay Company at their Emigration to New England* [1630]. Edited by Robert C. Winthrop. Boston: Little, Brown, 1869.

Woods, Gillian. "Catholicism and Conversion in *Love's Labour's Lost.*" In *How to Do Things with Shakespeare: New Approaches, New Essays,* edited by Laurie Maguire, 101–30. Malden, Mass.: Blackwell, 2008.

Wycliffe, John. *The Wycliffe Bible: John Wycliffe's Translation of the Holy Scriptures from the Latin Vulgate: Old and New Testament.* Winchester, Calif.: Lamp Post, 2009.

Young, R. V. *Doctrine and Devotion in Seventeenth-Century Poetry: Studies in Donne, Herbert, Crashaw, and Vaughan.* Suffolk, U.K.: D. S. Brewer, 2000.

Zwingli, Huldreich. *Ad Carolum Rom. Imperatorem, Fidei Huldrychi Zvingli ratio. Eiusdem quoq; ad illustrißimos Germaniae Principes Augustae congregatos Epistola.* Zurich: Ex Officina Froschoviana, 1530.

———. *Christian Fidei a Huldrycho Zvinglio Praedicatae, brevis et clara expositio.* Zurich: Christoph Froschauer D. A., 1536.

———. *Ejn klare Underrichtung vom Nachtmal Christi.* Zurich: Johannsen Hager, 1526.

———. *The Latin Works and the Correspondence of Huldreich Zwingli.* Edited by Clarence Nevin Heller, translated by Samuel Macauley Jackson. 3 vols. Philadelphia: Heidelberg, 1922.

Index

Page references in italics refer to illustrations

absence: of assurance, 83–84; of body of
    Christ, 54, 61; in devotional poetry, 144;
    divine, 21, 30, 141; in Herbert, 54; instabil-
    ities of, 158; objective reality of, 145; of
    presence, 29; in sacramental theology,
    193n40; of signified, 24, 33, 145
Adams, Robert, 119, 188n2, 192n33
Addison, Joseph, 171n56
aesthetics: of catechism, 48; of Catholic
    devotional poets, 4; Crashaw's, 32;
    Herbert's, 59, 60, 176n51; of immanence,
    51; post-Reformation, 149; of presence,
    162; Protestant, 168n4; Reformation,
    196n24; sacramental, 19, 146; theology
    and, 19, 147, 196n24
Altieri, Charles, 160, 161, 198n36
Ambrose of Milan: *De sacramentis*, 11–13;
    Donne's use of, 110; influence on transub-
    stantiation, 13
Andrewes, Lancelot, 20
Aristotle: influence on transubstantiation,
    13, 41; philosophies of matter, 173n13
art, symbolic action of, 19
Asals, Heather, 50–51, 59; on ontological
    language, 162
Ashton, Jennifer, 198n34
Augustine of Hippo: on allegory, 90; Bride/
    lover metaphor of, 179n19; Calvin's use of,
    170n35; sacramental theology of, 11, 12,
    14, 41, 68, 170n35; on signification,
    195n20. Works: *De Doctrina Christiana*,
    12; *In Iohannis evangelium*, 170n35

Barthes, Roland: on modern poetry, 161; on
    signs, 199n38

Bauer, Matthias, 53
Baumlin, James, 113, 193n40; on Donne,
    187n73
Bennett, Joan, 192n32
Bernard of Clairvaux, sacred eroticism of,
    179n19
Bernstein, Charles: on antiabsorptive poetics,
    23–24, 42, 160; on Postmodern poetry,
    161; use of Merleau-Ponty, 171n49
Bible: English translations of, 123; as generic
    sourcebook, 27; transmission of doctrine,
    197n26. *See also* Song of Songs
Blasing, Mutlu Konuk, 22–23, 159, 160, 163
body: as communicative instrument, 27; as
    distraction from spirit, 139; in Donne's
    works, 90–94; encounters with the divine,
    129, 138, 139; integrity with soul, 92; in
    sacramental worship, 32, 88; as site of spir-
    ituality, 138
body of Christ: in Crashaw, 120, 129, 131,
    135; in Donne, 95–97, 182n19; in Herbert,
    53, 59, 64; perceptual access to, 132; in
    sacramental worship, 10–11, 14–16, 26
Book of Common Prayer, Cranmer's revi-
    sions to, 34
books, material artifacts of, 158. *See also*
    print culture
Booth, Stephen, 162
bread: Christ's presence in, 2, 14, 16, 32, 36,
    86, 101, 111, 130; container of, 135; mate-
    riality of, 20, 35, 40, 108; as metaphor, 13;
    nourishment from, 8; sacramental element
    of, 17, 38, 99, 130–31; sensory encounter
    with, 58; as symbol, 18, 64, 100; Thomas
    Aquinas on, 58

Acknowledgments

Given that this study is so concerned with the ways in which presence is made manifest in the world, I take special pleasure in acknowledging the many people who were so manifestly present to me over the long course of this book's composition.

From the earliest days, my work on the research that would eventually become this book was sustained and encouraged by a wide range of friends, colleagues, and guides. I have endeavored elsewhere to express my appreciation for Donald M. Friedman; I echo that gratitude here. I was fortunate to have Paul Alpers and Stephen Booth as mentors early in this project's conception at the University of California at Berkeley, where it was also my privilege to be surrounded by a number of remarkable thinkers; for their encouragement and example during those years, I wish to thank Emily Anderson, Lorna Hutson, Jeff Knapp, and especially Kevis Goodman, whose nimble mind and gracious person continue to inspire me both on and off the page.

The argument of this book has been shaped by esteemed colleagues near and far. Jonathan Post gave his time and thought to my project in early incarnations. Michael Schoenfeldt provided invaluable guidance in early and late stages of writing, and his continued ministrations to the whole manuscript were augmented by generously thorough and rigorous responses from Molly Murray and Debora Shuger. Sections of this book have benefited tremendously from the attentive reading and suggestions of Sidney Gottlieb, Richard Strier, Edward Cutler, and Daniel Muhlestein. In the course of a single evening's conversation, Rob Watson helped me clarify for myself the position of my investigation in the wider critical field. Special thanks are due to Walter Benn Michaels and Jennifer Ashton, who urged me to write the book I wanted to write rather than the book I felt I was supposed to write. Though a zodiac of scholars have influenced my thinking, my appreciation for whom I hope is made clear in this project's conversation with its critical predecessors, I want in particular to recognize Ryan Netzley, whose work in its difference from mine has kept me specific about the claims I have hoped to make, and whose response to individual chapters in manuscript helped me refine my own focus. As my indefatigable research assistant and now virtual sister, Riley M. Lorimer trawled through a daunting pile of ancient texts with an alarming good humor; her wisdom has turned the mentoring tables on me completely.

Portions of this book's third chapter appeared as "Edward Taylor's 'Menstruous Cloth': Self-Feminization and the Problem of Assurance," in *From Anne Bradstreet to Abraham Lincoln: Puritanism in America*, volume 8 of *Studies in Puritan American Spirituality*, edited by Michael C. Schuldiner (Lewiston, N.Y.: Edwin Mellen, 2004). A section from this book's fifth chapter appeared as "Richard Crashaw's Indigestible Poetics," in *Modern Philology* 107.1, © 2009 by the University of Chicago, all rights reserved. I am grateful to those publishers for permission to reprint material from those essays.

My research was enriched by the helpful librarians at the Huntington Library and the Vatican Library. I extend special thanks to the American Academy in Rome for providing accommodation and a vibrant intellectual atmosphere while I conducted research in the Vatican Library's collections; I particularly wish to thank Chris Celenza for his encouragement and support, and Pina Pasquantonio for her guidance and expertise in the administrative protocols for conducting research in such a rarefied environment.

For support both tangible and intangible, I am grateful to Brigham Young University's Department of English and College of Humanities, and especially to Dean John Rosenberg, whose enthusiasm for my various projects has ever been unflagging. Also at BYU, the David M. Kennedy Center for International Studies granted me generous funding for research travel, and the Medieval and Renaissance Study group continues to provide a forum for challenging discussion.

Jerry Singerman, my editor at the University of Pennsylvania Press, impressed me from the first with his humanity and candor, a tricky balance in any profession but a pure relief in this one. Caroline Winschel and Noreen O'Connor-Abel answered my many pestering questions with clarity and patience. Throughout the publication process, I have received fine collegial support from Brooke Conti, James Marino, and Nancy Warren.

My family has always been my bedrock, the stable ground that made possible any precarious architecture I attempted to make of my life. My beloved Jay Hopler has adroitly managed his alternating roles as master of the revels and crisis counselor. I am most fortunate that my parents, Dean and Sondra Johnson, have always given me a safe place to try and to fail and to try again. My extended clan, an adorable collection of quirks and hilarities, help me keep perspective when I fall prey to the delusion that writing the next paragraph is the most important thing I will do in my entire life; I send a fist-pump of rockitude to Stephanie, David, Jack, and Elliot Ivers, Ryan and Janelle Johnson, Renae Taylor, and Kristin Matthews. With appreciation, I recognize that I would not be able to balance my professional endeavors and my real life without the supportive coparenting of Michael Greenfield.

Which brings me to my most profound acknowledgment of gratitude, though words must surely fail me. This project and my elder son were simultaneously embryonic, and his brother arrived as I began to reshape research into book. Through the various challenges and illuminations, stumblings and revisions, drafts and erasures, discouragements and victories of these years, Elijah and Bennett have been my most ardent cheerleaders. They make every moment present, every word gloriously immanent, and they manifest all the meaning in my world.